Models of Learning – Tools for Teaching

Third edition

Models of Learning – Tools for Teaching

Bruce Joyce, Booksend Laboratories, Saint Simons Island, Georgia, USA
Emily Calhoun, The Phoenix Alliance, Saint Simons Island, Georgia, USA
and
David Hopkins is the HSBL, Net Chair In International Leadership at the
University of London. Between 2002 and 2005 he served three Secretary of
States as the Chief Advisor on School Standards at the Department of Education
and Skills.

Open University Press

Open University Press
McGraw-Hill Education
McGraw-Hill House
Shoppenhangers Road
Maidenhead
Berkshire
England
SL6 2QL

email: enquiries@openup.co.uk
world wide web: www.openup.co.uk

and Two Penn Plaza, New York, NY 10121—2289, USA

first published 2009

Copyright © Bruce Joyce, Emily Calhoun and David Hopkins, 2009

A catalogue record of this book is available from the British Library

ISBN-13: 978-0-33-5234196 (pb)
ISBN-10: 0-33-523419-4 (pb)

Typeset by Kerrypress, Luton, Bedfordshire
Printed and bound by Bell and Bain Ltd, Glasgow

To Elinor and Joel Duncan

Contents

have to compare and contrast the items that belong to a category and those that don't and then build the new concept and study how they can better learn to organize and conceptualize data in all curriculum areas

We don't want to just CONVERGE on data, we want to expand on information to generate new ways of generating ideas (concepts), thinking through problems and keep ourselves from getting stale. Possibly the most delightful model of learning generates the playfulness and focused energy to break set when we are stuck with problem solving, writing, and living in a more open-ended manner

The picture–word inductive model (PWIM) draws on research on concept learning and on experience-based approaches to reading and is designed to teach young students to learn to read and write. It is also used as the base for curriculums for older struggling readers (see Chapter 8) and can be used in all the core curriculum areas to enhance inquiry and organises data

Learning how to learn with others has merit on its own right and enhances the strengths of the other models of learning. Cooperative inquiry means just that – working to seek knowledge and understanding and the skills that make working together a productive pleasure. We begin with dyads – pairs of students working together and introduce group investigation, the most powerful working-together model, which generates synergistic energy that can double content outcomes while helping students learn the most complex of social skills

Here we study multifaceted curriculums where secondary education students with learning disabilities and/or severe difficulties learning to read are taught how to learn in the core curriculum areas and build the literacy skills to enable them to succeed in school and in life. The University of Kansas SIM program and the Booksend Laboratories Read to Succeed Program are the centres of the chapter

Part 3 Learning to study oneself

Now, the content begins with the feelings and values of the students themselves. They study how to think about their selves and what they believe and to take hold of the reality that they have to take charge of who they are

9 Learning through counselling

A great deal of our capacity to learn has to do with how we feel about ourselves. The counselling model is centred around inquiry into oneself, particularly one's self-concept. The approach presented here is based on counselling sessions around current issues and problems. As we will see, the approach can be used with groups and class size gatherings as well as with individuals

10 Learning to study values

During our school years, we develop values quietly – with little notice taken. As we approach various problems those values come into play but almost unconsciously. Role playing helps surface values and enable them to be examined and helps students locate the sources of conflicts and how to resolve them

Part 4 Sources of developed models of learning

Going beyond this book, where can you find sources of models of learning and guidelines for using them? Here we examine the broad field of inquiry into learning and teaching and look into specific models and, finally, Robert Gagné's framework for looking at learning and instruction.

11 An inquiry into learning and teaching

Philosophers, researchers, and developers are in the hunt for ever better ways to help young people grow, in school and out. They provide not only models of learning but perspectives on growth and development and the societal purposes of education

Specific models and their developers are identified from personal, social, information processing and behavioural perspectives. Basically, this is a database from which to select models to learn

An insightful and eminently practical framework into levels of learning and the kinds of tasks that enable learners to achieve them. The framework is used to identify levels to be sought in instructional episodes and curriculums and the types of experience that have the greatest possibility of reaching them

We build the future of education on our present levels of knowledge and creative development. Here we look at a type of model that has been in development for 40 years and an innovation in early child education that has had dramatic effects on literacy

Simulation is a look at the past and a harbinger of the future. We can hardly believe that four decades have been past since development began in earnest on simulations. And, growth has been sporadic, but many are in existence and useful. Further work will parallel development in distance education which, like, simulations, depends on self-teaching ability

Many educational theorists have argued against teaching reading in the kindergarten years. But we believe that resistance is passé. Developments in models of learning and teaching have bypassed the controversies. We can build successful curriculums that will benefit the students in the primary grades, through school, and beyond. Here is a report of such a curriculum and its effects

We provide a simple formula for individuals, groups and whole school faculties

Acknowledgements

With appreciation to teachers who have developed illustrations drawn on throughout:

Lisa Mueller, Oketokes, Alberta, Canada. Associate with Booksend Laboratories
From the Literacy Teacher Cadre in Saskatoon, Saskatchewan, Canada
Lori Kindrachuk, Facilitator, Literacy for life
Mary Bishop and Sharon Champ, Literacy Teachers
From the Northern Lights School Division, Bonnyville, Alberta, Canada
Marilyn Hrycauk, Curriculum Director, retired, and
Walter Hyrcauk, Chairman, Board of Trustees

Foreword

Our collective ambition for our school systems has never been greater. Phrases like, 'allowing every child to reach their potential', 'no-one left behind', 'success for all' are mantras repeated by politicians of all political persuasions and accurately reflect the demands of parents and the public.

The economics of both are developed and the developing worlds have a seemingly endless need for higher and higher levels of skills; the expectation that public services will continually improve and the reality of global competitiveness have led to an unprecedented search for a school system that knows no failure.

One consequence is that the work to transform our schools has itself become an intenational, global effort. Education systems will always have a duty to transmit values and knowledge that reflect their own cultures but the activity of teaching and learning transcends national boundaries an we can work with and learn from each other.

Most of the school reforms since the end of the Second World War have focused on school level policy; comprehensive education, the characteristics of good schools, curriculum reform and assessment; school leadership. They have targeted school system change and together with the increased expenditure in education can claim significant credit for the progress we have seen. They are the bedrock for future developments.

Yet despite all the school improvement research and the considerable amount of extra resource allocated to education by Governments throughout the world, no one could claim that our aspirations are anywhere near being met. The performance of pupils in schools serving similar neighbourhoods is too varied as is the performance of individual pupils within the same school. The old argument that we just therefore need to do more of what we are already doing might be the answer; but I doubt it.

There is growing evidence – and it certainly explains the variation in performance – that what can make the difference is what happens in the classroom. The success or failure of some schools or of subject departments in the same school can't be explained by pupils' social background or financial investment.

It can be explained by the standard of teaching. If we are to accelerate improvements in our schools we must build on the school improvement reforms and build an evidence base about what works at classroom level. Pedagogy and class level reform should lead the next stage of reform.

In Models of Learning – tools for teaching, Bruce Joyce, Emily Calhoun and David Hopkins make an important contribution to this task. All three have been both classroom teachers and academics and among them they have an impressive record of research into teaching and learning.

In this book, the use their experience to bring together research and practice. The result is a description and analysis of a wide range of models of teaching all of which have then been developed in classrooms. The pedagogy is theoretically and academically underpined but practically proven with examples throughout.

There is no claim that the authors have found one answer to teaching and learning or that one pedagogical model is to be perferred over another. They all have their uses. There is, though, an underlining theme to the models. All emphasise the relationship between teacher and learner and remind us that one of the objectives of schools is to help pupils develop the skills of enquiry and independence that will stay with them beyond their school days.

In our search for 'an answer' to pupil underperformance we have on occasions been over prescriptive in what we asked teachers to do. There is though a strong case that teachers' professionalism is defined by their freedom to decide how to teach and their skill in making the right decisions.

Most teachers are natural innovators but too often lack the time and support to develop their ideas from existing evidence and evaluate what they do. We must do more to bring together the worlds of academic research and those practicing in our classrooms.

Models of learning – tools for teaching is an excellent example of what can be achieved when this happens. It provides teachers with a range of teaching models that will be an invaluable support in helping them make the hundreds of decisions that they are called on to make every lesson they teach.

Estelle Morris
formerly Secretary of State for Education
Presently Director, Institute for Effective Education, University of York

Part 1

Orientation

1 Learning how to learn: the (central?) goal of education

The missions of education are many and the priorities are often warmly debated. Laymen and professionals alike are well acquainted with the competing goals and the arguments about which to pursue with the greatest energy. Thinking about the possibilities with regard to one's *own* children arouses considerable affect, but considering what the schools should most emphasize in general often generates emotions, sometimes acutely.

Discussions are sometimes framed as if doing any given thing well will necessarily shortchange something else. As, if when we emphasize literature and writing in the literacy curriculum, we will lose attention to the 'basic' skills of reading and writing. Or, attention to scientific inquiry will reduce clarifying the major concepts of the sciences. Or, attention to contemporary social problems will result in a neglect of our historical heritages. We will argue that dichotomous arguments are often spurious – literature and basic skills can be taught together and compatibly and so on. There are approaches to schooling that override the dichotomies.

We have built our approach on a simple set of propositions. First, that a central focus of elementary/secondary education should be devoted to helping the students build their capacity to learn – essentially, learning how to learn. Note that we emphasize *both* elementary and secondary education. The secondary students are more mature and can learn more and more complex models and refine and consolidate ones they have explored while younger.

Second, that placing learning to learn at the centre of education will enhance, rather than diminish, the learning of content, skills, and processes in the core curriculum areas. The best curriculums are devoted to learning how to learn and the best schools make learning to learn central. As Vic Braden says with respect to playing doubles in tennis: 'It is your partner who will make you famous.' In our case, our partners are our students.

Third, the core mission of the student is to increase his/her learning capacity. The future is his/her oyster when the ability to learn and confidence to do so are well developed. Some students who appear to be outstanding in school can actually sit on their laurels and find that, in university and life, what served them well in Year 10 has serious shortcomings later. Some who seem to lag early increase their capacity and people begin to realize that their native ability has been greatly underestimated.

Is learning to learn obvious?

It is easy to say: 'Of course it is and always has been, at least at a certain level.' And, to a degree, learning to learn has always had some attention. Here, however, we will give learning to learn a central position and introduce models of learning – ways of teaching – that expand the ways we can increase learning capacity and do so across the curriculum and throughout the social climate of the school.

Introducing educators to models of learning that reconcile the need to build learning capacity and achievement within the core curriculum areas is extremely important. Teachers and schools have felt terrific pressure to 'cover' material and often have not known how to do that without sacrificing attention to the long-term learning needs of the students. We see students in algebra classes struggling to get through the content in such a way that they are not learning how to learn maths. Many adults readily confess that they took higher mathematics 'in order to forget it'.

Everyone is familiar with the dilemma. Here, we are making a frontal attack on solving it by dealing with ways of teaching and learning where building learning capacity and developing knowledge and skill are seamlessly integrated. All approaches to learning how to learn are inquiries because we have to observe the students carefully as they respond to the environments we create and the lessons we design and, then, the students will change as they learn. Students who were passive will become active seekers. Shy students will join their cohorts in cooperative inquiries.

We are getting new information about learning how to learn from the advances in distance education. To profit from distance education a student has to learn how to learn and many do – the alternative being to avoid the medium. And the results of distance courses and face-to-face instructor-managed courses are remarkably similar.

Let's begin by visiting a really lovely school and then some classrooms where learning to learn is the prominent theme.

2 Hempshill Hall School

"Wow!"

Bruce Joyce to Emily Calhoun, after a first visit

The following section was generated jointly by four people: Bruce Joyce and Emily Calhoun, who visited the school several times during October 1996 and made videotapes of lessons they taught while there; David Hopkins, who has an ongoing relationship with the school; and Marcia Puckey, the head teacher. Documents from the school files were drawn on extensively, as was the report from the Office for Standards in Education (Ofsted) on their inspection of the school. The Ofsted report was the product of the government inspection team responsible for assessing the quality of the school. The six-member team spent a week in the school; examined its documents pertaining to curriculum, instruction, management and assessments; observed 121 lessons or parts of lessons; watched assemblies; held discussions with teachers; interviewed the governors (school lay council); attended a meeting of 65 parents; examined the responses by 114 parents to a questionnaire; held planned discussions with students from Year 6; and listened to a range of pupils read.

The school serves about 350 children from the working-class community of Bulwell, in Nottinghamshire. About 60 per cent of the children live in the catchment (immediate neighbourhood), a pleasant area of tidy homes. Within the catchment, most families are two-parent households. The majority of the fathers have marketable skills and their employment provides a comfortable living. Most of the mothers left school early, married young and have few skills that are marketable in today's workplaces, although they will be quite young when their children reach the age where intensive parenting consumes less and less time.

About 40 per cent of the students who attend Hempshill Hall come from outside the neighbourhood. The economic and family situation of these children who live outside the catchment area is quite different. The majority of these children come from households where the mother raises the children alone and many are in public housing. Few of their mothers have marketable skills.

About 30 per cent of the children in the school, most of them from the homes outside the catchment, receive free (government-subsidized) lunches.

The school has a head and 10 full-time teaching staff. There are four paid teaching assistants. In addition there are five assistants-in-training under a programme developed by the head, who capitalized on the need by many of the mothers to begin to develop marketable skills.

In addition, the head has made arrangements with several teacher education programmes to provide experience for student teachers. There are usually half a dozen student teachers working in some capacity in the school.

Perhaps most importantly, 60 parent volunteers work in the school each week for about half a day to 2 days each. Again, the head has capitalized on the nature of the community, drawing into the school those parents who have the willingness and time to be a major part of the school community. As the head put it: 'You must be totally inclusive. Lots of people can help out if you will only provide the avenues and make them welcome.'

The school as a social system: collaboration, inquiry, responsibility

Hempshill Hall is packed with activity, much too much to report in less than a full-length book devoted only to the school, although a remarkable proportion is relevant to our theme.

Mrs Puckey has worked with the staff and parents to develop a thoroughgoing process for building a collaborative, energetic social system – one in which school staff, parents and students share responsibility for excellence in academic, social and personal development of the children. From the letter to parents: 'We are all equal partners at Hempshill Hall. We welcome parents who want to be fully involved in school life.'

The social system has many dimensions. Here are a few of them.

Orientation of the parents and children to the school

Meetings between parents, children and school begin before the children have reached school age. In the autumn of each year there are a series of meetings designed to build the student–parent–school partnership.

The Thursday club

Parents in the community who have children not yet in school are invited to bring their children to the school on Thursdays so that both parents and children can become accustomed to the school. Importantly, the Thursday Club inaugurates the orientation process; it provides families with opportunities to 'talk' to the school.

The staff has organized its actions to ensure that parents are welcomed into the school. Parents evidently do feel like an integral part of the school community because approximately one person from every six families is successfully recruited to work as an assistant to the teachers.

School assemblies

Two or three times a week the entire school gathers as an assembly, led by Stuart Harrison who is the deputy head, and a play is presented by a group of students. Many of the plays involve a considerable amount of improvisation and have slowly developing story lines. The assembly brings together the students as a whole-school community, provides an opportunity to develop them into a civil, polite audience, and, incidentally, means that each year they are participants in or audience to about 70 plays. The Ofsted report comments:

> Spiritual development is encouraged in the broadest sense and permeates the life of the school in a pervasive yet unobtrusive manner. Opportunities are taken to bring out spiritual issues during lessons, as they occur. Regular, well-prepared school and class assemblies take place, often using stories that illustrate values or have a moral content. The assemblies contribute effectively to the school's overall ethos and values.

Communication and the home–school connection

The reading wallet

Every child in the school is provided with a red vinyl briefcase, called a 'reading wallet', that they carry between home and school. The wallet contains real books and children's work. Parents are encouraged to provide time for their child to read the books at home and are helped in learning how to support their child's reading.

The comment book

An important communication document in each reading wallet is a 'comment book', a notebook in which teachers and parents write back and forth to each other on a weekly basis. If either makes a comment, the other responds. The comments discuss aspects of the children's academic and social progress and ways of helping them move forward.

To get the flavour of the interaction, let's look at the comments between the parents and teacher of one 5 year old:

> *4 September* [first day of school]
>
> [*Teacher*] Jessica has chosen some books to share with you: *The Greatest Show on Earth*, *Brown Bear* and *Not Now, Bernard*. She could just concentrate on one or read them all equally. She can keep these as long as she wants – I will probably next share them with her next Monday. [This last comment is a reference to the twice-weekly conference with individual students about books they are reading.]

4 September

[*Father*] I read *The Greatest Show* with Jessica and her brothers, Jeroen and Dylan. We discussed the story and tried to find out what was happening from the pictures. Jessica enjoyed the story and understood all the pictures.

5 September

[*Mother*] Jessica read Dylan and me the *Brown Bear* book without much help. She also read Jeroen's book *The Red Fox*.

6 September

[*Teacher*] Thank you. Jessica now has her poetry folder and a poem to share with you.

9 September

[*Mother*] Jessica and her younger brother, Dylan, read the poem and she showed us how to shout 'all join in'. They both enjoyed it, so we read it a few times. She also read us the *Brown Bea*r again.

[*Teacher*] I am pleased Jessica and Dylan enjoyed the poem. Also, it is interesting to learn what other books she is sharing with you. Jessica read *Brown Bear* with me together and she had remembered it really well. On the few occasions she had forgotten what came next, I just needed to jog her memory by beginning the next word and she remembered and carried on. She is bringing home two new books to share.

14 September

[*Father*] Jessica, her brothers and I read *Bill and Pete* ... Jessica and I read the story and Dylan told us what was happening in the pictures.

[*Mother*] Jessica, Dylan and Jeroen read *Would You Rather* and enjoyed it.

17 September

[*Teacher*] Jessica shared *Would You Rather* with me today and she remembered quite a lot of it, using the pictures efficiently to help.

18 September

[*Mother*] Jessica played a matching game with Jeroen with words such as *the*, *they*; *is*, *in*; *come, comes*. After that, she read his book, *The Book Shop*.

It is easy to see that the interchange is relatively dense as parents and teachers try to talk to one another over the common objective – helping the child become a successful reader. The teachers feel that the interchanges help extend the influence of the school into reading/writing activities in the home. The parents feel that the process keeps them in close touch with the student–teacher–parent triad that makes education work.

To make the nature of this connection more vivid, here are some excerpts from an interview with the mother:

> The comments make a real difference. They are one of the best things about having my daughter in Hempshill Hall. It really keeps you in touch and also keeps pressure on you as a parent. You feel that you have to read with the children every day because the teacher comments so regularly. It also is interesting to see how Jessica is learning to read. Yesterday, when I asked her about reading her newest book, she said that she could read it 'because all the words were in my head'. What we do now with Jessica adds about three hours a week to her concentration on learning to read.

The curriculum framework

The curriculum is academically rich and integrative. Everything is taught as the achievement of literacy. Reading is taught through real books. School subjects are divided into units that are tackled as experiential and reading/writing inquiries. The curriculum is naturally rather than artificially integrated, i.e. it is organized around related concepts, not around topics. The curriculum, as stated in the letter to parents, is 'based on the programmes of study in the National Curriculum Core Subjects of Mathematics, Science, English and Technology'.

Teaching, learning and working together

A general inquiry model dominates teaching and learning. All teachers and all children follow a scheme where material to be mastered and problems to be solved are presented; children, organized into groups, get to grips with the material and problems. Thus collaborative inquiry is the hallmark of the process, but individual children have responsibility for many strands of learning and individual differences in achievement are closely monitored. The school as a whole is the educative unit. In this the school is very different from the typical setting where schools assign children to classes in which teachers, working as individuals in miniature schools, progress through the curriculum. At Hempshill Hall everybody is responsible for all the children working toward common goals and using common strategies.

Every effort is made to help the children feel that they are capable and that each is responsible for the learning of all. From the letter to parents: 'We provide a warm, caring, "family style" environment where your child can feel valued, living in harmony with friends – a real extended family unit.' Within the context of the curriculum units, the children and teachers work together to plan specific activities. In a real sense, learning to cooperate, learning to live democratically and learning to collaborate as inquirers – as scholars – fit together in a comfortable whole.

The mode of collaborative inquiry pervasive at Hempshill Hall also greatly diminishes the disciplinary problems typical of the 'chalk and talk, drill and recite' school. 'Discipline' is a matter of bringing the children into the social norms of cooperation, inquiry and mutual respect. Thus the mode is socialization, rather than the enforcement of a code only tangentially relevant to the teaching/learning process.

The operation of the school is relevant to contemporary discussions about 'whole class' and 'cooperative group' activity. In a very real sense, the entirety of Hempshill Hall primary is a 'class' whose members cooperate as a whole and within which cooperative groups work within a common framework to pursue excellence. Personal, social and academic growth are perceived to be part of a whole. From the letter to parents: 'Hempshill Hall School has a mission – that all our children shall be happy, live in harmony and achieve success.'

Classes are not isolated educational settings. The classes operate as units where several teachers work together to plan and carry out their project plans and day-to-day inquiries. The familiar image of 'chalk and talk, drill and recite' is absent. Goals are made clear and the whole class works towards common substantive objectives. On a day-to-day basis, the children work from three-quarters to nine-tenths of the time in collaborative groups and as individuals to master those goals and develop their capacity as learners.

Reading and writing are taught from experience records and real books through-out the curriculum. This practice contrasts sharply with that of most schools, where the language arts are taught as a subject, with the product applied in the other curriculum areas. Reading and writing are pervasive activities at Hempshill Hall.

Similarly, technology is a tool to support learning, not an activity in itself. The computer is integrated in the learning of all subjects. Parents are urged to purchase laptop computers for their children and they are extensively used, as are about 40 computers in the school.

Staff planning

The staff work in teams to develop schemes of work that reflect the National Curriculum. However, each scheme is developed as a research activity for the children and first-hand experiences such as field trips and secondary experiences such as videotapes and films are combined with extensive reading. Products of research are expressed in writing, multimedia presentations and enactments.

Individual learning and responsibility

Individual responsibility and excellence is expected and supported. Individual students do the learning in all schools. In this case, individual projects are included in the curricular units as offshoots of the collaborative inquiry. Unlike some collabora-tive schools, Hempshill Hall does not make the mistake of generating 'group products' that are not an amalgam of individual inquiries. In addition, individual children develop their own inquiries, doing personal research and developing and testing their own hypotheses.

The tending of individual needs at all levels is a fluid part of the conduct of teaching. Every week, each child has two personal, one-on-one conferences with an adult over his or her individual reading and receives help in setting personal goals and in resolving problems. In the spring of the year, children in Year 2 who have not progressed above Level 1 in reading are identified and receive intensive assistance. In the spring of 1996, 10 children out of 52 were so identified. By the end of the school year, only four had not reached Level 2, the stage where children can read simple books independently.

At Hempshill Hall, parents are very much a part of the educational process on a daily basis. The regular exchange of written communication between parents and teachers and the daily carrying home of books to be read and pieces being written reinforces everyone's responsibility for educating the child. And, on an average day, about 10 parent volunteers will be in the school working alongside the teachers.

Ofsted inspection report

What do the authorities think of Hempshill Hall? Whenever a school deviates from the 'chalk and talk, drill and recite' mode, people in both the UK and the United States ask, sceptically, whether the 'basics' are being neglected. Largely, this scepticism is a product of the culturally normative image of teaching that persists despite its terrifying inefficiency. Of course, most people have had more experience with the CTDR model of teaching – the provision of information, oral or written, followed by queries to which one makes oral or written responses – than any other model, and it 'worked' for them.

Sometimes the dominance of recitation is seriously underestimated. Inefficiency in education is frequently laid at the door of a supposed drift away from its use toward the use of permissive, flaccid modes of teaching, modes commonly thought to be promoted by educational reformers working at a distance from the school. There are continuous calls to reassert recitation and drill as the major method of primary education and to eliminate the 'distractions' of inquiry and group work. These beliefs are held by many members of the public, despite the long recorded and current dominance of the recitation model in English-language countries. The tested alternatives such as those described in this book are largely unknown to a public whose experience as schoolchildren was largely in the environment of the recitation. Whenever a school uses a different model it is liable to nearly automatic criticism.

Consequently, the opinion of external examiners and the evidence of examination or test results become very important whenever a school strives for excellence through collaborative inquiry models. This is the case, even when a school asserts, as Hempshill Hall does in its letter to parents, that: 'Although our [academic] aims are traditional, our methods are not always so, and you may find that your children will be taught very differently to the way you were taught at their age. We respect individual differences, and do not normally "drill" whole classes together, regardless of ability.'

With this cultural context in mind, here are some of the products of the external examination of Hempshill Hall primary school, from the Ofsted inspection report:

Standards in reading, writing and speaking and listening, and in number and information technology, are good and sometimes outstanding ... Pupils use text effectively for learning. They read widely and value reading as a source of information. They read accurately, expressively, and with understanding. Pupils enjoy books and speak warmly of the pleasures of reading ... Pupils write with the coherence, fluency, and accuracy which is appropriate for their age and ability and often beyond. As they move through the school, they tackle successfully an increasing range of written work and plan, develop, and re-write their own text where appropriate. They are able to narrate, explain, describe, hypothesise, analyse, assert, compare, question, and deduce. They listen well to others and respond appropriately and sensitively [...]

Pupils handle number well across the curriculum, mentally and in writing. They use measurement effectively in a range of different contexts, particularly in science, technology and history. They have well-developed calculator skills and interpret statistical data effectively in their work in humanities.

Standards in information technology are good and sometimes outstanding. Pupils create, modify, and present information in English, art, history and mathematics. They use databases to enhance the quality of their work in history. By Year 6, pupils build and study computer models confidently and control movement and other physical effects in technology.

At the Key Stage 2 assessment, conducted when 10 to 11 year olds are leaving Year 6, the percentage of pupils achieving Levels 4 and 5 in English was 70, compared with a national average of 48. In maths, the percentage reaching Levels 4 and 5 was 82, compared with a national average of 44.

The school staff has continued to generate improvements, large and small, in the curriculum and in the relationship between school and home. Reading and writing have clearly been pervasive activities at Hempshill Hall. So much so, that when the head heard about an American approach to supporting reading throughout the school community, she adopted it enthusiastically. The 'Just Read' programme is designed to increase the number of books read by students in and outside school (Joyce and Calhoun 1996: Ch. 4). The research on Just Read suggests that community involvement in encouraging students to read has multiple benefits. These range from increased ability in literacy on the part of students, through an enhanced involvement in schooling on the part of parents, to an increasing commitment to education from the community (Joyce and Calhoun 1998: 154–70). The number of books read by students at Hempshill Hall each week almost doubled following the first 2 months of implementation and remained consistent at that level thereafter.

An analysis of test scores for the past 3 years at ages 7 and 11 illustrates a consistent upward trend in the key curriculum areas at a level at least 10 per cent above national averages.

Reflections

So much of this scenario is self-explanatory that we need to be careful not to overdo our reflections and diminish the narrative. Very few schools reach the comprehensive learning to learn level that Hempshill Hall has reached. A distinction is the inclusion of *everybody* in some aspect of learning for themselves. Unusual and outstanding are the opportunities for the young, ill-educated female parents who are drawn into an environment where they have a chance of developing marketable skills.

Hempshill Hall gives us a signature model for this book.

Part 2

Learning to process information

3 Learning to think inductively

"Thinking inductively is inborn and lawful. This [school renewal] is revolutionary work, because schools have decided to teach in a lawless fashion, subverting inborn capacity."

Hilda Taba to a group sitting on the steps of the Lincoln Memorial

Learning to process information inductively has a vital place in teaching students how to learn better. And no area illustrates better the oxymoronic character of helping students to learn. As Taba said, so many years ago, babies are born with the capacity to classify and they begin to use it right away. Within a few months we can see their learning in two ways: one is in the development of categories about their immediate environment and the second is in language development.

Very soon they can distinguish the cat from the cuddly toy and things that float in the bath from things that sink.

Not long after, the little people are recognizing words and trying to use them. By age 3 or so, they have learned an astonishing number of categories of words. In primitive speech, they will put the subject before the word and inflect the end of a question.

We want to unfetter their cognitive birthright – in a sense to get out of the way of the inborn capacity. Also, however, and this is important, we want to help our young to enhance their skills – to become more and more self-consciously capable. *And, that does not happen automatically.* Curiously, the classification skill that serves so well during the first 4 or 5 years can be arrested in the school years as the child tries to imitate adult learning rather than continuing the process of inventing concepts and skills that dominates the delightful infant and early childhood years. And, through inquiry, we have refined ways of classifying and can help the students explore them and enhance their learning during the later childhood, pre-adolescent, adolescent and young adulthood years. As Taba indicated, there are curriculums and ways of teaching that actually subvert and can even derail, this major part of humanness. Available to us are versions of the inductive model of learning – ways of helping our children enhance their tools for building and using categories. In these pages, we will concentrate on one of them – one that has been researched and polished to make it viable. Let's begin by examining a simple example.

Scenario 1: the Seamus Inquiry

Eight-year-old Seamus is apparently playing in his kitchen. In front of him are a number of plates. On one is a potato, cut in quarters. Another contains an apple, similarly cut. The others contain a variety of fruits and vegetables. Seamus pushes into the segments of potato a number of copper and zinc plates that are wired together and to a tiny light bulb. He nods with satisfaction when the bulb begins to glow. He disconnects the bulb, attaches a voltmeter, examines it briefly and then reattaches the bulb. He repeats the process with the apple, examining the bulb and voltmeter once again. Then come the raspberries, lemon, carrot and so on. His father enters the room and Seamus looks up. 'I was right about the raspberries', he says, 'we can use them as in a battery. But some of these other things …'

Seamus is, of course, classifying fruits and vegetables in terms of whether they can interact with metals to produce electric current.

Reflection: the Seamus Inquiry

Before this inquiry was initiated, Seamus has had a good deal of experience with the classification process. He has classified the characteristics of animals and their habitats (see later). He has classified words and sentences and the titles of books. In fact, the last is what led to the inquiry with fruits, vegetables, and batteries after he found a little book on the basics of electricity. With the help of his parents, he set up a study of metals that would and would not become electromagnets when surrounded with a coil. And, then they found a kit with tiny lights, voltmeters and the copper and zinc plates and he began to classify the groceries according to whether and how much they generated electricity.

This little scenario illustrates how direct the components of classification are:

- We need a set of data relative to some content domain.
- We need to examine the items in the set, noting their attributes. To do so thoroughly, we may need to operate on the dataset (in this case collecting the further information about the production of electricity. And, we may need a measurement device (as the little light and the voltmeter).
- And we need to make notes of some kind or, possibly, here, make piles of the groceries depending on the results.
- Then, reflecting on what is learned leads to a clarification of the concepts and, importantly, the development of names for them. What shall we call the fruit that generates the most electricity? Will dictionary or encyclopedia help us – or other non-fiction books on electricity?

As we continue to explore the learning process, note that, although this illustration focuses on a single child, a classroom or laboratory can be set up so that larger numbers of students can carry on the same type of inquiry that Seamus did. We will proceed to a first grade class on the first day of school where the schooling process begins with classification with no need for special equipment.

Scenario 2: the Diane Inquiry

Diane Schuetz provided each of her first grade children with sets of tulip bulbs – each had a dozen or so on their little desks. She asked them to examine the bulbs carefully. Then she asked them to make categories (move the bulbs around into groups, putting similar ones together etc.). All this on the first day at school.

Gradually, the students formed groups according to characteristics like size (putting big and little ones together), whether were joined together ('some have babies on them said some of the children'), whether they had 'coats' or whether they had the beginnings of what look like roots.

Diane led the children to share their ideas, moving around their set as the others shared (as putting those with 'babies' or 'coats' in a temporary pile).

Diane had set up a number of boxes, half-filled with potting soil and the other half with water. Above the boxes she arrayed ultraviolet lights.

She then organized the children to plant half of their bulbs and sit the other half in stones in the water. As they planted them, she made cards with their hypotheses written on them, such as: 'Will the big ones [bulbs] grow bigger?' 'Will the babies grow on their own?' 'Will the ones in soil do better?' and so on. She has designed the science curriculum area around the basic processes of building categories, making predictions and testing them.

Reflection: the Diane Inquiry

Again we can see the essentials of learning to develop and use categories. Repeating ourselves somewhat:

- We need a set of data relative to some content domain. In this case, the bulbs make up the dataset and the domain is growth from bulb to plant.
- We need to examine the items in the set, noting their attributes. Here, the students can use their eyes and hands to take in the attributes.
- And, we need to make notes of some kind or, as here, make piles of the bulbs as classification proceeds.
- Then, reflecting on what is learned leads to a clarification of the concepts and the development of questions – hypotheses by these little people.

Given that this is the first day of school for these children, you can imagine that thinking will be the theme of the curriculum. Diane will use other models of learning, as we will see later, but she is unafraid to lead her students to explore their content with their good heads. By the way, how many first grades have the depth and relevance hers is going to develop? And, as they make their observations and dictate them to her, can we expect that a healthy part of the literacy (reading and writing) curriculum will develop over inquiries into content?

Scenario 3: biology in India with Bharati Baveja

At the Motilal Nehru School of Sports in the state of Haryana, India, two groups of 15 year olds are engaged in the study of a botany unit that focuses on the structure of plant life. One group is studying the textbook with the tutorial help of their instructor, who illustrates the structures with plants found in the grounds of the school. We will call this group the presentation/illustration group. The other group, which we will call the inductive group, is taught by Dr Bharati Baveja, an instructor at Delhi University. This group is presented with a large number of labelled plants. Working in pairs, Bharati's students build classifications of the plants based on the structural characteristics of their roots, stems and leaves. Periodically the pairs share their classifications and generate labels for them.

Occasionally Mrs Baveja employs concept attainment (see Chapter 4) to introduce a concept designed to expand the students' frame of reference and induce more complex classification. She also supplies the scientific names for the categories the students invent. Eventually Mrs Baveja presents the students with some new specimens and asks them to see if they can predict the structure of one part of the plant from the observation of another part (as predicting the root structure from the observation of the leaves). Finally, she asks them to collect some more specimens and fit them to the categories they have developed so they can determine how comprehensive their categories have become. They discover that most of the new plants will fit into existing categories but that new categories have to be invented to hold some of them.

Reflections on the Baveja experience

After 2 weeks of study, the two groups take a test over the content of the unit and are asked to analyse more specimens and name their structural characteristics.

The inductive group has gained twice as much on the test of knowledge and can correctly identify the structure of eight times more specimens than the presentation/illustration group. Inductive teaching and learning has a strong base of research that fits with the Baveja results.

Scenario 4: classifying with Sharon Champ

We now take the reader into an exploration of a dataset generated by a wonderful teacher for her students in the Saskatoon, Saskatchewan, public schools. Rather than describe how she led her students, we invite the reader to examine the dataset and form concepts. Sharon Champ is a literacy trainer in the Saskatoon public schools. She decided to build a set where several concepts about syntactic structures of sentences are built in so that they might be discovered as the students build their categories. The content objective is to increase the students' study of sentences and how they are structured to convey particular types of meanings. Let's look at the structural characteristics of 21 of the sentences.

> In the grass, the spider patiently weaves her web.
> In the trees, birds gather to eat berries.
> In the forest, a squirrel leaps from tree to tree.

In the space shuttle, the astronauts complete their experiment.
In the burrow, the rabbit family nestles together to keep warm.
In the cockpit, the pilot carefully checks his instrument panel.
In the icy water, a penguin dives and splashes.

Under the sea, large sharks circle the school of fish.
Near the trees, lion cubs scamper in the tall grass.
Under the water, the diver silently searches for a dolphin.
Under the snow, a hungry mouse burrows deep looking for food.
Beside the school, two small boys play catch with a bright red ball.
Behind the mountain tops, dark storm clouds are gathering.
Between the trees, a small monkey wrestles with its mother.

Beside the river, a bear cub scrambles on the rocks.
Between the rocks, a snake slithers to search for food.
On the surface of the pond, a loon floats peacefully.
Hidden under leaves, a spotted frog hides from the sun's brilliant rays.
Deep in the forest, a black panther patiently waits to pounce on her prey.
High in the sky, the lone eagle glides gracefully.
Far below the earth's surface, molten lava rumbles and boils.

From a formal perspective, each of these sentences contains a prepositional phrase that provides information about *where* the action is taking place.

Sharon reasons that if the students can build a category that contains those attributes (prepositional phrases and their attributes and the meaningful content, '*where*'), they can use the category as they read, looking for structures that provide particular meanings and, as they write, building a tool for giving their readers information about, in this case, *where*.

So, the rest of the set contains prepositional phrases that do *not* tell us where:

Penguins have huge appetites.
This bird is a rockhopper penguin.
You would not want to fight a grizzly bear!
Clouds come in all shapes and sizes.
A blue whale is not a fish.
This tough bird is an emperor penguin.
The small dog yapped impatiently.

In the day, bats sleep upside down.
At twilight, bat's sharp cries fill the air.
At night, the owl hunts silently for mice and rabbits.
In the winter, most bears hibernate in caves.
Some frogs lay their eggs on land.
A duck makes its nest in the reeds.
The young penguin stays beside his mother.

Many desert animals live underground.
Many plants and animals live beside lakes.

A woman is standing between her children.

The woodpecker searches for insects under the bark of the aspen tree.

They build their nests on steep, rocky cliffs and hillsides.

Snow leopards live high on snowy mountain sides.

Yaks live on some of the tallest mountains in the world.

These last sentences are mixed with the first 21 as Sharon presents the set to her sixth grade students. She asks them to look at characteristics of the sentences and the kind of information that is conveyed. She asks them to focus not on specific bits of information (as where the yak lives) but on general information conveyed by a particular characteristic of the sentences.

Clearly, this is not the first lesson on sentence structure and purpose, but part of a long unit dealing with comprehension in reading and ways of conveying information in writing.

What do you think? What categories do you suppose the students formed in their inquiry?

The classification core: inductive thinking as a model of learning

The scenarios that introduce this chapter illustrate the inductive model in operation. The inductive model has a long history. Inductive thinking has been written about since the classical Greek period and the model has been polished and studied formally during the last 30 years. Very important to current classroom use was the work of Hilda Taba (1966, 1967), who was largely responsible for popularizing the term *teaching strategy* and for shaping the inductive model so that it could be conveniently used to design curriculums and lessons. (See also Joyce and Calhoun 1998.)

The inductive model causes students to collect information and examine it closely, to organize it into concepts and to learn to manipulate those concepts. Used regularly, this strategy increases students' abilities to form concepts efficiently and increases the range of perspectives from which they can view information.

If students in a group regularly engage in inductive activity, the group can be taught to use a wider range of sources of data. The students can learn to examine data from many sides and to scrutinize all aspects of objects and events. For example, imagine students studying communities. We can expect that at first their data will be superficial, but their increasingly sophisticated inquiry will turn up more and more attributes that they can use for classifying the information they are gathering. Also, if a classroom of students works in groups to form concepts and data and then the groups share the categories they develop, they will stimulate each other to look at the information from different perspectives.

Phases of the model

Think about the scenarios at the beginning of the chapter as you review the phases of the inductive model of teaching and learning. The flow of the inductive process is made up of several types of inquiry that overlap considerably:

- identifying an area of study – a domain that contains conceptual or actual territory to be explored
- collecting and sifting information relevant to that area or domain of inquiry; sometimes the students create the dataset, sometimes it is the instructor
- constructing ideas, particularly categories, that provide conceptual control over territories of information
- generating hypotheses to be explored in an effort to understand relationships within that domain or to provide solutions to problems
- testing hypotheses, including the conversion of knowledge into skills that have practical application
- applying concepts and skills, practising them and developing 'executive control' over them so that they are available for use.

In this flow of cognitive operations, we find the definition of *induction*, for, in these types of inquiry, *the student constructs knowledge and then tests that knowledge through experience and against the knowledge of experts. Induction*, rooted in the analysis of information, is often contrasted with *deduction*, where one builds knowledge by starting with ideas and proceedings to infer further ideas by logical reasoning.

Although it is convenient to imagine a prototype inquiry that begins with data collection and organization and proceeds to the development of categories, the generation and testing of hypotheses, and perhaps then to the development of skills, the inductive process may begin at any of these stages or phases. Now, consider how the inductive process emerges.

Coverage and conceptualization

Although much research on information processing models has been focused on how to increase students' ability to form and use concepts and hypotheses, a number of questions asked by both practitioners and laymen are particularly relevant here. The questions mainly reflect the concern we have mentioned earlier – that a concentration on thinking might inhibit the mastery of content.

Teachers put the question something like this: 'I have much content to cover. If I devote energy to the teaching of thinking, won't the students miss out on the basic skills and content that are the "core" of the curriculum?'

Several reviews of research have addressed this question. El-Nemr (1979) concentrated on the teaching of biology as inquiry in high schools and colleges. He looked at the effects on student achievement, on the development of process skills and on attitudes toward science. The experimentally oriented biology curricula achieved positive effects on all three outcomes. Bredderman's (1983) analysis included a broader range of science programmes and included the elementary grades. He also reported positive effects for information acquisition, creativity, science process and, in addition, on intelligence tests where they were included. Hillocks' (1987) review of the teaching of writing produced similar results. In short, the inductive inquiry-oriented approaches to the teaching of writing produced average effect sizes of about 0.60 compared to treatments that covered the same material, but without the inductive approaches to the teaching/learning process.

Some other researchers have approached the question of 'coverage' in terms of the transfer of the teaching of thinking from one curriculum to another, and found that inquiry-oriented curriculums appear to stimulate growth in other, apparently unconnected, areas. For example, Smith's (1980) analysis of aesthetics curricula shows that the implementation of the arts-oriented curricula was accompanied by gains in the basic skills areas.

The question of time and efficiency has been addressed recently in a number of large-scale field studies in the basic curriculum areas. An example has been provided by the 190 elementary school teachers of an Iowa school district. The teachers and administrators in this district focused on improving the quality of writing of their students by using the inductive model of teaching to help students explore the techniques used by published authors to accomplish such tasks as introducing characters, establishing settings and describing action. At intervals teachers collected samples of the children's writing and those samples were scored by experts who did not know the identity of the children.

By the end of the year, student writing had improved dramatically. In the fourth grade, for example, their end-of-year scores for writing quality were higher than the end-of-year scores for eighth grade students the previous year! Students had made greater gains in 1 year than were normally achieved by comparable students over a period of 4 years. Moreover, students at all levels of writing quality had gained substantially – from the ones who started with the poorest writing skills to the ones who began with the most developed skills. The 'gender gap' in writing (males often lag behind females in developing writing skills) narrowed significantly (Joyce et al. 1994, 1996).

Chapter 15 is a contemporary report describing a multiple-model early years curriculum and reporting benefits across gender, socioeconomic groups and ethnic groups. Chapter 8 contains another report of an inductive curriculum designed for older, struggling readers.

That the same type of curriculum reached all the categories of students is surprising to many people but it is a typical finding in studies of teaching and teaching strategies. Teachers who reach the students with poor histories of learning and help them out of their rut also propel the best students into states of growth higher than they have been accustomed to.

We stress that students are natural conceptualizers. Humans conceptualize all the time, comparing and contrasting objects, events, emotions – everything. To capitalize on this natural tendency, we arrange the learning environment and give tasks to students to increase their effectiveness in forming and using concepts and we help them consciously develop their skills for doing so. Over the years we have generated guidelines for shaping the environment and creating tasks that facilitate concept formation. As students become more skilled in inductive learning, we modulate our behaviour, helping them create appropriate environments and tasks. Learning how to think inductively is the critical goal and the students need to practise it, not just be led through it. The guidelines for shaping the environment (designing lessons and units) are straightforward.

One is *focus* – helping the students concentrate on a domain (an area of inquiry) they can master, without constricting them so much that they can't use their full abilities to generate ideas. At first we do this by presenting the students with datasets that provide information in the domain that will be the focus of the lesson or unit and by asking them to study the attributes of the items in the set. A simple example is to present kindergarten or first grade students with cards containing several letters from the alphabet and ask them to examine them closely and describe their attributes. The domain is *the alphabet: letters and their names*. Another example is to present fifth or sixth grade students with a dataset containing statistical data on the countries from a region of the world, say, Latin America, and ask the students to study the data on each country carefully. The domain is *Latin American countries*, with the subdomain of *statistical data*.

Second is *conceptual control* – helping the students develop conceptual mastery of the domain. In the case of the alphabet, the goal is to distinguish the letters from one another and to develop categories by grouping letters that have many, but not all, attributes in common. The students will learn to see the alphabet in terms of similarities and differences. They will also find those letters in words and, when they have made categories of letters with the same shape (as putting half a dozen 'b's together), will learn the names of those letters as we supply them. The letters will be placed on charts in the classroom along with words that contain them. In the case of the Latin American countries, the students will classify the countries according to the demographic data provided in the set, moving from single-attribute categories such as population and per capita income to multiple-attribute categories such as determining whether variables like education levels, fertility and income are related. They will be able to see Latin America in terms of those categories, a step toward the conceptual control that will emerge as they add more data to their set and develop advanced categories, gaining *meta control* by developing hierarchies of concepts to gain further mastery of the domain.

The third guideline is converting conceptual understanding to *skill*. In the case of the alphabet, this is exploring letter–sound relationships and how to use them in reading and spelling, where recognition evolves to conscious application in word identification. In the case of the Latin American countries, the skills are in the development of multiple-attribute categories and generating and testing hypotheses (such as studying whether per capita income is related to fertility rates or education levels).

The environment is made up of the development of the learning community, the creation of the datasets and the learning tasks – classification, reclassification and development of hypotheses. Also, the teacher observes the students and scaffolds their inquiry by helping them elaborate and extend their concepts. In the alphabet example, tasks such as 'which letters are most like the "a" and are most likely to be confused with it' would be generated. In the Latin American example, tasks like 'what other variables might be correlated with levels of literacy' would be generated.

As the students learn to build and extend categories (concepts), they take on increased responsibility for the process. For example, they learn to build datasets that are relevant to the domains being studied. Our kindergarten/first grade students use their word charts to develop datasets, at first with explicit guidance ('Here are three words that begin the same. Can you add to my list?') and later by looking at the list and sorting the words independently according to how they begin and end. Our young scholars on Latin America learn to add variables to the database using statistical sources and expository sources like encyclopedias. As their study of nations proceeds, they will be able to create datasets on regions and sets that enable them to compare and contrast entire regions.

The inductive model leads students to collect information and examine it closely, to organize the information into concepts and to learn to manipulate those concepts Used regularly, this strategy increases students' abilities to form concepts efficiently and increases the range of perspectives from which they can view information.

4 Learning to explore concepts

"What that kid did made the point so everybody could hear it. Four times last week he was in concept attainment lessons taught by the student teachers. So he said we owed him one. If we'd get him some second graders to teach, he'd make a dataset and teach the same kind of lesson. And he wanted to be videotaped like the student teachers were. So we got him the kids and he taught the lesson and he did a great job. So now everybody understands that the whole point is to teach the kids the model and practice will do it."

Kay Vandergrift to Bruce Joyce, November 1969

The centre of learning to improve inductive capacity is practice with datasets, including the development of hypotheses and terms, with guidance from us to assist in the development of more sophisticated ways of learning.

Now we will examine a model of learning derived from the model of teaching that is called 'concept attainment'. This model of learning is highly structured and used both to teach specific concepts and how to form and attain concepts. Instructors develop datasets that include examples and non-examples of a concept. The students compare and contrast the positive and negative examples and arrive at the concept, which is then manipulated and dealt with in much the same way as the inductive model of learning. The outcome is concepts and ways of thinking and, importantly, a new dimension of how to learn – how the students form and attain concepts is surfaced and improved.

We'll begin with a series of lessons developed by Lori Kindrachuk, a leading staff development provider in the Saskatoon, Saskatchewan, public schools.

Lori scenario 1: the Whoopee lessons

The set was built for sixth grade students who are struggling readers and writers (see the description of 'Read to Succeed' on page 89). The lesson was part of a series to help the students read more discerningly – many, when reading aloud, read with little inflection, indicating a lack of comprehension of devices such as interjections. In addition, the series was put together to help them add devices to their repertoire when writing.

Lori's notes clarify the concept as she built the lesson:

This first lesson is built around the concept: Interjections, directed at improving comprehension and leading the students to use more animated inflections in their reading and more descriptive words in their writing.

Definition: An interjection is a word added to a sentence to convey emotion. It has no grammatical function in the construction of a sentence. Interjections are usually used when quoting spoken words and should be avoided in business writing.

Punctuation: Either a comma or an exclamation mark can follow an interjection. A comma is used for a mild interjection; where as, an exclamation mark is used for a more abrupt display of surprise, emotion, or deep feeling:

1   All positive exemplars begin with an interjection (a word added to convey emotion)
2   All positive exemplars have a short phrase or sentence following the interjection that quotes spoken words.

She has developed a set of sentences, some of which contain the attributes of interjections and some of which do not. The students are to arrive at the concept by comparing the positive exemplars (called 'yeses' by most teachers and students) and negative exemplars (called 'nos' by most teachers and students).

The students are presented with the sentences, one by one, after Lori makes a statement to them to help them focus.

Focus statement

In this concept attainment lesson all of the positive exemplars (yeses) have two common attributes or characteristics. For one of the attributes you are looking for something in the way the statement is written, for the other one you will need to think about the meaning of the statement (what it actually says). Note that interjections have more than one attribute in common.

She presents the dataset in pairs. The first pair is:

Whooppee! We won! (yes)
We won the game. (no)

The students ponder the differences and make notes.

The next pair is:

Ouch! That hurt! (yes)
It hurt when the needle poked me. (no)

The first set of positive sentences are very clear examples of interjection

Again, the students reflect and Lori asks them to compare the differences between the positive and negative exemplars in the two pairs.

In the next examples an exclamation mark follows the interjection. The sentence following the interjection does not have an exclamation mark and does not have the same level of surprise emotion or feeling as in the first set of sentences

The next pairs are:

Whoa! Hold your horses!
Try to slow down and be patient.

Wow! That is a giant pumpkin!
That is a very big pumpkin.

Hey! Put that down!
You shouldn't touch things that don't belong to you.

Yikes! There's a fire in the oven!
The grease is on fire!

Now Lori asks the students if they have a hypothesis about the attributes that separate the positive and negative exemplars (yeses and nos). They do not share their hypotheses orally – we'll discuss why not presently.

But now she presents another series of pairs where the differences are not as dramatic as in the first pairs:

The paired sentences end with an exclamation mark and convey emotion, but they do not start with an interjection

These sentences are written to partner with the first positive examples but with less emotion

Hurry! The bus is about to leave.
The bus is leaving!

Phew! I'm not trying that again.
I'll never do that again!

Oh! You're here.
You're finally here!

And several others. Now, she asks the students whether they have new hypotheses. And, she asks them to try to change some positives into negatives, for instance 'Please remove the part of the sentence that makes these positives ...' as

Ah, now I understand.
Gosh, I'm tired.

And then to make some negatives into positives, as:

You mean the exam is today!
That was a real surprise!

In the seven examples, the interjection is not followed by an exclamation mark and becomes a part of the sentence. These examples can easily be changed to negative exemplars by removing the interjection. The sentence left behind still conveys the same meaning

If the students can do these tasks, then they are probably beginning to attain the concept.

Then, Lori gives them a short story whose prose contains a good many interjections and asks them to try to locate them all.

The inquiry will continue. By the way, this kind of lesson frequently stretches over several days and, importantly, is part of a long unit in which the students are studying reading and writing.

The datasets and tasks are organized into the contrasting pairs, leading the students to compare the positive and negative exemplars until the penny drops and they attain the concept.

After she is satisfied that the students *can* find examples in the prose she gives them, Lori asks them to provide definitions and to label the concept.

The students decide to call them 'Whoopees' after the one in the first pair of sentences. Then, as they read, they can say: 'I found a Whoopee!' As they generate sentences, they can debate whether a Whoopee is appropriate or not.

For sure, they are using stronger inflections when they encounter an interjection or another type of word that conveys emotion and they are able to discuss why the inflection is important a part of the reading process.

The datasets developed for the concept model of learning are loaded toward the selected concept. They can be used in the inductive learning model, but will draw students toward the embedded concept.

Lori scenario 2: attaining phonics concepts

Lori generated this unit after learning that a number of second grade students were having problems with some structural analysis/phonics concepts. The following is an example: 'Students had overgeneralized the "hard" sound of *g*. They would read or spell *page* as "paggey".'

This was not their only structural/phonics problem and Lori wished to draw the students into an inquiry that would help them straighten out the concepts that govern sounds in the context of words.

Her notes indicate how she selected the items in the set:

All positive exemplars contain two attributes:

- g follows e – as ge
- the ge must represent the /j/ sound.

Her presentation begins with seven pairs in which the differences are relatively unambiguous. She asks the students to compare the positive and negative exemplars and try to develop hypotheses about the attributes that the positives have that are not shared by their partners. The pairs are presented one by one.

The first seven words all end with **ge**. I purposely chose one-syllable words using the same word family (and vowel) to make it easier for the students

	Positive exemplars	*Negative exemplars*
1	age	ace
2	cage	came
3	page	plate
4	rage	rate
5	wage	wade
6	sage	sale
7	stage	grade

Lori asks the students to reflect on any hypotheses they may have developed, but not to share them with the other students, because each student needs to develop their own and, once someone else shares an idea, students tend to stop their independent thinking and try to test the hypothesis of the one who has shared.

Now she presents another set of seven pairs.

The next seven words continue to end in **ge**. They are still one syllable long, but they now have different vowels and mixed word families

8	bridge	gate
9	huge	game
10	range	gave
11	hedge	gale
12	urge	grape
13	large	grade
14	dodge	great

In this group, the placement of the letters is prominent. The negatives have both *g* and *e* but they are not together in sequence. The idea is for the students to refine their hypotheses as they see that the /j/ sound is generated when the g and e *are* together in sequence.

In her next set of positive exemplars placement is changed, showing that the *g e* combination is associated with the /j/ sound whether at the beginning or middle of the word and in multiple-syllable words.

ge is at the beginning of the first three words. By the fourth word **ge** has moved to the middle of the word. The last four words have two syllables. My students were able to change agent to angry, urgent to rent and digest to dig to make them into negatives

15	germ
16	gel
17	gem
18	angel
19	agent
20	urgent
21	digest

And, finally, Lori presents some negative exemplars where the g–e combination are in sequence, but the 'hard *g*' sound is produced. What is the difference?

The last seven words all contain **ge** in succession, however, the **ge** makes the hard sound of /g/. The last four examples are specifically chosen as they are easy to turn into a positive (ragged/rage, anger/angel, forget/forge, singer/singe)

15	getting
16	together
17	forget
18	ragged
19	anger
20	forget
21	singer

Here, we see that bringing the students into inquiry, even in the structure of words and the association of letter combinations with sounds, involves attaining concepts that are not just that simple, but where the development of sequences of sets can help the students gain control of the concepts and develop the skills to employ them.

Scenario 3

Mrs Stern's eighth grade class in Houston, Texas, has been studying the characteristics of the 14 largest cities in the United States. They have collected data on size, ethnicity of population, types of industry, location and proximity to natural resources.

Working in pairs, the students have collected information and summarized it on a series of charts now pasted up around the room. One Wednesday in November, Mrs Stern says:

> Today, let's try a series of exercises designed to help us understand these cities better. I have identified a number of concepts that help us compare and contrast them. I am going to label our charts either *yes* or *no*. If you look at the information we have and think about the populations and the other characteristics, you will identify the ideas that I have in mind. I'm going to start with the city that's a *yes* and then one that's a *no*, and so forth. Think about what the yeses have in common. Then write down after the second *yes* the idea that you think connects those two places and keep testing those ideas as we go along. Let's begin with our own city. Houston is a yes.

The students look at the information about Houston: its size, industries, location, ethnic composition. Then Mrs Stern points to Baltimore, Maryland. 'Baltimore is a no', she says. Then she points to San José, California. 'Here is another yes', she comments.

The students look for a moment at the information about San José. Two or three raise their hands. 'I think I know what it is', one offers. 'Hold on to your idea', she replies. 'See if you're right.' She then selects another yes – Seattle, Washington; Detroit, Michigan, is a no; but Miami, Florida, is a yes. After each city is presented, she allows students time to study their information. She continues until all students think they know what the concept is, and then they begin to share concepts.

'What do you think it is, Jill?' 'The *yeses* all have mild climates', says Jill. 'That is, it doesn't get very cold in any of them.' 'It gets pretty cold in Salt Lake City!', objects another. 'Yes, but not as cold as in Chicago, Detroit or Baltimore', another student counters.

'I think the *yeses* are all rapidly growing cities. Each one of them increased more than 10 per cent during the last 10 years.' There is some student discussion about whether this is accurate.

'All the *yeses* have lots of different industries', volunteers another. 'That's true, but almost all of these cities do', replies another student.

Finally, the students decide the *yeses* are all cities that are growing very fast and have relatively mild climates. 'That's right', agrees Mrs Stern. 'That's exactly what I had in mind. Now let's do this again. This time I want to begin with Baltimore, Maryland, and now it is a *yes*.'

The exercise is repeated several times. Students learn that Mrs Stern has grouped the cities on the basis of their relationship to waterways, natural resources, ethnic composition and several other dimensions.

The students are beginning to see patterns in their data. Finally, Mrs Stern says:

'Now, each of you try to group the cities in a way that *you* think is important. Then take turns and lead us through this exercise, helping us to see which ones you place in which category. Then we'll discuss the ways we can look at cities and how we can use different categories for different purposes. Finally, we'll use the inductive model and you can see how many relationships you can find.'

Scenario 4

In Robin Lees' Year 8 English lesson, the pupils are given 20 sentences to compare. Each sentence is labelled either A or B. Examples of these sentences are as follows:

A The sun was an *orb of light*. **B** The sun shone brightly.

A The moon was a *diamond of the night*. **B** The moon looked like a diamond.

A *Ice-cold pain* stabbed at his heart. **B** It was a pain like frozen ice.

Individually, the pupils are told to scrutinize the sentences and to pay particular attention to the words in italics. They are also told that the A sentences are positive exemplars and that the B sentences are negative exemplars. They are also told that the positive exemplars have something in common in terms of the work they do in the sentence. The negative examples do not have these features.

Robin then asks the pupils to make notes about what they believe the exemplars have in common. Again, this is undertaken individually. Robin then presents more sets of examples and asks the pupils whether they still have the same idea. Examples continue to be presented until most of the pupils have an idea that they think will withstand questioning. Pupils are asked to raise their hands if they are sure they know what the sentences have in common. At that point, Robin asks individual pupils to provide their explanation. One pupil says: 'The B sentences are all very descriptive', another suggests that the sentences 'describe things as if they were other things'. Another pupil suggests that the A sentences 'are more accurate descriptions as they say what the things are like'.

Robin uses the ideas offered by the pupils to illuminate what a metaphor is and how it is used. He then provides the name of the concept (*metaphor*) and asks the pupils to agree on a definition. Robin concludes the lesson by asking the pupils to share their thinking about how they arrived at the concept and to describe how they used the information to arrive at a conclusion.

Concept attainment as a model of learning and teaching

Whereas *concept formation*, which is the basis of the inductive model described in the previous chapter, requires the students to decide the basis on which they will build categories, *concept attainment* requires a student to figure out the attributes of a category that is already formed in another person's mind by comparing and contrasting examples (called *exemplars*) that contain the characteristics (called *attributes*) of the concept with examples that do not contain those attributes.

Simultaneously, the students study their strategies for building and attaining concepts and using them.

To create such lessons, we need to have our category clearly in mind. Lori's were built around the category 'interjection' for 'average beginning readers' and a phonics concept for second year students.

The adjective

Let's think through building a unit on the concept *adjective*.

Adjectives are words, so we select some words that are adjectives (these become the positive exemplars) and some that are not (these become negative exemplars – the ones that do not have the attributes of the category *adjective*). We present the words to the students in pairs. Consider the following four pairs:

triumphant	triumph
large	chair
broken	laugh
painful	pain

It is probably best to present the words in sentences to provide more information, because adjectives function in the context of a sentence. So we generate sentences (or find them in books):

Yes— Our *triumphant* team returned home after winning the state championship.
No— After his *triumph*, Senator Jones gave a gracious speech.
Yes— The *large* truck backed slowly into the barn.
No— He sank gratefully into the *chair*.
Yes— The *broken* arm healed slowly.

No— His *laugh* filled the room.
Yes— The *painful* separation had to be endured.
No— He felt a sharp *pain* in his ankle.

To carry on the model, we need about 20 pairs in all – we would need more pairs of positive and negative exemplars if the concept were more complex than our current example of *adjective*. Usually people have to compare and contrast about seven pairs before an idea about the category begins to emerge. The study of another seven consolidates the idea – or it may be rejected with the further information and the student will have to review all 14.

We begin the process by asking the students to scrutinize the sentences and to pay particular attention to the words in italics. Then we instruct them to compare and contrast the functions of the positive and negative exemplars: 'The positive exemplars have something in common in the work they do in the sentence. The negative exemplars do different work.'

We ask the students to make notes about what they believe the exemplars have in common. Then we present more sets of exemplars and ask them whether they still have the same idea. If not, we ask what they now think. We continue to present exemplars until most of the students have an idea they think will withstand scrutiny. At that point, we ask one of the students to share his or her idea and how he or she arrived at it. One possible response is as follows: 'Well, at first I thought that the positive words were longer. Then some of the negatives were longer, so I gave that idea up. Now, I think that the positive ones always come next to some other word and do something to it. I'm not sure just what.'

Then other students share their ideas. We provide some more examples. Gradually, the students agree that each positive exemplar adds something to the meaning of a word that stands for an object or a person, or qualifies it in some way.

We continue by providing some more sentences and by asking the students to identify the words that belong to our concept. When they can do that, we provide them with the name of the concept (*adjective*) and ask them to agree on a definition.

The final activity is to ask the students to describe their thinking as they arrived at the concepts and to share how they used the information that was given.

For homework, we ask the students to find adjectives in a short story we assign them to read. We will then examine the exemplars they come up with to be sure that they have a clear picture of the concept.

This process ensures that the students learn the attributes that define a concept (the defining attributes) and can distinguish those from other important attributes that do not form the definition. All the words, for example, are composed of letters, but the presence of letters does not define the part of speech. Letters are important characteristics of all items in the dataset, but are not critical in defining the category known as *adjective*. The students learn that it is the function of the word that is the essence of the concept, not what it denotes. *Pain* and *painful* both refer to trauma, but only one is an adjective.

Applying the concept to writing is obviously another important part of the transfer process – putting the concept to work knowledgeably.

The dreadful silent 'e'

Now let's think through another example where a teacher leads students into an understanding of the process.

The teacher presents 6-year-old children with the following list of words labelled *yes* or *no*:

fat (*yes*)	fate (*no*)
mat (*yes*)	mate (*no*)
rat (*yes*)	rate (*no*)

'I have a list of words here. Notice that some have *yes* by them and some have *no* by them. [Children observe and comment on the format. Teacher puts the list aside for a moment.] Now, I have an idea in my head and I want you to try to guess what I'm thinking of. Remember the list I showed you. [Picks up the list.] This will help you guess my idea because each of these is a clue. The clues work this way: if a word has a *yes* by it [points to first word], then it is an example of what I'm thinking. If it has a *no* by it, then it is not an example.'

The teacher continues to work with the children so that they understand the procedures of the lesson and then turns over the task of working out the concept to them.

Teacher: 'Can you come up with a name for my idea? Do you know what my idea is?' [The children decide what they think the teacher's idea is. She continues the lesson.]

Teacher: 'Let's see if your idea is correct by testing it. I'll give you some examples and you tell me if they are a *yes* or a *no*, based on your idea.' [She gives them more examples. This time the children supply the *nos* and *yeses*.]

cat (*yes*)	kite (*no*)
hat (*yes*)	hate (*no*)

'Well, you seem to have it. Now think up some words you believe are yeses. The rest of us will tell you whether your example is right. You tell us if we guessed correctly.' [The exercise ends with the children generating their own examples and telling how they arrived at the concept.]

In this lesson, if the children simply identified the concept as the *at* vowel–consonant phonogram and correctly recognized *cat* and *hat* as a *yes*, they have attained the concept on a simple level. If they verbalized the distinguishing features (essential attributes) of the *at* sound, they attained the concept on a more advanced level. There are different levels of attainment: correctly distinguishing examples from non-examples is easier than verbalizing the attributes of the concept. Students will probably be able to distinguish examples correctly before they will be able to explain verbally either the concept name or its essential characteristics.

Terms

We have used terms such as *exemplar* and *attribute* to describe categorizing activity and concept attainment. Each term has a special meaning and function in all forms of conceptual learning.

Exemplars are a subset of a collection of data or a dataset. The category is the subset or collection of samples that share one or more characteristics that are missing in the others. It is by comparing the positive exemplars and contrasting them with the negative ones that the concept or category is learned.

Attributes are features of the data. Nations, for example, have areas with agreed-on boundaries, people and governments that can deal with other nations. Cities have boundaries, people and governments also, but they cannot independently deal with other countries. Distinguishing nations from cities depends on locating the attribute of international relations.

Essential attributes are those that are critical to the domain under consideration. Exemplars of a category have many other attributes that may not be relevant to the category itself. For example, nations have trees and flowers also, but these are not relevant to the definition of nation; although they, too, represent important domains and can also be categorized and subcategorized. However, with respect to the category *nation*, trees and flowers are not essential.

Once a category is established, it is named so that we can refer to it symbolically. As the students name the categories, they should do so in terms of attributes. Thus in the scenario at the very beginning of the chapter, they will describe the category as words beginning with *cl* and *sounding like* [imagine the sound of *cl* at the beginning of a word]. Then if there is a technical term (*adjective* in one of our earlier examples), we supply it. However, the concept attainment process is not one of guessing names. It is used to get the attributes of a category clear. Then the name can be created or supplied. Thus the name is merely the term given to a category. *Fruit, dog, government, ghetto* are all names given to a class of experiences, objects, configurations or processes. Although the items commonly grouped together in a single category may differ from one another in certain respects (dogs, for example, vary greatly), the common features cause them to be referred to by the same general term.

Often we teach ideas that students already know intuitively without knowing the name itself. For instance, young children often put pictures of fruit together for the reason that they are 'all things you can eat'. They are using one characteristic to describe the concept instead of the name or label. If students know a concept, however, they can easily learn the name for it and their verbal expression will be more articulate. Part of knowing a concept is recognizing positive instances of it and also distinguishing closely related, but negative, examples. Just knowing terms will not suffice for this. Many people know the terms *metaphor* and *simile* but have never clarified the attributes of each well enough to tell them apart or apply them in their own writing. One cannot knowingly employ metaphoric language without a clear understanding of its attributes.

Multiple attributes are another consideration in clarifying concepts. Concepts range from cases in which the mere presence of a single attribute is sufficient for membership in a category to those in which the presence of several attributes is necessary. Membership in the category *boy* requires maleness and youth. Membership in the category *red-haired boy* requires the presence of maleness, youth and red hair. *Intelligent, gregarious, athletic red-haired boys* is a concept that requires the presence of several attributes simultaneously.

In literature, social studies and science we deal with numerous concepts that are defined by the presence of multiple attributes and sometimes attribute value is a consideration also. Consider the theatrical concept *romantic comedy*. A positive example must be a play or film, must have enough humorous values to qualify as a comedy and must be romantic as well. Negative exemplars include plays that are neither funny nor romantic, are funny but not romantic and are romantic but not funny.

To teach a concept we have to be very clear about its defining attributes and about whether attribute values are a consideration. We must also select our negative exemplars so that items with some but not all the attributes can be ruled out.

Let's close this inquiry with another dataset developed by Lori Kindrachuk.

Lori's third set

This time we will ask *you* to look at lists of positive and negative exemplars and draw your own conclusions about the concept.

Here are her notes about the concept. We have omitted her definition.

Focus statement

In this lesson all of the positive exemplars (yeses) have a common attribute. As you read each sentence, focus on its content and the information it provides.

And, now, the sets of positive and negative exemplars:

Concept attainment lesson positive exemplars

1   It was October 31, 1997 and Danny knew he had the best Halloween costume ever.
2   In 2001, Valentine's Day fell on a Friday and Joanne had her cards ready to deliver the night before.
3   Easter Sunday, 1952, fell on April 14th, giving Sam five more days to finish decorating the eggs.
4   Mark had just celebrated his twelfth birthday, January 29, 1999, the same day as the super bowl game.
5   The spring of 1981 was hot and dry; June 7th, graduation day was no exception.
6   On a Saturday morning, in August of 1862, he left on his first trip.
7   Cold, damp and wet that was March of 1965.

The first seven sentences name specific dates and times

Negative exemplars paired with the positive ones above

8   The day after Pearl Harbor had been hit, the air was still filled with smoke from the fires.

9   As he read the headline he realized the *Titanic* had gone down the day before yesterday.

10 The church service this morning marked one year since the events of 911.

11 This devastating time in America became known as the Civil War.

12 As Hitler's forces pressed forward, Cal listened to the reports each day, wishing he were old enough to join the fight.

13 After the crash of the stockmarket, times were tough; they were surviving the years that would become known as the 'dirty 30s'.

14 Tom had always wanted to be a pilot, last summer a man had walked on the moon for the first time, who knew what the future would hold.

Positives

15 Jake sat down in front of the computer and scanned his email.

16 The crowd roared as the gladiator entered the arena on a chariot trimmed with gold.

17 Mark's new iPod had been stolen out of his locker last week.

18 The covered wagon would be their home during the long trip to the new settlement.

19 With cell phone in one hand and snowboard in the other, Tanis made her way towards the hill.

20 Interplanetary travel was still quite new and they hadn't yet worked out all of the kinks in the booking system.

21 They had arrived by horse and carriage the night before, as it was the fastest and most comfortable way he could think of to get the entire family home.

Negative exemplars

1   Sarah was taller than her sister but they shared the same red hair and freckles.

2   The child in the picture wore a bright blue dress and had ribbons in her hair.

3   June's favourite band was going to play for the dance.

4   He knew that he should help put out the fire, but he couldn't seem to move.

5   She was his second cousin and they had always been good friends.

6   Mrs Thompson worked in the store and taught piano lessons in her spare time.

7   If they won the game, they would advance to the semi-final.

Positives

8   Last month they saw each other three times.

9   She had talked to him yesterday.

10   Two more weeks until the big day!

11   She had only heard the news 3 days before.

12   In 2 more hours the celebration would begin.

13   They were still 15 minutes away from the nearest help.

14   During half-time the players would discuss a new strategy.

Negatives

15   The sale will be 3 weeks from Saturday.

16   The deal was final at midnight on the 25th.

17   They would attend the lessons the next three Wednesdays in a row.

18   March, April and May were her favourite months.

19   They always had fish for supper on Friday.

20   Autumn always brought the smells of pumpkin pie and decaying leaves.

21   Next spring they planned to start building their new home.

Well, what did you find? What do you think the concept is? Share with someone and see if you agree with one another.

What *are* the major attributes of the category?

5 Learning to think metaphorically with synectics

"Of all the models, synectics has got to give the most immediate pleasure when you're leading the exercises. We've been teaching kids (both elementary and secondary) to lead synectics. I have to admit that I always have a little touch of green when I turn it over to them, because they're going to have the fun, now."

Letter from Bruce Joyce to Bill Gordon

Now that we are learning to form and attain concepts, we consider how we can broaden our understandings and learn to build ideas and language by building metaphors. The processes of synectics are developed from a set of assumptions about the psychology of creativity:

- First, by bringing the creative process to consciousness and by developing explicit aids to creativity, we can directly increase the creative capacity of both individuals and groups.
- A second assumption is that the 'emotional component is more important than the intellectual, the irrational more important than the rational' (Gordon, 1961: 6). Creativity is the development of new mental patterns. Non-rational interplay leaves room for open-ended thoughts that can lead to a mental state in which new ideas are possible. The basis for decisions, however, is always the rational. The analogistic state is the best mental environment for exploring and expanding ideas, but it is not a decision-making stage. Gordon does not undervalue the linear intellect; he assumes that a logic is used in decision making and that technical competence is necessary to the formation of ideas in many areas. But he believes that creativity is essentially an *emotional* process, one that requires elements of irrationality and emotion to enhance intellectual processes. Much problem solving is rational and intellectual, but by adding the irrational we increase the likelihood that we will generate fresh ideas.
- The third assumption is that the 'emotional, irrational elements must be understood in order to increase the probability of success in a problem solving situation' (Gordon, 1961: 1). In other words, the analysis of certain irrational and emotional processes can help the individual and the group increase their creativity by using irrationality constructively. Aspects of the

irrational can be understood and consciously controlled. Achievement of this control, through the deliberate use of metaphor and analogy, is the object of synectics.

Scenario: Lisa Mueller introduces third graders to synectics

Day one

Lisa has conducted two sessions with the students using 'stretching' exercises where they have been introduced to direct, personal and compressed conflict analogies. Now she begins by asking them to study the picture in Figure 5.1. Lisa says: 'We are going to study this picture for these 3 days. As you study this picture, what are the major things that are going on in it?'

Figure 5.1 Boat picture

Some of their responses are as follows:

'There are people pushing very hard …'

'It is on a beach – they are pushing a boat onto the beach –'

'It looks very hot …'.

Lisa adds that the people are dressed for the weather.

'They are pushing the boat on to the shore …'

'There are leaves on the sand ...'.

'It looks like hard work ...'

'They are leaning really hard ...'

'There is teamwork ...'

Now, at the end of this first session, Lisa asks the students to write whatever ideas are most in their mind at this time.

The students try to write – something. Here are some of their products at the end of Day one:

'People are pushing.'

'The water is on the beach.'

''The water is shiny.'

'Men pushing a boat together.'

In sum, the students are describing what they see *in literal terms*.

Day two

Now Lisa opens up the metaphorical dimension – trying to make synectics accessible to the students. 'We will begin with direct analogies – I will ask you questions like "How is a teacher like a computer?" 'Then, we will explore personal analogies. I will ask you questions like "How do you feel as tennis balls when the day is over and you are put back in the can?" '

'Let's go — 'How is a cracker like toast?'

The students respond with 'Crunchy.' 'Bits of stuff.' And other remarks.

'How is a videotape like a book?'

The students respond with 'They have stories in them.' 'They unwind in your head.' And other comments.

Lisa continues to ask the students to create analogies, working within analogies that are relatively easy to generate.

'How is a spoon like a shovel?' 'How is a rose like a cactus?'

And, then she moved to personal analogies, such as 'Now, become a pencil. Pencils, you have to write a laundry list. How do you feel?'

'Scared.'

'I have to use my head to write with ...'

'It hurts to write.'

'How is a traffic light like an alarm clock?'

'It gets you going.'

'They both tell time.'

'How is an earring like a Christmas ornament?' 'How is a button like a nail?' 'How is riding an elevator like climbing a tree?'
Lisa continues with personal analogies:

'Be a cellphone.'

'What would you like to control?'

'If you could pick a ring tone, what would you pick?'

'Who would you want talking on you?'

The students respond with a variety of thoughts as they are being brought into a metaphoric stance:

'I control the world.'

'I want to play my own rap.'

'I want to talk to my friends, but I'd like to say a few things to the PM.'

Then Lisa switches back to direct analogies: 'How is tying your shoes like locking the front door?'

'They are both like locking something up.'

'How is a map like a skeleton?'

'It looks like one. Like the body of a place.'

And, then, Lisa closes the session: 'Tomorrow, we will take all these words and do something else with them.'

Day three

Lisa has prepared a display that shows the words that have been generated during Day two. She warms the students up with a few direct and personal analogy stems and then asks them to try to generate compressed conflicts from the words that have been generated. [In a previous session, she has taught the students the concept of compressed conflicts in concept attainment lessons.]
Lisa gives the students a few examples:

beautiful nightmare
silent sound
honest liar

Then she says: 'Today we are going to learn to make some of these and use them to guide our writing. First, let's play with analogies a bit. How is a turtle like a helmet?'

'Shells and helmets protect something.'

'How is a recipe like a jogging trail?'

'You can use both to get somewhere.'

'How is the moon like a mirror?'

'They both shine.'

And now she asks the students to generate compressed conflicts. 'Now, I want you to look at all of the words we came up with yesterday [these are displayed on a chart] and look for ones that don't quite fit together.'

Here are some of the products:

happy hurt

tickly hard

noisily bored

crazy wind

crazy control

crumbly shelter

crazy energy

tired energy

correct mistake

delicate metal

And, then Lisa says: 'Now, I want you to think of the ones that have the most tension between them – that don't fit together.'

After some discussion, 'tired energy' is selected and Lisa says: 'Now, I want you to write about this picture again – using tired energy.'

And they do. Here are some of the products:

'Tired energy fits with the picture because if people push the boat on the shore it looks heavy.'

'The men are out of energy because they are working hard.'

'First they have energy and then they use all the energy.'

'The men are tired because they are pushing so hard.'

In sum

Lisa is just beginning to teach the students to think in analogies. However, even in this first training exercise, you can see that the students have moved from fragmentary descriptions of the scene to the development of sentences built around the compressed conflict. An increase in fluency and conceptualization is a typical outcome even of the early experiences with the metaphoric way of thinking. The students generated 2.8 sentences in the second writing, compared with 1.6 in the first descriptive passages.

Scenario: Abramowitz class – experienced with synectics

Abramowitz's seventh grade class is preparing a campaign in opposition to a change in Forest Service regulations that would permit a large grove of redwood trees to be cut down as part of a lumbering operation. They have made posters that they intend to display around their community and send to the members of the state legislature. They have the rough sketches for the posters and their captions, and they are examining them.

'Well, what do you think?' asks Priscilla.

'Well, they're OK', says Tommy. 'They sure say where we stand. Actually, though, I think they're a little dull.'

'So do I', adds Maryann. 'A couple of them are OK, but the others are real preachy and stiff.'

'There's nothing really wrong with them', chimes in another, 'they're just not very zingy.'

'Also, they don't build any bridges with our opponents. They present our side, but I'm not sure they'll reach anybody but people who already agree with us.'

After some discussion, it is obvious that nearly everybody feels the same way. They decide that two or three of the posters are well designed and convey their message, but they need some others that would be more poignant.

'Let's try synectics', suggests one of them.

'With pictures and captions?' asks one of the other children. 'I thought we could only use synectics with poetry. Can we use synectics with stuff like this?'

'Why sure we can', says Priscilla. 'I don't know why I didn't think of it. We've been doing it with poetry all year long.'

'Well, we sure have nothing to lose', adds Tommy. 'How would it work?'

'Well', says Priscilla, 'we could see these posters we've done as the beginning point and then go through a synectics training exercise and see if it gives us some ideas for pictures and captions. We could think of redwood trees in terms of various personal and direct analogies and compressed conflicts.'

'Well let's try it', chimes in George.

'Let's start right now', says Sally. 'We could go through our exercises and then have lunchtime to think about the posters.'

'Can I be the leader?' asks Nancy. 'I've got some super ideas for some stretching exercises.'

'Is that OK?' says Priscilla.

The others agree and Nancy begins.

'How is a redwood tree like a toothpick?' she asks.

'You use the tree to pick the teeth of the gods,' laughs George. Everyone joins in the laughter and they are off.

It's clear that Mr Abramowitz has spent enough time using synectics that the students internalized the process and purpose. They can proceed on their own, drawing on the model when they find it helpful.

A metaphoric model of learning

Gordon grounds synectics in four ideas that challenge conventional views about creativity. First, creativity is important in everyday activities. Most of us associate the creative process with the development of great works of art or music or perhaps with a clever new invention. Gordon emphasizes creativity as a part of our daily work and leisure lives. His model is designed to increase problem-solving capacity, creative expression, empathy and insight into social relations. He also stresses that the meanings of ideas can be enhanced through creative activity by helping us see things more richly.

Second, the creative process is not at all mysterious. It can be described and it is possible to train people directly to increase their creativity. Traditionally, creativity is viewed as a mysterious, innate and personal capacity that can be destroyed if its processes are probed too deeply. In contrast, Gordon believes that if individuals understand the *basis* of the creative process, they can learn to use that understanding to increase the creativity with which they live and work, independently and as members of groups. Gordon's view that creativity is enhanced by conscious analysis led him to describe it and create training procedures that can be applied in schools and other settings.

Third, creative invention is similar in all fields – the arts, the sciences, engineering – and is characterized by the same underlying intellectual processes. This idea is contrary to common belief. In fact, to many people, creativity is confined to the arts. In engineering and the sciences, however, it is simply called by another name: *invention*. Gordon maintains that the link between generative thinking in the arts and in the sciences is quite strong.

Gordon's fourth assumption is that individual and group invention (creative thinking) are very similar. Individuals and groups generate ideas and products in much the same fashion. Again, this is very different from the stance that creativity is an intensely personal experience, not to be shared.

The creative state and the synectics process: Metaphoric activity

Through the metaphoric activity of the synectics model, creativity becomes a conscious process. Metaphors establish a relationship of likeness, the comparison of one object or idea with another object or idea by using one in place of the other.

Through these substitutions the creative process occurs, connecting the familiar with the unfamiliar or creating a new idea from familiar ideas.

Metaphor introduces conceptual distance between the people and the object or subject matter and prompts original thoughts. For example, by asking students to think of their textbook as an old shoe or as a river, we provide a structure, a metaphor, with which the students can think about something familiar in a new way. Conversely, we can ask students to think about a new topic, say the human body, in an old way by asking them to compare it to the transportation system. Metaphoric activity thus depends on and draws from the students' knowledge, helping them connect ideas from familiar content to those from new content or view familiar content from a new perspective. Synectics strategies using metaphoric activity are designed, then, to provide a structure through which people can free themselves to develop imagination and insight into everyday activities. Three types of analogy are used as the basis of synectics exercises: personal analogy, direct analogy and compressed conflict.

Personal analogies

To make personal analogies requires students to empathize with the ideas or objects to be compared. Students must feel they have become part of the physical elements of the problem. The identification may be with a person, plant, animal or nonliving thing. For example, students may be instructed: 'Be an automobile engine. What do you feel like? Describe how you feel when you are started in the morning; when your battery goes dead; when you come to a stoplight.'

The essence of personal analogy is on empathetic involvement. Gordon gives the example of a problem situation in which the chemist personally identifies with the molecules in action. He might ask, 'How would I feel if I were a molecule?' and then feel himself being part of the 'stream of dancing molecules'. Making personal analogies requires loss of self as one transports oneself into another space or object. The greater the conceptual distance created by loss of self, the more likely it is that the analogy is new and that the students have been creative or innovative. Gordon identifies four levels of involvement in personal analogizing:

1 *First-person description of facts.* The person recites a list of well-known facts but presents no new way of viewing the object or animal and shows no empathetic involvement. In terms of the car engine, the person might say: 'I feel greasy.' 'I feel hot.'

2 *First-person identification with emotion.* The person recites common emotions but does not present new insights: 'I feel powerful' [as the car engine].

3 *Empathetic identification with a living thing.* The student identifies emotionally and kinaesthetically with the subject of the analogy: 'When you smile like that, I smile all over.'

4 *Empathetic identification with a nonliving object.* This level requires the most commitment. The person sees himself or herself as an inorganic object and

tries to explore the problem from a sympathetic point of view: 'I feel exploited. I cannot determine when I start and stop. Someone does that for me' [as the car engine].

The purpose of introducing these levels of personal analogy is not to identify forms of metaphoric activity but to provide guidelines for how well conceptual distance has been established. Gordon believes that the usefulness of analogies is directly proportional to the distance created. The greater the distance, the more likely the student is to come up with new ideas.

Direct analogies

Direct analogy is the comparison of two objects or concepts. The comparison does not have to be identical in all respects. Its function is simply to transpose the conditions of the real topic or problem situation to another situation in order to present a new view of an idea or problem. This involves identification with a person, plant, animal or nonliving thing. Gordon cites the experience of the engineer watching a shipworm tunnelling into a timber. As the worm ate its way into the timber by constructing a tube for itself and moving forward, the engineer, Sir Marce Isambard Brunel, got the notion of using caissons to construct underwater tunnels (Gordon 1961: 40–1). Another example of direct analogy occurred when a group was attempting to devise a can with a top that could be used to cover the can once it had been opened. In this instance, the analogy of the peapod gradually emerged, which produced the idea of a seam placed a distance below the top of the can, thus permitting a removable lid.

Compressed conflicts

The third metaphorical form is compressed conflict, generally a two-word phrase in which the words seem to contradict one another. *Tiredly aggressive* and *friendly foe* are two examples. Gordon's examples are *life-saving destroyer* and *nourishing flame*. He also cites Pasteur's expression, 'safe attack'. Compressed conflicts, according to Gordon, provide the broadest insight into a new subject. They reflect the student's ability to incorporate two frames of reference with respect to a single object. The greater the distance between frames of reference, the greater the mental flexibility.

Direct analogies are elicited with questions that ask for a direct comparison, such as:

An orange is like what living thing?

How is a school like a salad?

How are polar bears like frozen yogurt?

Which is softer – a whisper or a kitten's fur?

Personal analogies are elicited by asking people to pretend to be an object, action, idea or event, such as:

> Be a cloud. Where are you? What are you doing?

> How do you feel when the sun comes out and dries you up?

> Pretend you are your favourite book. Describe yourself.

> What are your three wishes?

Compressed conflict practice is elicited by presenting some questions and asking people to manipulate them, such as:

> How is a computer shy and aggressive?

> What machine is like a smile and a frown?

Broadening our perspective of a concept

Abstract ideas such as culture, prejudice and economy are difficult to internalize because we cannot see them in the same way we can see a table or building, yet we frequently use them in our language. Synectics is a good way to make a familiar idea 'strange' and thereby obtain another perspective on it.

We have found that synectics can be used with all ages, although with very young children it is best to stick to stretching exercises. Beyond this, adjustments are the same as for any other approach to teaching – take care to work within their experience, make rich use of concrete materials, attentive pacing and pay attention to pacing and explicit outlining of procedures.

The model often works effectively with students who withdraw from more 'academic' learning activities because they are not willing to risk being wrong. Conversely, high-achieving students who are only comfortable giving a response they are sure is 'right' often feel reluctant to participate. We believe that for these reasons alone, synectics is valuable to everyone.

Synectics combines easily with other models. It can stretch concepts being explored with the information processing family; open up dimensions of social issues explored through role playing, group investigation, or jurisprudential thinking; and expand the richness of problems and feelings opened up by other models in the personal family.

The most effective use of synectics develops over time. It has short-term results in stretching views of concepts and problems, but when students are exposed to it repeatedly, they can learn how to use it with increasing skill – and they learn to enter a metaphoric mode with increasing ease and completeness.

Using synectics in the curriculum

Synectics is designed to increase the creativity of both individuals and groups. Sharing the synectics experience can build a feeling of community among students.

Students learn about their fellow classmates as they watch them react to an idea or problem. Thoughts are valued for their potential contribution to the group process, while synectics procedures help create a community of equals in which simply having a thought is the sole basis for status. This norm and that of playfulness quickly give support to even the most timid participant.

Synectics procedures may be used with students in all areas of the curriculum, the sciences as well as the arts. They can be applied to both teacher–student discussion in the classroom and to teacher-made materials for the students. The products or vehicles of synectics activity need not always be written: they can be oral, or they can take the form of role plays, paintings and graphics or simply changes in behaviour.

Scenario: following an individual

Devin: seeking metaphors in the familiar

This scenario was developed by Dixie K. Keyes (Keyes 2006) whose excellent study of the processes by which teachers and students work their ways into metaphoric ways of thinking gives us new insight into Bill Gordon's ways of thinking and working.

Devin plays soccer and he is very successful at it. His name is often heard over the intercom during second period announcements as the high scorer for our high school team. Devin is not so successful in writing; he often takes half the class to simply forget distractions so he can concentrate on the topic at hand. Once he sparks with a clever idea, he writes quickly and even stays after class to finish. As good athletes often do, he has a drive to be successful. As the class brainstormed metaphors and their connections for the adversity essay, Devin had trouble with the 'connection column'. I guided him by asking him questions about soccer. (Does the other team intercept passes? Is dribbling down the field against the defence full of pressure? Is there stress to keep the ball? Do you look for opportunities to score?) The process of questioning allowed him to proceed in his writing, using his experience in soccer as a conceptual, metaphorical hook in which to discuss a difficult time in his life. Devin's strong relationship to soccer and his knowledge of the systems involved in playing a soccer game provided him that specific 'search pattern'. With only a few simple questions from my rudimentary knowledge of soccer, Devin actively began to write his essay. Soccer is a very visual game with a goal on each end of the field and a brightly clothed goalie protecting each one. The yardage stripes are bright white and serve as symbols for progression down the field. Besides those visual aspects, Devin had built up visual memories of specific instances during soccer games. He used these important experiences to detail his story of adversity. Note how Devin used soccer as a conceptual hook in the beginning of his essay:

> There's a lot of problems in life you have to deal with. Just when you think
> that everything is alright trouble comes and intercepts your good time. Just
> like in soccer, if you're making good passes and then the other team

> intercepts it you start feeling bad. It was just like that time my brother and me had to take care of my mom. We thought we were gonna do that forever.

Not only did Devin connect the idea of 'trouble' and 'feeling bad' with an interception during a soccer game, but he also related this feeling directly to a similar feeling during a difficult family situation. By using experiences in soccer, Devin developed a pattern throughout the rest of the essay, where, in subsequent paragraphs, Devin continued using the soccer 'peg' and images from soccer game events. In the second paragraph of his essay, he wrote:

> So me and my brother had to take care of her for 2 months. Right away I got real worried because it was going to be hard work. So the pressure was on us. I felt like the pressure you have when your playing soccer to not lose the ball.

He continued this pattern in the third paragraph:

> But my brother and me defended ourselves against adversity. We did everything possible to make it better for my mom. It sort of like when the other team in soccer has a free kick and you have to defend your goal. We didn't let adversity take over us.

Finally, in writing his conclusion he found a way to end optimistically, again taking on the attitude of a successful competitor in a soccer game.

> What I learned was that no matter if difficulties come your way, we should always look for options to score. Don't let anything put you down in life. It's going to be hard but you have to learn how to deal with problems. It's like in soccer: no matter if your opponents come your way, you have to keep on dribbling while looking for options to score.

Although the overarching conceptual metaphors, 'sport is a war' or 'life is a game', that seem to belong to Devin's metaphor are conventional, Devin used his metaphor unconventionally; his efforts were original, relying on his unique experiences. An example is Ross Perot's comment about America's high medical costs. 'We're buying a front row box seat and we're not even getting to see a bad show from the bleachers.' Although Perot's version is unconventional, the conventional metaphor for this linguistic expression is 'life is a sporting game'. Kövecses states: 'While it is easy to find unconventionalized metaphorical linguistic expressions that realize conventional conceptual metaphors, it is less easy to find unconventional conceptual metaphors for a given target domain' (2002: 31–2). Devin used the target of 'adversity', found his source domain (a soccer game) and used it in unconventional ways, mostly for the images soccer provided him and also for the conceptual peg to spatially describe the steps of progress he and his brother made in helping their mother. Those steps matched the steps of progression to a successful soccer game.

Another aspect found in Devin's conceptual metaphor is emotional value. Such phrases as 'feeling bad', 'the pressure was on us' and 'we defended ourselves against adversity' suggest emotions about this incident, just as there are emotional occurrences in the game of soccer.

Conclusions: invention and cognition

Devin used the larger metaphor 'adversity is like the game of soccer' to find the specific metaphorical ideas for each paragraph of his essay. His understanding and reflection of his own personal growth during the time he took care of his mother developed through his experiences with soccer. He seemed to be reaching for feelings of success and achievement as he described how he and his brother worked hard to ensure their mother's safekeeping during her illness. Because of success in his specialty sport, he had a conceptual peg that assisted him in detailing the events of an adverse time in his life. Devin wanted others to empathize with his plight, to feel the pressure of his situation. He believes everyone loves soccer as he does; therefore, soccer was his vehicle for sharing his narrative of adversity. His is not the only activity to be a metaphoric peg. In an unlikely example, Johnson writes of a hooker who justified her actions on the streets. Just as the hooker tried to 'justify herself morally in terms of the values and practices of her culture', Devin tried to share his story to 'resolve an indeterminate situation' to share how he solved a problem and to set the 'standards of narrative explanation' so the community around him could understand. Since several of Devin's English classmates play soccer, he knew they would react affirmatively to his writing.

Reflections

Participation in a synectics group invariably creates a unique shared experience that fosters interpersonal understanding and a sense of community. Members learn about one another as each person reacts to the common event in his or her unique way. Individuals become acutely aware of their dependence on the various perceptions of other group members. Each thought, no matter how prosaic, is valued for its potential catalytic effect on one's own thoughts.

6 Learning to read and write with the picture–word inductive model

"It's inquiry, INQUIRY, INQUIRY! Do I sound like a broken record? We must have students inquire into how language works. Thelen was right! It's inquiry, not activity!"

Emily Calhoun to Bruce Joyce, for the thousandth time.

The picture–word inductive model (PWIM) focuses on learning to read and write through inquiry. Teaching the students how to learn to read gives them the key to learn the culture, to reach into its writings, to succeed not just in school, which it does. Notice the difference between trying to teach reading and teaching the students how to teach themselves. They have a lot to learn about learning to read, but when they possess it, wow!

Scenario 1: Lisa teaches with PWIM and studies the effects

We are in Lisa Mueller's first grade class in the Vera M. Welsh Elementary School in the town of Lac La Biche, included in the Northern Lights School Division #69 in Alberta, Canada. This narrative is taken from Lisa's log, which describes a picture–word inductive model (PWIM) cycle in which her 23 students were engaged for 22 sessions, each 50 minutes long, during the second month of school: October 2–30.

The picture in Figure 6.1 shows a carriage entering a street in front of Buckingham Palace. At the beginning of the cycle, Lisa asks the students to study the picture and take turns identifying items and actions: 'You have had a couple of days to look at the picture and identify things in it and things that are going on. Let's take turns putting words to some of the things you have found.' As each item is named, Lisa draws a line from the item to a place on the background paper where she prints the word, spells it and then has the students spell it and say it. The students review the words frequently, spelling them, saying them and tracing the line from the word to the picture, learning how to use the chart as a picture dictionary. During the first session, 24 words are 'shaken out' of the picture.

These words are tapped into a computer and printed out on cards, a set of which is given to each child. Three activities alternate during the next few days. One

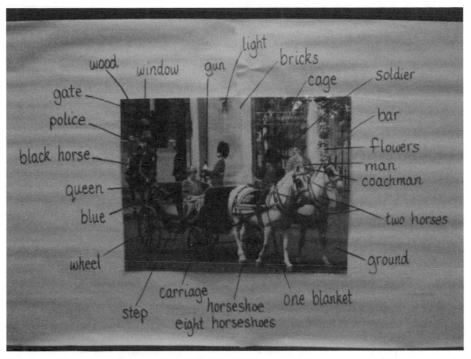

Figure 6.1 Buckingham Palace

is review of the words as a class, looking at the PWIM chart, selecting a word, tracing it to the element in the picture to which it refers, spelling the word and then moving on to another word. 'Look at your cards, one by one. If you can say the word on a card, then look at the picture chart, find the word, trace it to the picture and make sure you are right.' Second, each student looks at the cards, decides whether they recognize the word correctly and, if not, goes to the PWIM chart to figure it out. Third, the students classify the words, manipulating their cards into groups containing common attributes. 'Look carefully at the words. Then make groups of ones that have something in common.' During classification, several categories of word family emerge, particularly words with common endings. Singulars and plurals also emerge (e.g. *horse* and *horses*). Lisa prints some of those categories on large cards and the students discuss what they have in common and think of other words that might fit into the categories – an additional 16 words appear (among them *to*, *two* and *too*, *slight*, *might*, *tight* and *night*).

At the beginning of the second week of the PWIM cycle, the children are asked to generate titles for the picture: 'I'm going to show you some other pictures and titles I've made for them. Then I want you to make up a title for our picture. Try to make a title that would help a visitor find our picture from among the other pictures in the room.' Lisa models some sample titles and asks the students to examine the titles of several books as further models. Each student creates a title, which is printed on newsprint. Fourteen words are added to the list and more families of words are discovered (e.g. *as*, *marching*, *pulling*, *watching*) as the students continue to classify their words. Throughout the second week, the children continue to study the words, using the picture–word dictionary and classifying the words on their word cards.

At the beginning of the third week, Lisa presents a series of sentences she has written about the picture, modelling several sentence structures (e.g. 'We found a _____ in the picture'. During the week the students dictate their own sentences, using the words they shook out of the picture plus other words that are needed to make sentences (e.g. *the*). Altogether, 16 more words were identified as the sentences were dictated by the children, many of them 'little useful words' (e.g. *is, are, by* and *from*).

One week after the words are shaken out, Lisa and her teaching assistant, Cecile, check the students' knowledge of the words out of the context of the picture (or titles or sentences) by presenting the words to the students on cards where only one word appears. Nine students could read correctly between 11 and 17 of the words. Six students identified only between one and seven correctly at the end of the week.

In week three, the students continue to study the words and read the sentences. At the end of the week, Lisa and Cecile test the recognition of the words again. During that week there was a considerable gain in words recognized – most students were able to read 20 or more. Only one student showed no improvement. Most students were able to read the titles and sentences without assistance.

During the last week Lisa selects one of the titles and constructs a paragraph using modifications of the sentences the students had created (see Figure 6.2). The paragraph was printed on a card programme, making a booklet the students could take home and read to their parents.

Figure 6.2 Lisa checking child

Studying student learning

During the 2000–2001 school year, Lisa conducted several studies, including sight word acquisition and retention, an analysis of the degree to which high frequency words were included in the body of words, the development of phonetic and structural analysis skills, books read independently and reading levels attained.

Sight words learned

Altogether, as a class, the students encountered 1,029 words during the year, aside from the words encountered by individuals in their reading. Of these, 377 words came from the initial weeks of the PWIM cycles. Retention of those words was assessed in May and again in September. On average, the students recognized 91 per cent of the words in out-of-context assessments in May and in September. The lowest student retained 59 per cent.

Sight words learned as 'high-frequency' words

Lisa tested the students' recognition of the Dolch lists of the high frequency words appearing in typical books through third grade. On average, the students recognized 87 per cent of the words, with a range of 49 to 100 per cent. Fifteen of the 22 students recognized 90 per cent of the words or more. This finding has importance because this curriculum does not introduce the sight words systematically according to predetermined lists. Despite that, the high-frequency words appear regularly, which is logical, and these first grade students appear to be learning them at a good rate.

Skill in phonics

PWIM does not introduce phonetic skills one at a time in a predetermined manner. The students analyse words and develop phonics concepts inductively or are led by the teacher to explore beginning and ending sounds and structural properties of words as words containing those attributes are encountered. In May, Lisa administered the names test to the students. (In the test, the students try to decode unfamiliar words that, among them, contain all the basic combinations.) A perfect score on the test indicates that all basic letter–sound relationships have been used correctly when decoding the words. The average score was 81 per cent. The lowest was 62 per cent. Four students scored 95 per cent or better. This picture is considerably better than the typical performance of first grade classes assessed in this manner.

Levels of reading achieved

By the end of the year, 22 students who had been enrolled throughout the year were administered the Alberta Diagnostic Test, which provided estimates of reading achievement in terms of grade levels. Twelve of the students were well above the 'ending grade' level. Two were at the mid-sixth grade level, three at mid-fourth grade, six at beginning of third grade and two at the end of second grade level. Six scored at ending first grade or beginning of second grade and three at the mid-first grade level. The average was a little above the ending of second grade level, where typical exiting second grade students score.

Lisa Mueller is a very fine teacher/researcher, teaching strongly, learning new models of teaching and how to use them and studying student progress. In addition to the studies discussed here, she also studied the amounts of books read by her students during the year – remembering that many of these are at the 'picture story' book level, no student read fewer than two books a week and some as many as five.

In Chapter 8, we will discuss a study where PWIM was used as one of the central components to help students from fourth to twelfth grade who are struggling readers (essentially beginning readers). Then, in Chapter 15, we will discuss another study where PWIM was used to turn around low levels of reading in several schools in the Canadian district where Lisa Mueller was working.

Rationale: the picture–word inductive model

Let's begin with a series of propositions.

First, children learn to listen and speak the languages spoken to them in a most natural way. In an Arabic-speaking household, they learn to hear and reproduce Arabic; they would learn French in a French household. In homes where large vocabularies and complex syntaxes are used, they develop large vocabularies and complex syntaxes. Importantly, the process is *natural*.

Second, inductive thinking is built into their brains. Children classify from birth, sorting out the world. They are natural conceptualizers. And they can get better at building concepts.

Third, they seek meaning. They want to understand their world by organizing what they perceive and they reach toward language as a source of meaning.

Fourth, interaction with adults and peers is the natural avenue to socialization. Interaction through reading is an important part of socialization as the young reader encounters information and ideas. The depth of socialization is enormously affected by literacy. Non-readers have a serious disadvantage in learning the culture and a serious deprivation of the pleasure that accompanies learning through interaction with authors.

All this is not to assert that reading and writing are natural biological processes, but it is to say that the natural ways children approach the learning of language can be capitalized on. A challenge for us is to design curriculums that will take advantage of these natural abilities so as to make the learning of reading and writing an extension of what our children are born to do naturally.

The PWIM was designed to meet this challenge and its conceptual underpinnings drew on the body of research about how literacy is acquired and on the bodies of research underlying several of the models of learning we have been describing in the previous chapters. Although the model addresses literacy across all the core academic curriculum areas, the concentration here will be on its application to the reading/writing curriculum in the early years of schooling. Later, we will discuss its use as a dimension of a successful curriculum for older students who have not responded well to the prevailing curriculums in the language arts.

The model was designed to be a major component of language arts curriculums for primary-level beginning readers and older beginning or early-stage readers. The core is to help students inquire into language and learn to build generalizations about how letters, words, phrases, sentences and longer text work together. The model also contains a number of tools to help teachers and students to study progress. In fact, using the PWIM effectively requires an action research frame of reference, for you don't just adopt or buy into the PWIM, you inquire into its theory and rationale, its structure and its effects on your students, including their learning how to learn.

Children's development of language

The model of learning is based on children's natural acquisition of language. By the time most children in developed countries are 5 years old they are able to listen to and speak between 4,000 and 6,000 words with understanding, and have developed the basic syntactical structure of the language (Chall 1983; Clark and Clark 1977). They can listen with understanding to complex sentences and longer communications. They produce sentences that include prepositions and conjunctions and make causal connections, such as: 'If we go to the store now, we could watch *Thomas* when we get back.' They gobble up words, play with them and have conversations with stuffed animals and dolls – composing ideas and manipulating words, as they will again later when they write. Children's natural acquisition of language is one of the most exciting inductions into their culture and brings with it a great sense of personal power and satisfaction. It is convenient to study PWIM in terms of cycles of inquiry that are built around pictures that bring information to the children.

The PWIM cycle begins when the students are presented with pictures of scenes that are understandable to them, although the pictures may have been taken in any number of settings and cultures. Studying the picture, the students 'shake out' the words from the picture by identifying objects, actions and qualities they recognize. A line is drawn from the object to the chart paper, where the word or phrase is written, thus connecting the items identified to words already in their naturally developed listening/speaking vocabularies as in the scenario in Lisa Mueller's lessons (see Figure 6.3).

These connections between the items and actions in the picture and the children's language enable them to make the transition naturally from spoken (listened to and spoken) language to written (read and written) language. They see these transformations. They watch the words being spelled and spell them with the teacher. They connect something in the picture with a word and then watch that

Figure 6.3 Traci Poirier

word appear in print. They can now read that word. Soon they will learn that we always spell that word the same way. They identify a dog in the picture, see *dog* written, hear it spelled, spell it themselves and on the way home from school they see a 'Lost dog' sign on the street corner and read 'dog'.

Thus, a major principle of the model is to build on children's growing storehouse of words and syntactic forms and to facilitate the transition to print. Most children want to 'make sense' of the language around them and they will engage with us eagerly in unlocking its mysteries. A corollary principle is that the approach respects the children's language development: their words are used and their ability to make connections is central.

The process of learning to read and write

Much remains to be learned about the almost magical process whereby children make connections between their naturally developing language and the world of print – surely a cognitive marvel. Our understanding at this time is that several types of learning need to be accomplished as reading and writing develop.

To learn to read and write, children need to *build a substantial 'sight' vocabulary* – that is, a storehouse of words they can recognize instantly by their spellings. About 400 to 500 words are necessary to bring children to the stage where picture story books are available to them, although, as we will see, even 100 to 150 words bring very simple books like *Go, Dog, Go* (Eastman 1961) and *Ten in the Bed* (Dale 1988) within reach. Also, once students have about 50 sight words their study of phonics is greatly facilitated, as are many other aspects of learning, including the development of more vocabulary (Graves 1992).

PWIM approaches this development of sight vocabulary directly. First, the students read and spell the words as they are 'shaken out' of the picture. Then, these words are placed on large vocabulary cards that they can look at and the teacher can use for group instruction. Students also get their own set of smaller vocabulary cards. They sort these words and consult the picture dictionary to check their understanding and refresh the meaning of the words. The students keep their word cards in 'word banks' or word boxes, consulting them as they wish and eventually arranging them to compose sentences.

Today, it is again recognized that the development of sight vocabulary is an essential channel to literacy (Ehri 1994). The PWIM addresses this development as well as the problem of retention of words and how to move them into long-term memory and make them available for the study of how the English-language alphabet works (Adams and Huggins 1985; Graves 1992; Swanborn and de Glopper 1999).

Build concepts about the conventions used in language to connect sounds and structures to print forms

With respect to sound/print forms (phonetic, often called sound/symbol or letter –sound relationships), children need to learn that nearly all the words that begin with a particular sound begin with particular letters representing those sounds. Periodically, a teacher using the PWIM will ask students to pull out all the words they have in their word bank that contain the letter *b* and they will concentrate on that letter for a while. Another time, all the words with *at* will get attention. After the students have learned to read most of the words on the picture chart, the teacher may ask them to pull out all the words in which they can hear an /s/ sound.

With respect to the structure of words, students need to build an understanding of inflection: the change in form that words 'undergo' to indicate number, gender, person, tense, case, mood and voice. While it may seem impossible to believe, these structural conventions that have developed over time do eventually result in more rapid and accurate communication of ideas. Students notice the similarities and differences between singular and plural words (as in how *book* and *books* are both alike and different).

PWIM induces students to classify their new words, building the concepts that will enable them to unlock words they have not seen before. The English language has about 44 sounds represented in more than 200 forms – some say as many as 250 forms (Morris 1997) – because some have multiple representations (/sh/ut, na/tion/). As students work with their words, they will develop many categories: these words all begin like *boy*, these all have two *d*s in the middle like *ladder*. They will develop word families (*bat*, *cat*, *hat*) that they will use to read and spell words they have not memorized previously (*mat*). And they will learn that the generalizations they make will enable them to unlock about 70 per cent of the new words they encounter.

Students will be amused at some of the ways we spell words (*ate*, *eight*), and, like the rest of us before them, they will sigh occasionally at our insistence that they learn the peculiarities our language has developed. They will be perplexed by *see* and *sea* and want to know why we 'made them sound alike'; at times, all we can say is what some of our teachers said to us: 'You'll just have to memorize them.'

In summary, the PWIM capitalizes on children's ability to think inductively. It enables them to build generalizations that form the basis of structural and phonetic analysis. And it respects their ability to think. Thus a major principle of the model is that students have the capability to make those generalizations that reveal to them the conventions of language.

The reading/writing connection

As the students mine a picture for words, those words are spelled correctly by the teacher and written on the picture dictionary, which launches the students into the early stages of formal writing. Later, the students will be asked to make up sentences about the picture and, with the help of the teacher, they begin to write longer pieces. Through much repetition, the words in the sentences are added to their storehouse of knowledge and perhaps even physically to their word banks. Gradually, as they read more and more trade books, the students learn to analyse how other authors write and they use the devices of these authors to enhance their ability to express themselves. Essentially, they come to use our great literature and prose base (the library of the world) as models for learning about writing as a tool to share and communicate ideas. As they read more picture story books and short informative books, they will discuss them, in a sense 'making up sentences' about the book they are reading or have just read. Many will come to feel that the reading of a book is not complete until they have said something about it in their own words, completing the communication loop between the writer (author) and the reader in constructing meaning.

From the early years on, the students and the teacher work together building words and sentences and paragraphs and little books. As they build paragraphs, they will select and discuss titles. The teacher will lead metacognitive discussions on using this title or that title: talking to the students about which title is most comprehensive, which title might be most interesting to one audience or another, which sentences would go with one title, which with another. When writing a paragraph, or creating a title, the teacher will help the students focus on the essence of communication: what do we want to say to our readers, to ourselves. The students will use the reading/ writing connection as the teacher helps them think about what they want to share, what they most want the reader to know and how they will 'help' the reader 'get' this information. Finally, did the class group, as writers, share what they wished? The teacher will continue to work on this link until it becomes explicit and accessible for the students' use as independent learners.

Thus, another major principle at work in the PWIM is that reading and writing are naturally connected and can be learned simultaneously and later can be used together to rapidly and powerfully advance one's growth in language use. Relational concepts are critical. If singular nouns are connected to singular verbs in speech, should they be so connected when writing? If authors write titles that promise readers the content and approach to content, beginning writers learn to promise readers content and approach as they shape titles.

Structure

Each cycle of the PWIM uses a large photograph as a common stimulus for the generation of words and sentences. The teacher, working with the whole class or small groups of students, uses the moves that comprise a PWIM cycle to support students' building of vocabulary; forming and using phonetic and structural analysis generalizations; reading comprehension at the word, phrase, sentence, paragraph and extended text levels; composing at the word, sentence, paragraph and extended text levels; and observing and verifying data using reference sources. The PWIM cycles generally last 2 to 6 weeks. The sequence begins with the picture, usually a photograph, whose contents (both the central elements and details) include many things that students can describe using their developed listening–speaking language. The students study the picture and then 'shake out the words'. What this means is that the students identify things they see in the picture and the teacher draws a line from those things to a place outside the picture, reiterates the word and writes and spells the word or phrase aloud. The students repeat the word and its spelling. What emerges is an illustrated picture–word dictionary as in Figure 6.4.

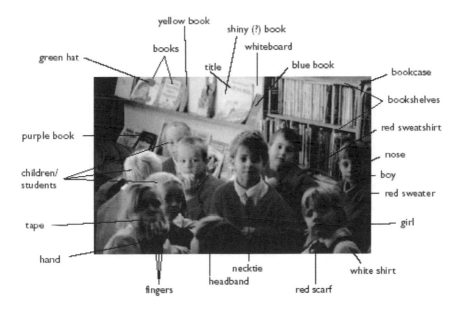

Figure 6.4 Children and picture–word chart

The next phase of the PWIM involves providing students with their individual sets of word cards. They check whether they can 'recognize' the words immediately or decode them if necessary, using the picture–word dictionary if they have difficulty.

It's easy to assess students' ability to read the words as the teacher moves among the students. As students begin to read the words, the next phase of the model comes into play: students classify the words in terms of phonetic, structural or content properties and share their categories and why they put a particular set of words together. The categorization activity occurs several times during the PWIM cycle.

The pace of lessons during a picture–word cycle depends on the reading level of the students and the curriculum objectives of the teacher, but after the classification of words, students are asked to generate factual sentences about the picture. New words from the sentences may be added to students' vocabulary banks and the categorization activity repeated, possibly several times. As soon as students begin to read the sentences they are asked to classify them (however they wish, by content or common patterns of syntax or structure) into groups and provide reasons for their classifications.

Next, the teacher selects one of the students' sentence categories (content) and models writing a well-organized paragraph, sharing their thinking about how they use the ideas in the sentences and modify the structures, if needed, to form the message about the picture that they wish to share with their readers. In whatever way is appropriate to the developmental level of the students (e.g. a combination of drawing and writing, pieces dictated to an older student friend), students are asked to use other categories and generate their own paragraphs. The PWIM cycle ends at any time after the paragraph development stage.

Closing scenario

We drop in on Nancy Werner and her second grade class during the third week of school. Nancy has 22 students, eight of whom entered school with limited English proficiency. This is the students' second picture–word inductive model unit and Nancy is still teaching them the moves of the model.

She is using the picture of the children in Figure 6.4.

Pinned to the bulletin board and centred in the middle of two large strips of light blue paper is a 24- by 30-inch picture of a classroom where a group of children is gathered. Nancy gathers the students in front of the picture. As they seat themselves on the rug, she says: 'Make sure you have your personal space around you and that you can see the picture.' She takes a minute to help students adjust their spaces. 'We're going to work with this picture for the next few days, just like we did with the picture of the school. We'll shake a lot of words out, learn to read and spell those words, and maybe we'll write about the picture so we can practise our writing. Now, be ready to tell us something you recognize in the picture.'

Nancy waits about a minute until most hands are up and calls on Dylan: 'What's something you see in this picture?'

Dylan points to a necktie one of the children in the picture is wearing and says: 'That's a necktie.'

Nancy draws a line from the necktie to a spot on the paper and says 'Necktie. Now, I want you to listen while I spell *necktie* first and then we'll spell it together so that you get lots of practice on your spelling.' The children listen while Nancy says, 'n-e-c-k-t-i-e', writing the letters as she says them. Then again: 'N-e-c-k-t-i-e spells *necktie*. Now, all together.'

The children chorus the spelling as the teacher points to each letter. 'Now, that spells ...?'

'Necktie!'

Nancy next calls on Marianna. Marianna points to a piece of tape in the picture and says, 'tape'. The teacher draws a line from the piece of tape to the paper and says: 'Now, let's learn how to spell *tape*.' She spells it, then has the students spell it as she points to each letter and says 'Now, t-a-p-e spells ...?'

'Tape', the children say, almost in unison.

For the next 20 minutes, the group continues to shake words out of the picture. *Gold letters*, *books*, *whiteboard* and *children* are quickly identified. Each time, the teacher spells the word and pronounces it again and the children spell and pronounce it. As in their first unit, they are building a picture dictionary.

'T-shirt' is volunteered and Nancy spells it *'tee shirt'*. Harry bursts out with: 'That's not T-shirt. It's spelled with a big T!' She adds *T-shirt* to the chart as well. She has students read both versions, but they only spell *shirt* with her. She says: 'I'll have to check and see if both spellings are correct. See what you can find out too.' Altogether, about 25 words appear.

Nancy reviews all the words with the children, then leads them into a discussion of the picture. 'Now, several of you asked me where these children are. Where do *you* think they are?' She calls on Marta.

'School.'

'How many of you agree with Marta? And what makes you think they are in school?'

'Well, it could be a family, but there are too many children.'

One student asks: 'Why are they all wearing red?' Nancy has them speculate for a while and ideas like 'special class' and 'their school makes them do it' surface.

Robert suggests that it's probably a school because there's a whiteboard and most houses don't have whiteboards.

Francesca suggests that the presence of a big library corner makes it more likely that the picture is of a group of students at school.

Paul says it can't be a home because there are too many books. Anna adds: 'And homes don't have bookcases.' There's some discussion about this.

Finally, Nancy confirms that it is a school, that in this school students wear uniforms, that the school is in Nottingham, England, and that these are 5-year-old students. She pulls the map down and asks Sarah to come up and put her hand on Nottingham. 'Tomorrow we'll continue with our picture. When you have a little time today, practise reading our words. If you have trouble reading a word, what do you do?'

'Trace the line to the picture', they chorus.

The next day the students gather around the picture at 9 am and Nancy announces: 'We're going to work on silent reading before I give you your set of new word cards.' She points to a word and about half the children read it aloud. She says:

'Let's all read it again … silently. Don't let any letter sounds or words escape your mouth. Here we go, just practise reading it in your mind.' She points to a word, holding her hand against her lips. Everyone is silent. She traces the line: 'Now, out loud.'

And the process continues, with Nancy pointing to words, the students reading them silently; then she traces the line so they can check their reading and they read the word out loud. Then she gives them their envelopes with the words from yesterday's work and says: 'For the next 15 minutes I want everyone to work individually on reading your set of words. Use the picture chart when you need to.'

They begin the third lesson the next morning with a quick review of the chart. After all the words are read, Nancy takes a number of pattern blocks in her hand and begins to prepare students for the process of classification. She picks up a yellow plastic bucket and shakes it. 'What's this?' They – respond: 'Our math bucket.' 'Our pattern blocks.' 'Our shapes.' Then she says: 'I'm going to select some pattern blocks from this bucket. I'm going to sort out some and put them together. I want you to think about why I put them together. See if you can come up with at least two reasons.' She pulls out five pattern blocks and holds them so students can see them. Then she calls on Kyrinas, who says: 'You put them together because they're all red.'

'How many of you agree with Kyrinas that these are all red?' Hands go up. 'Does anyone have another reason?' Scott volunteers that they each have four sides. Again, Nancy asks who agrees. They all do. Serena then volunteers: 'You put them together because they are red, have four sides and are square.' Nancy says: 'Serena just gave us three reasons why I might have put these pattern blocks together. Who agrees with all three reasons?' Some students who saw only one attribute come to recognize that Nancy made her category one in which the objects have several attributes in common.

She says: 'Now, let's switch to words. I want you to learn to study words carefully and put them together in groups based on how they are spelled or on what they mean.' She places three word cards in the large pocket chart with the words turned away from the students. 'I want you to do the same kind of detective work with these words that you just did with our pattern blocks.' She turns the cards over. 'Everyone read them silently.' Then she demonstrates checking your reading by taking each card and placing it under the matching word on the chart and running her finger down the line to the item(s).

purple

person

pictures

'Now, why do you think I might have put these words together?'

She calls on Marloes, who shyly ventures the reason is that all three words begin with the letter *p*.

'Who agrees? These three words begin with the letter *p*.' Nancy pauses for the students to study the words for a few seconds.

'Now, let's read the words together and see if you can come up with another reason why I might have put them together.' They read them, first silently, then out loud, as she points to them. 'Now, I am going to read them aloud and you listen. See if you can think of another reason. You were right: one reason was they all begin with the letter *p*.'

She pronounces *purple*, *person*, and *pictures* carefully and several hands go up. She calls on Annelle.

'They all have *e* in them.'

'That's correct. What else can you discover? Read them silently and think about them. Jueron?'

'Person and purple sound alike at the beginning, but they have different letters.'

'Good thinking, Jueron. The *r* often works like that when it follows vowels. Here it makes the *er* and *ur* sound alike at the beginning of *person* and *purple*. 'Can you think of anything else?' Nancy calls on Christina.

'It's like they're two words.'

'Say more about that, Christina. What do you mean when you say 'it's like they're two words'?'

'You know, like two parts, two pieces.'

Nancy says: 'Everyone listen carefully' and she pronounces the three words, slightly emphasizing the two syllables. 'Good thinking. You discovered both reasons I put those words together: they all begin with *p and* they all have two parts or *syllables*. Would the word *paper* (writing it on the board as she says it) fit in this group?' The students assure her it would. 'How about *pen*?' she asks as she writes it. There is some disagreement about whether *pen* would belong, so Nancy uses the difference between *pen* and *pencil* for a little more practice.

'Good detective work. Today, I want you to sort the words in your envelope any way you want to and be prepared to share your groups and tell us why you put the words together.' She passes out the envelopes, helps the students spread out and they get to work. Nancy circulates, observing the groups being formed, checking to be sure the students can read the words, sending some students to the chart to check their reading and asking students to tell her why they put words together.

Lots of categories emerge. As would be expected, many students have similar groups; however, there is much variety in what they 'see' in the words and what they can articulate. Some students attend more to letters and sounds, some to the meanings of words and some to a combination. Here are a few of their categories and the reasons expressed by the students:

- *book, boy, board* ('All begin with *b*.' 'All have the same two first letters.')
- *picture, people, person* ('All have *p*s.' 'All have *p*s at the beginning.' "All have *p*s as the first letter and two parts.' 'All have *p*s at the beginning and they all have *e*s.')
- *girl, boy, child, children, people, person* ('They are all humans.' 'They are all names for people when we don't know their names.' 'They are all people.')
- *black book, yellow book, blue book* ('They all have *book*.' 'All have the colour of the book.' 'They all have *book* and they all have two *o*s.')

Nancy ends this lesson by commenting on several categories then uses her large word cards to share the category with *book*, *board* and *boy*. They discuss initial *b* sound and the varying sounds of *oo*, *oa* and *oy*. Homework is to see if they can find at least six words that begin with the two letters *bo*, list them on a piece of paper and drop them in the picture–word box in the morning.

On Thursday, they begin with a quick review of the words and add a few new words to the picture–word chart. Then Nancy selects some of the words from the homework papers for a short lesson on *oo*, *oa* and *oy*. Part of the content generated by students during this segment includes a list of words that rhyme with *book* and *boy* and a discussion of the influence of *r* on vowels. Then she asks students to reclassify their words to see if they can identify any new groups and to make sure they can read every word on the chart. Homework is to see if they can find any more words that stand for 'people when we don't know their names'.

During Friday's lesson, Nancy begins working on titles and sentences. As the students gather around the picture, she says: 'Who remembers what a title does?' The responses circle around: 'Names of books.' 'Names of stories.' 'Covers of books.' 'Tells us what the story's about.' Then Nancy says: 'Study our picture carefully. See if you can think of a good title for our picture.' She gives them a minute to think, then collects about 10 titles. As students volunteer titles, she asks them how the various titles relate to the picture. Some are comprehensive and accurate, some are less so and some are sentences. Here are a few of their responses:

> 'I think the picture should be called "all colors", because there are so many colors in it.'

> ' "Children in uniforms", cause they're all wearing red uniforms.'

> ' "Shiny books", there are lots of shiny books in their school.'

> ' "Kids in school." They are *at* school.'

After listening to a few of the titles, Nancy decides she wants to pull out a few informative books – a couple she has read to them and a few new ones – and talk with them about length, content and promises to the reader represented by informative titles. They move on to sentences for now.

Nancy writes the word *sentence* on the board and under it two of the sentences she heard during discussion:

1   The students are all wearing uniforms.
2   They're young kids all gathered around their teacher.

She asks the students to read the sentences silently, reading as many words as they can; then they read the sentences together.

'Remember, we helped Renata turn the first sentence into the title, "Students wearing uniforms", because Renata said "The students are all wearing uniforms." And George came up with "Children around their teacher", for sentence number two. Well, that is good thinking. Later, we'll work on titles again. For journal time, you may want to write something that goes with your title. Study our picture sometime today and pretend you are going to write a letter describing the picture to someone who has not seen it. Be ready on Monday to share something from your pretend letter.'

On Monday morning, when it's picture–word time, Nancy has the overhead projector set up near their work area. They begin the lesson with a quick reading of the picture–word chart, they work on two target sight words and they add a few more *oo*, *oa* and *oy* words to the wall charts. Then Nancy says: 'All right. Sentence time. Who's ready?' They spend the next 2 days generating and recording sentences describing things in the picture.

The sentences cover most everything. Here are a few of them:

'Gold letters are on the uniform.' [began as 'gold letters'. Nancy asks: 'Where are the letters, Maryanne?' 'On the uniform.']

'They like school because they're smiling.'

'The tops of the uniforms are all alike, but the bottoms are different for boys and girls.'

When students give something that is not obvious or that requires some interpretation, Nancy asks them for their evidence.

'The children are learning by listening to the teacher.'

'Why do you say that?' Nancy asks.

'They are all being quiet, sort of leaning close to the teacher and it doesn't look like they're talking.'

Serena adds: 'They are learning because they're good listeners and they read lots of books.'

'They look like they are happy.'

'Why do you think so?' asks Nancy.

'Most of them are smiling. They look like they're happy working together.'

'These kids are learning how to read and write.'

'How do you know? They could be getting ready for music,' Nancy adds.

'I see their work, and they have a chart up too!'

On Wednesday, the students get copies of all the sentences printed front and back on light green paper. Their work time the next few lessons is on learning to read the sentences. As Nancy walks around listening to them read their sentences, she targets some high-frequency words (*in*, *on*, *the/the*, *they/they*) to work on.

The following week they begin classifying their sentences. They work in partners and they spend several days reading and classifying. At first, Nancy just observes and listens to their categories; she wants to find out how they are thinking and be sure their reasons for grouping are accurate. About half the students put sentences together based on how they are written: 'These all begin with *they*.' 'These all begin with *they are*.' One student describes her category thus: 'These all have five words and they all have our work word *the* in them.' About half the students put sentences together based on a topic or what they are about: 'These are about students in uniforms.' 'My sentences are all about what's in the room.'

After the second session of reading sentences and classifying them however they wish, Nancy selects one of the topical categories she has seen several times and uses it as a demonstration of grouping sentences by content. She encourages every partnership to find at least one group of sentences that go together because of what they are about. Before they begin working as partners, she does a quick drill with them on *an, and, are, all*, high-frequency words she's heard some students confuse and that she wants every student to master.

Nancy is preparing her students for work on writing informative paragraphs about a single topic and main idea and how an accurate brief description of their category can provide a good title. For their next lesson, she will take one of their groups, put together a paragraph and discuss how she put the paragraph together.

On Thursday, she begins the PWIM lesson by saying:

> You've put together a number of good categories with our sentences. Some of you put – together sentences about uniforms; some about all the colors in the picture; some about the books, where they were and how they were being used; and some about what the students were doing. Several of you put together three or four different categories and some of you have written your own piece about what you were most interested in.
>
> I took one of your groups and wrote a paragraph about our picture.
>
> She places four of their sentences one below the other in the large pocket chart. Let's read these sentences; then I'll share my paragraph.
>
> The students have many talents.
>
> They are learning how to write words and spell.
>
> They are learning by listening to the teacher and by reading lots of books.
>
> They look like they are happy working together.

Nancy continues: 'There are lots of good groups we could write about, but I selected this one because when I asked why you put them together, you talked about kids learning. And that's one of the things I think is special when I look at our picture and that's what I wanted to write about.'

Then, she displays this paragraph on the overhead projector:

All Kids Learning

These young students have many talents. They're learning how to write words and how to spell. Reading lots of books and listening to the teacher helps them learn. They look like they're happy working together.

She gives students time to read the paragraph silently; then she reads it aloud and talks about how she structured the paragraph, telling the reader who (young students), what (learning happily), how (by reading lots of books, by listening to the teacher, by working together, and because they have many talents) and where (in a classroom).

She keeps the pace up but includes, among other things, why she changed the first *they* to *these young students*, why she added the second *how to* in the second sentence and so forth. She puts her first draft on the projector as she talks about a couple of the changes she made in word order and sentence order, and students ask her about a few of the changes from the original sentences.

We have been visiting with Nancy and her students for 3 weeks of picture–word lessons. Most of the lessons lasted around 30 minutes, a few around 45 minutes. This picture–word cycle will continue for at least another week. They will write a group paragraph about uniforms because that is one of the more interesting topics to many of them and students will write individual paragraphs about at least one of their categories. They will continue to add words to the chart and to their word wall, to work on spelling and phonics patterns and Nancy will continue to listen to them, to observe what they are producing and to model and demonstrate and talk about how the English language works.

Taking PWIM further

As we close the chapter, let's take you to a classroom of sixth grade students where the students are studying life in three cities (see Figures 6.5, 6.6 and 6.7).

Figure 6.5 House in Saskatoon

Figure 6.6 House in Des Moines

Figure 6.7 House in Willemstad

One is their own city, Saskatoon, a modern Canadian city on the prairies. The second is Des Moines, Iowa, a United States city on the prairie. The third is Willemstad, in the Dutch Antilles. They study many aspects of life in the three cities, gathering demographic information, narratives from a variety of sources and using the picture–word strategy to analyse information from pictures. The three pictures were taken in 2006 and show residences in suburban neighbourhoods. As you look at them, do your own analysis – shake out the information. And ask yourselves whether these houses are more alike or more different and what are the implications for life today in the three environments?

7   Learning to learn through cooperative inquiry

"The most stunning thing about teaching people to help kids learn cooperatively is that people don't know how to do it as a consequence of their own schooling and life in this society. And, if anything is genetically driven, it's a social instinct. If it weren't for each other, we wouldn't even know who we are."

Herbert Thelen to Bruce Joyce, circa 1964

Again, we examine a model of learning that fits our nature closely. Note that all these models capitalize on our nature, rather than altering it. We begin life cooperating with our caretakers, learn to talk with our pets and cuddly toys, are educated in social settings, work in social environments, play and recreate with others and, finally, learn to mate and, in time, to help initiate the lifecycle for our successors.

Learning to cooperate with others is an essential for a productive and happy life in family, in school and in adult life. Folks who don't absorb the models of cooperate inquiry are terribly handicapped. Weirdly, however, the educational practices that stem from when common education was established often run counter to cooperative life. Studies of teaching have documented that most school assignments are directed at individuals (read this, write that) and instruction, more often than not, is an administration of chalk and talk to the whole class, followed by questions (the infamous recitation approach). In many schools, students are pitted against one another. We know teachers and parents who want it that way, as perverse as it seems and as unproductive as it is.

A model with many varietals

There is not one single, defined model for cooperative learning but a collection of ways of organizing our students and helping them learn how to inquire together. The common element – learning how to inquire with others – is powerful and unifying. Models that look quite different superficially share that common element.

In previous chapters, we have seen cooperative settings in the inductive model, in concept attainment, in synectics and in the picture–word inductive model, If those models of learning were explored as we have depicted them, the students would have learned an orientation toward cooperation and a good sized repertoire of cooperative inquiry skills that were embedded in the process of building learning communities. In other words, each of those models of learning generates forms of cooperative inquiry.

Let's begin by looking at one simple, straightforward approach to cooperative learning and one complex mode of cooperative inquiry.

Scenario 1: basics

As the children enter Kelly Farmer's Year 5 classroom on the first day of the school year, they find the class list on each desk. She smiles at her pupils and says:

> Let's start by learning all our names and one of the ways we will be working together this year. You'll notice I've arranged the desks in pairs and the persons sitting at each pair will be partners in today's activities. I want each partnership to take our class list and classify the first names by how they sound. Then we will share the groupings or categories each partnership makes. This will help us learn one another's names. It will also introduce you to one of the ways we will study spelling and several other subjects this year. I know from Mrs Annis that you worked inductively last year so you know how to classify information, but let me know if you have any problems.

The children *do* know what to do and within a few minutes they are ready to share their classifications:

> 'We put Nancy and Sally together because they end in *y*.'

> 'We put George and Jerry together because they sound the same at the beginning although they're spelled differently.'

> 'We put the three Kevins together.'

A few minutes later the pairs are murmuring together as they help one another learn to spell the list of names.

Kelly has started the year by organizing the children into a 'cooperative set', by which we mean an organization for cooperative learning. She will teach the children to work in dyads and triads, which can be combined into groups of five or six. (Taskgroups or workgroups larger than that generally have low productivity.) The partnerships will change for various activities. The children will learn to accept any member of the class as their partner and that they are to work with each other to try to ensure that everyone achieves the objectives of each activity.

Let's pause on this point. The students need to learn to work with all their cohorts, not just friends or ones with similar learning styles. This is an 'all-for-one-and-one-for-all approach'. A major part of learning how to cooperate is learning how much it benefits every partner in an inquiry. By working with someone else we help ourselves! (Not in all things, however. There are many tasks best done by individuals, even if the products are shared later. For example, the building of concepts in the concept attainment model *does not* involve sharing until the very end.

Also, when students are able to take notes, *all* should be recorders and no one appointed to do that job. When all record, all learn better!

Back to Kelly. She begins with pairs because that is the simplest social organization. In fact, much of the early training in cooperative activity will be conducted in groups of two and three because the interaction is simpler than in larger groups. She also uses fairly straightforward and familiar cognitive tasks for the initial training for the same reason – it is easier for children to learn to work together when they are not mastering complex activities at the same time. For example, she asks them to change partners, for the new partnerships to quiz each other on simple knowledge (such as of the states and their capitals) and tutor one another. She may change partnerships again and ask them to categorize sets of fractions by size. Each pupil learns how to work with any and all of the other children in a variety of tasks. Later she will teach the children to respond to the cognitive tasks of the more complex information processing models of teaching as well as more complex cooperative sets. By the end of October, she expects the children to be skilful enough to be introduced to group investigation.

Scenario 2: a complex inductive inquiry into poetry

Mary Thomas opens the course in her Year 10 English class by presenting the students with 12 poems that she has selected from a set of 100 poems representing the works of prominent contemporary poets. She organizes the students into pairs, asks them to read the poems and then to classify them by structure, style and themes. As they classify the poems, they also prepare to report their categories to the other students so that each pair can compare their classifications with those of the other students.

Working together, the class accumulates a list of the ways they have discriminated structure, style and theme. Then Ms Thomas presents the pairs of students with another dozen poems which they examine, fitting them into their existing categories and expanding the categories as necessary. This process is repeated until all students are familiar with nearly 50 poems.

She then gives the students several other tasks: one is to decide how particular themes are handled by style and structure and vice versa (whether style and structure are correlated with each other and with themes). Another task is to build hypotheses about whether some groups of poems were written by particular authors using distinctive combinations of style, structure and theme.

Only then does she pass out the anthologies and books of critical analysis that are used as the textbooks of the course, asking students to test their hypotheses about authorship and also to find out if the scholars of poetry employ the same categories they have been developing as pairs.

Scenario 3: inching toward group investigation

Collette Singleton's Year 11 class on world geography has been studying demographic data taken from a computer program of nations of the world. Each of the nine groups of four students has analysed the data on about 20 nations and searched for correlations among the following variables: population, per capita GNP (gross national product), birth rate, life expectancy, education, healthcare services, industrial base, agricultural production, transportation systems, foreign debt, balance of payments, women's rights and natural resources.

The groups reported back what they had discovered – and what had begun as a purely academic exercise suddenly took off:

> 'People born in some countries have a life expectancy 20 years less than people in other countries.'

> 'We didn't find a relationship between levels of education and per capita wealth!'

> 'Some rich countries spend more on military facilities and personnel than some large poor ones spend on healthcare!'

> 'Women's rights don't correlate with type of government! Some democracies are less liberal than some dictatorships!'

> 'Some little countries are relatively wealthy because of commerce and industry. Some others just have one mineral that is valuable.'

> 'The United States owes other countries an awful lot of money.'

The time is ripe to lead the students into group investigation. Ms Singleton carefully leads the students to record their reactions to the data. They make a decision to bring together the data on all the countries and find out if the groups' conclusions will apply over the entire dataset. They also decide that they need to find a way of getting in-depth information about selected countries to flesh out their statistical data. But which countries? How will they test their hypotheses?

One student wonders out loud about world organizations and how they relate to the social situation of the world. They have heard of the United Nations and the European Union but are vague about how they function. One has heard about the 'Committee of Eight', but the others have not. Several have heard of NATO but are not sure how it operates. Some wonder about UNESCO, others about India and China and their immense populations and how they fit into the global picture.

Clearly, deciding priorities for the inquiry will not be easy. However, the conditions for group investigation are present. The students are puzzled. They react differently to the various questions. They need information and information sources are available. Ms Singleton smiles at her brood of young furrowed brows. 'Let's get organized. There is information we all need and let's start with that. Then let's prioritize our questions and divide the labour to get information that will help us.'

Reflections

All the simpler forms of cooperative learning, as seen in Scenario 1, are preparations for the more rigorous, active and integrative collective action required in very complex inductive activity as seen in Scenario 2. Then we introduce students to the beginning versions of group investigation, the most complex of the cooperative learning models for learning. All three teachers have embarked on the task of building learning communities. They will teach the students to work together impersonally but positively, to gather and analyse information, to build and test hypotheses and to coach one another as they develop skills. The difference in maturity between the classes will affect the degree of sophistication of their inquiry, but the basic teaching/learning process will be the same.

Each of these teachers has a variety of strategies for helping her students learn to work productively together. Each teacher is studying her students, learning how effectively they cooperate and deciding how to design the next activities to teach them to work more effectively together.

Assumptions

The assumptions that underlie the development of cooperative learning communities are straightforward:

1   The synergy generated in cooperative settings generates more motivation than do individualistic, competitive environments. Integrative social groups are, in effect, more than the sum of their parts. The feelings of connectedness produce positive energy.

2   The members of cooperative groups learn from one another. Each learner has more helping hands than in a structure that generates isolation.

3   Interacting with one another produces cognitive as well as social complexity, creating more intellectual activity that increases learning when contrasted with solitary study.

4   Cooperation increases positive feelings toward one another, reduces alienation and loneliness, builds relationships and provides affirmative views of other people.

5   Cooperation increases self-esteem not only through increased learning but through the feeling of being respected and cared for by others in the environment.

6   Students can respond to experience in tasks requiring cooperation by increasing their capacity to work together productively. In other words, the more children are given the opportunity to work together, the better they get at it, with benefit to their general social skills.

7   Students, including primary schoolchildren, can learn from training to increase their ability to work together.

The results of cooperative arrangements can be very large. Joyce et al. (1989) combined cooperative learning with several other models of teaching to obtain dramatic (30 to 95 per cent) increases in promotion rates with at-risk students. There were also correspondingly large decreases in disruptive activity, an obvious reciprocal of increases in cooperative and integrative behaviour.

For those teachers for whom cooperative learning is an innovation, an attractive feature is that it is so very easy to organize students into pairs and triads. And it gets effects immediately. The combination of social support and the increase in cognitive complexity caused by the social interaction have mild but rapid effects on the learning of content and skills. In addition, partnerships in learning provide a pleasant laboratory in which to develop social skills and empathy for others. Off-task and disruptive behaviour diminish substantially. Students feel good in cooperative settings and positive feelings toward self and others are enhanced.

Another positive feature is that the students with poorer academic histories benefit so quickly. Partnerships increase involvement, and the concentration on cooperation has the side-effect of reducing self-absorption and increasing responsibility for personal learning. Whereas the effect sizes on academic learning are modest but consistent, the effects on social learning and personal esteem can be considerable when comparisons are made with individualistic classroom organization.

Curiously, we have found that some parents and teachers believe that students who are the most successful in individualistic environments will not profit from cooperative environments. Sometimes this belief is expressed as 'gifted students prefer to work alone'. A mass of evidence contradicts that belief (Joyce 1991; Slavin 1991). Perhaps a misunderstanding about the relationship between individual and cooperative study contributes to the persistence of the belief. Developing partnerships does not imply that individual effort is not required. In Scenario 4 at the beginning of the book, all the individuals in Mary Thomas's Year 10 class read the poems. When classifying poems together, each individual contributed ideas and studied the ideas of others. Individuals are not submerged, but are enhanced by partnerships with others. Successful students are not inherently less cooperative. In highly individualistic environments, they are sometimes taught disdain for less successful students, to their detriment as students and people, both in school and in the future.

Increasing the efficiency of partnerships: training for cooperation

For reasons not entirely clear to us, the initial reaction of some people to the proposition that students be organized to study together is one of concern that they will not know how to work together productively. In fact, partnerships over simple tasks are not very demanding of social skills. Most students are quite capable of cooperating when they are clear about what has been asked of them. However, developing more efficient ways of working together is clearly important and there are some guidelines for helping students become more practised and efficient: group size, complexity and practice.

To teach basic cooperative skills, we use simple dyadic partnerships over clear cognitive tasks. The reason is that the pair or dyad is the simplest form of social organization. One way to help students learn to work cooperatively is to provide practice in the simpler settings of twos and threes. Assuming we regulate complexity through the tasks we give and the sizes of groups we form, if students are unaccustomed to cooperative work, it makes sense to give the smallest size groups simple or familiar tasks to permit them to gain the experience that will enable them to work in groups of larger sizes. However, task groups larger than six persons are clumsy and require skilled leadership which students cannot provide to one another without experience or training. Actually partnerships of two, three or four are the most effective in most situations.

Practice results in increased efficiency. If we begin learning with just two partners and simply provide practice for a few weeks, we will find that the students become increasingly productive.

Training for efficiency

There are also methods for training the students for more efficient cooperation and 'positive interdependence' (see Johnson and Johnson 1994; Kagan 1990). Simple hand signals can be used to get the attention of busy groups. One of the common procedures is to teach the students that when the instructors raise their hands, anyone who notices is to give their attention to the instructor and raise their hand also. Other students notice and raise their hands and soon the entire instructional group is attending. This type of procedure is constructive because it works while avoiding shouting above the hubbub of the busy partnerships; it also teaches the students to participate in the management process.

Also, for tasks for which it is appropriate, pretests may be given. An example might be a list of words to learn to spell. After the pretest a number of tasks might be given to help the students study the words. Then an interval might be provided for the students to tutor one another, followed by a posttest. Each group would then calculate their gain scores (the number correct on the posttest minus the number correct on the pretest), giving all members a stake in everyone's learning. Also, cooperative learning aside, the procedure makes clear that it is learning as expressed in *gain* that is the purpose of the exercise. When posttests only are used, it is not clear whether anyone has actually *learned* – students can receive high marks for a score no higher than they would have achieved in a pretest.

Sets of training tasks can help students learn to be more effective partnerships, to increase their stake in one another and to work assiduously for learning by all.

Training for interdependence

In addition to practice and training for more efficient cooperative behaviour, procedures for helping students to become truly interdependent are available. The least complex procedures involve reflection on the group process and discussions about ways of working together most effectively. The more complex procedures involve the provision of tasks that require interdependent behaviour. For example, there are card games where success depends on 'giving up' valuable cards to another player and communication games where success requires taking the position of another. Familiar games like charades and Pictionary are popular because they increase cohesion and the ability to put oneself in the place of the other. There are also procedures for rotating tasks so that each person moves from subordinate to superordinate tasks and where members take turns as coordinators.

The Johnsons (1994) have demonstrated that sets of these tasks can increase interdependence, empathy and role-taking ability and that students can become quite expert at analysing group dynamics and learning to create group climates that foster mutuality and collective responsibility. The role-playing model of teaching, discussed in the next chapter, is designed to help students analyse their values and to work together to develop interactive frames of reference.

Cooperative or competitive goal structures

As we have already noted, some developers organize teams to compete against one another while others emphasize cooperative goals and minimize team competition. Johnson and Johnson (1993) have analysed the research and argue that the evidence favours cooperative goal structures, while Slavin (1983) argues that competition between teams benefits learning. The fundamental question is whether students are oriented toward competing with one another or with a goal. Recently several of our colleagues have organized whole classes to work cooperatively toward a goal. For example, the science department of a high school began the year in chemistry by organizing the students to master the essential features of the table of elements. In teams, they built mnemonics that were used by all the students. Within 2 weeks all students knew the table backward and forward and that information served as the structural organizer for the entire course.

In a group of fifth grade classes, the exploration of social studies began with memorization of the states, large cities, river and mountain systems and other basic information about the geography of the United States. Class scores were computed (for example, 50 states times 30 students is 1,500 items). The goal was for the class as a whole to achieve a perfect score. The classes reached scores over 1,450 within a week, leaving individuals with very few items to master to reach a perfect score for the class.

Motivation: from extrinsic to intrinsic?

The issue about how much to emphasize cooperative or individualistic goal structures relates to conceptions of motivation. Sharan (1990) has argued that cooperative learning increases learning partly because it causes motivational orientation to move from the external to the internal. In other words, when students cooperate over learning tasks they become more interested in learning for its own sake rather than for external rewards. Thus students engage in learning for intrinsic satisfaction and become less dependent on praise from teachers or other authorities. The internal motivation is more powerful than the external, resulting in increased learning rates and retention of information and skills.

The frame of reference of the cooperative learning community is a direct challenge to the principles that many schools have used to guide their use of tests and rewards to students for achievement. Unquestionably, one of the fundamental purposes of general education is to increase internal motivation to learn and to encourage students to generate learning for the sheer satisfaction in growing. If cooperative learning procedures (among others) succeed partly because they contribute to this goal, then the testing and reward structures that prevail in most school environments may actually retard learning. As we turn to group investigation – a powerful model that radically changes the learning environment – let us consider how different are the tasks, cooperative structures and principles of motivation we observe in many contemporary schools.

Group investigation: phases of the model

Group investigation begins by confronting the students with a stimulating problem. The confrontation may be presented verbally or it may be an actual experience; it may arise naturally or it may be provided by a teacher. If the students react, the teacher draws their attention to the differences in their reactions – what stances they take, what they perceive, how they organize things and what they feel. As the students become interested in their differences in reaction, the teacher draws them toward formulating and structuring the problem for themselves. Next, students analyse the required roles, organize themselves, act and report their results. Finally, the group evaluates its solution in terms of its original purposes. The cycle repeats itself, either with another confrontation or with a new problem growing out of the investigation itself.

The teacher's role in group investigation is one of counsellor, consultant and friendly critic. He or she must guide and reflect the group experience over three levels: the problem-solving or task level (What is the nature of the problem? What are the factors involved?); the group management level (What information do we need now? How can we organize ourselves to get it?); and the level of individual meaning (How do you feel about these conclusions? What would you do differently as a result of knowing about …? (Thelen 1954: 52–3). This teaching role is a very difficult and sensitive one, because the essence of inquiry is student activity – problems cannot be imposed. At the same time, the teacher needs to:

- facilitate the group process
- intervene in the group to channel its energy into potentially educative activities
- supervise these educative activities so that personal meaning comes from the experience (p. 13).

Intervention by the teacher should be minimal unless the group bogs down seriously.

How do students respond to the model and what does the teaching/learning interaction look like? The students react to the puzzling situation and examine the nature of their common and different reactions. They determine what kinds of information they need to approach the problem and proceed to collect relevant data. They generate hypotheses and gather the information needed to test them. They evaluate their products and continue their inquiry or begin a new line of inquiry. The central teaching moves build the cooperative social environment and teach students the skills of negotiation and conflict resolution necessary for democratic problem solving. In addition, the teacher needs to guide the students in methods of data collection and analysis, help them frame testable hypotheses and decide what would constitute a reasonable test of a hypothesis. Because groups vary considerably in their need for structure (Hunt 1971) and their cohesiveness (Thelen 1967), the teacher cannot behave mechanically but must 'read' the students' social and academic behaviour and provide the assistance that keeps the inquiry moving without squelching it.

Group investigation requires the use of multiple sources of information. The school needs to be equipped with a first-class library that provides information and opinion through a wide variety of media; it should also be able to provide access to outside resources as well. Children should be encouraged to investigate and to contact resource people beyond the school walls. One reason cooperative inquiry of this sort has been relatively rare is that the information and support systems were not adequate to maintain the level of inquiry; nowadays, this should not be a problem.

Group investigation also requires flexibility from the teacher and the classroom organization. If students have not had an opportunity to experience the kind of social interaction, decision making and independent inquiry called for in this model, it may take some time before they function at a high level. By the same token, students who have participated in classroom meetings and/or self-directed, inquiry-oriented learning will probably have an easier time. In any case, it is probably useful for the teacher to remember that the social aspects of the model may be as unfamiliar to students as the intellectual aspects and may be as demanding in terms of skill acquisition.

With young children or students new to group investigation, fairly small-scale investigations are possible; the initial confrontation can provide a narrow range of topics, issues, information and alternative activities. For example, providing an evening's entertainment for the school is more focused than resolving the energy crisis. Deciding who will care for the classroom pet, and how, is even narrower. Of course, the nature of the inquiry depends on the interests and ages of the students. Older students tend to be concerned with more complex issues. However, the skilful teacher can design inquiries appropriate to the students' abilities and to his or her own ability to manage the investigation.

Results

A group of secondary school teachers in Israel, led by Shlomo Sharan and Hana Shachar (1988), demonstrated the rapid acceleration of student learning when they studied and first began to use group investigation. These teachers worked with classes in which the children of the poor (referred to as 'low SES', which is shorthand for 'lower socioeconomic status') were mixed with the children of middle-class parents (referred to as 'high SES', for 'higher socioeconomic status'). In a year-long course on the social studies, the teachers gave pretests of knowledge to the students as well as final examinations, so that they could measure gains in academic learning and compare them with students taught by the 'whole-class' format most common in Israeli schools. The results point to several interesting comparisons. First, in the pretests the lower SES students scored significantly lower than their higher SES counterparts. (Typically, socioeconomic status is related to the knowledge students bring to the instructional situation and these students were no exception.) The lower SES students taught by group investigation achieved average gains nearly two and a half times those of the lower SES students taught by the whole-class method *and* exceeded the scores made by the higher SES students taught with the 'whole-class' format. In other words, the 'socially disadvantaged' students taught with group investigation learned at rates above those of the 'socially advantaged' students taught by teachers who did not have the repertoire provided by group investigation. Finally, the 'advantaged' students also learned more through group investigation. Their average gain was twice that of their whole-class counterparts. Thus the model was effective by a large margin for students from both backgrounds. Essentially, the model enabled the students' learning capability to flourish.

8 Building multidimensional curriculums for learning disabled and literacy-challenged secondary school students

Models of learning can be combined in various ways to enhance them and to enable us to devise new curriculums in the general education programme, for special curriculum areas and populations needing unusual help.

Here we will discuss two many-sided curriculums designed to help struggling adolescent learners – a very challenging population because those students have not responded to several years of education and, in many instances, have come to believe that they can fight off teachers and curriculum. Also, schools and teachers have become very discouraged as they watch these students fail and leave school. Here we discuss two curriculums that have had considerable success with these students.

One is an innovative curriculum, the strategic instructional model (SIM) that is directed at learning disabled secondary students. The second is a fresh curriculum directed at what we call 'overage beginning readers', that is, adolescent students who are poorly developed in reading skills and are consequently unable to profit from secondary education. The first approach concentrates on teaching students learning strategies that will mitigate their disabilities as they approach the core secondary school curriculum areas and focuses them on generating success in the basic curriculum. The second treats the students as beginning readers and builds the vocabulary, skills, and basic writing skills that help them dig themselves out of the deficit world they have inhabited.

A many-sided curriculum for adolescents with disabilities: achievements of the strategic instructional model (SIM)

Over the last 25 years at the University of Kansas Center for Learning a team headed by Donald Deshler and Jean Schumaker has been developing a many-sided curriculum model for teaching adolescents with disabilities (see, for example, Deshler and Schumaker 2006).

In the United States, adolescent students who have mild to moderate learning disabilities (we are not talking about *profound* disabilities here, such as blindness, deafness and serious orthopaedic handicaps) are unlikely to have productive high school years. Many students with learning disabilities do not finish school and few go on to any form of post-secondary education. The situation in some districts and even states is frightening. For example, in Florida, fewer than 50 per cent finish high school. And, despite the huge investment in specialist teachers in the treatment of learning disabilities, the situation has not got better. In the more than 15,000 school districts in the United States, districts that house nearly 50,000 schools and more than 400 million students, about one-seventh of the students are receiving special services on any given day. Unfortunately, very narrow curriculums have been the diet for most special education programmes and few students have made significant progress. A good many of the struggling secondary education student simply give up.

Undaunted by the problems with ordinary curriculums for students with learning disabilities, the Kansas team has developed a comprehensive curriculum that combines an approach to learning disabilities by teaching the students learning strategies and applying the strategic instructional model (SIM) to the core curriculum areas. The SIM team has implemented its approach in many settings and researched it intensively. Were you to consider failing high school students with learning disabilities and to ask the SIM staff to help you, the help would come in the form of aiding you to learn two things: how to help those students to learn more effectively and how to help them and their teachers to engage in the core curriculum subjects more powerfully. This is very important. In many special education programmes, students are taught remedial learning skills and then have to apply them in the core subjects on their own. In SIM, students are taught learning strategies and also how to apply those strategies to the basic secondary curriculum.

In other words, the students learn how to learn and how to get to work to study learn the curriculum areas. Teachers study how to teach learning strategies and how to find, generate and modify curriculum materials to make knowledge and skills more accessible to the students, including modifying existing materials – the curriculum is in no way 'dumbed down'.

Rationales

As we consider the rationales, we discover how radical they are with respect to the norms of the subfield of education that deals with learning disabilities. The normative practice has been to tutor students in a step-by-step coverage of the basic skills of reading and mathematics. Instruction for low-achieving economically poor students has been similar. The rationale of the normative field has been that the students are limited and that instruction has to proceed in a parsimonious way that accommodates their limited capabilities and covers curriculum areas specifically and very slowly. Freeing them to learn better is a better course.

The five points of the SIM rationale (see Deshler and Schumaker 2006: 122 ff), here in any prose and interpretations, are as follows:

1   First is that *these* adolescents who are labelled as learning disabled come to secondary school without the skills to enable them to perform adequately. Although Deshler and Schumaker are discreet, we are less so. These students have been in school for 8 or 9 years and, over that near decade have had service by 'experts' in special education. And still they are left without the tools of learning to enable them to profit from secondary education.

2   Second, these students do not naturally develop productive learning strategies. In fact, a good many develop unproductive strategies, ones that make learning difficult. They need productive learning strategies. In many cases, the interface with school instruction has not been enhancing. They are born with the tools for learning, such as classification abilities and cooperative capacities that should have carried them through. But, they have, in a sense, learned to 'hide' those skills, pushed away instruction and the companionship of their peers and fallen further and further behind.

3   Although they have many disadvantages as learners in secondary education, they are more mature cognitively than when they were younger – one can actually teach them more easily than when they were, say, 7 or 8. This fact is often overlooked because they look more like the class that the Sidney Poitier character faced in *To Sir, With Love*, than the friendly, often goofy, but generally cheerful demeanours of their cohorts.

4   They *have* to learn to be independent learners – high school is the 'last chance' for them to prepare themselves for a life in which learning capacity is a crucial variable.

5   These students have to learn to take responsibility for their learning – they need to accept responsibility for learning effective learning strategies. One reason for the failure of previous interventions is that the teacher is put in the position of taking responsibility – the students become more and more passive and willing to 'leave it to the teacher' to motivate and teach.

Thus, to be effective a curriculum has to address their terrible self-concepts, their need to learn how to learn. They have to learn to approach the curriculum areas that have frightened them for years and to understand that *they* have to do the learning – that withdrawing from education is not a productive option and that, against all odds, THEY CAN DO IT.

Why a multidimensional model?

There is no single model of learning that can solve the complex of problems carried by these students. Thus, the curriculum *has* to be built with several dimensions: 'The curriculum is organized into three major strands that correspond to three categories of demands presented by mainstream secondary and post-secondary curricula' (Deshler and Schumaker 2006: 124).

Thus:

1   The first strand is composed of 'strategies that help students get information from written material' (p. 124) and 'store that information'. [Sounds like concept formation and attainment, doesn't it?]

2 The second strand is 'strategies that enable students to identify, organize, and store important information' (p. 125). [Sounds like mnemonics, concept formation, concept attainment and ...]
3 The third is 'strategies for facilitating written expression' (p. 125). [Has more than a little in common with the picture–word inductive model and the other inquiry models.]

If you think about the demands of secondary and higher education – being able to approach written material productively, organize and store information and write decently – a student is in pretty good shape if these goals are achieved.

Grounding in research and good clinical information

To build these strands, the Kansas team studied a wide variety of sources on how these three types of inquiry have been studied and synthesized the results into the sets of learning strategies that comprise the three strands.

For example, within the strand where students get, store and express information from written material, the storage strand includes three components:

1 a first-letter mnemonic strategy
2 a paired-associates strategy
3 a vocabulary-learning strategy.

Thus, the students are taught research and inquiry-based strategies throughout the strategic inquiry model, just as the general models of learning approach provides teachers with grounded learning strategies that they can teach their students.

A strategy for teaching the strands to learning-disabled students

Again, the Kansas group has developed a very careful strategy that is designed to help students learn the strategies and to transfer them to curricular tasks and commit themselves to generate higher rates of learning.

Rather than confining the SIM model only to special education practitioners, the SIM approach extends to secondary teachers of the core subjects, helping them to take on the capability to teach learning strategies and to plan and execute ways of helping those students become successful learners.

Learning to acquire, store and apply information is part of the job of all students and if students with learning disabilities are in the classes with other students, no harm will be done but, rather, all students should benefit from these strategies. And these approaches include helping the students learn how to apply the content of their courses to solve problems in and out of school, rather than regarding the 'school content' as irrelevant to real life.

There is nothing frivolous about the Kansas City team. That team has shown what multiple models can do for a population that many others virtually write off, largely because they simply do not know how to help.

A felicitous comparison: a second chance to learn to read

Emily and Bruce have developed a curriculum for 'overage beginning readers', students from fourth to twelfth grades who are struggling readers. About half of them have been diagnosed as having learning disabilities. We have called this curriculum 'A Second Chance to Learn to Read', and some school districts have called it 'Read to Succeed', a term invented by the Northern Lights school district in Alberta (see Joyce et al. 2001). Second Chance is a multidimensioned approach that teaches students to develop sight vocabulary, inquire into the structure of words, read extensively and write to learn to read. Prior to engagement with Second Chance, the students' average GLE gain in their history is about 0.5 GLE. When they exit the fourth grade, their average is about 2.5 against a national average of about 5.0. During their first year in Read to Succeed, the average gains for both 'regular' (those not diagnosed as having learning disabilities) struggling readers and those with learning disabilities is about GLE 2.0. In other words, their fifth grade exit score is about 4.5 against a national average of 6.0. As with SIM, these pre-adolescent and adolescent failing students are being brought into a new and optimistic world of achievement. A major difference with SIM is that learning disabilities are not addressed, neither are applications to the core curriculum areas, although non-fiction is used extensively, much of it related to the core areas. The 90-minute a day focus is on reading and writing. The following is adapted from one of our reports, written by Bruce and Emily with Marilyn Hrycauk, then the curriculum director of Northern Lights School Division #69 in Alberta, Canada.

The 'overage' beginning reader: an action research test of a multidimensional approach

Whether one judges by examining the studies reported as the National Assessment of Educational Progress (2004), the studies by state and provincial departments of education or examines the information available in school districts, the picture is the same: somewhere around one-third of our students have not reached the level of competence needed to educate themselves by accessing the learning resources used in the upper elementary, middle and high schools. Further, the situation gets worse for those students as their competence falls further behind their peers and the massive programmes directed at categories of student, whether special education, programmes for the economically poor, second-language initiatives and early years initiatives have in general been able to do little to alleviate the problem (McGill-Franzen and Allington 1991).

Consequently, nearly all school districts face a situation where a substantial proportion of their students in fourth to twelfth grades are virtually 'beginning' readers, essentially having only the knowledge and skills characteristic of early or middle primary grade students. In some settings, interventions made in the pre-school, kindergarten and primary years have reduced the number (see Slavin et al. 1994), but in most districts the number continues to be sizeable and the interventions after the primary grades are largely ineffective.

Perspective

Yet the research on how to teach reading is substantial and lays a base from which we can construct curriculums that we believe will make a considerable difference. However, these curriculums are not built around off-the-shelf packages of materials that can be adopted with minimal training. To implement those curriculums requires extensive inquiry-oriented staff development. To implement radically different curriculums requires considerable study because implementing them thoroughly requires considerable expansion of the repertoire of most teachers. The staff need to study the research, acquire new teaching strategies and study student learning on a formative as well as a summative basis.

In a number of reviews (Calhoun 1997; Joyce 1999; Showers et al. 1998) we have theorized that a multidimensional curriculum containing the following components has a reasonable chance of helping overage beginning readers to accelerate their growth in literacy, regain lost self-esteem and get in reach of academic success and the capability of teaching themselves through reading and writing. The components include:

- development of sight vocabulary from the developed listening – speaking vocabulary through the picture – word inductive model (Calhoun 1997; see also Chapter 6) or an experience-record approach (Stauffer 1969) and the study of words encountered through wide reading (Nagy and Anderson 1984)
- wide reading at the developed level (Duke and Pearson undated)
- the study of word patterns, including spelling (Ehri 1994)
- regular (several times daily) writing and the study of writing (Englert et al. 1991)
- the study of comprehension strategies (Garner 1987; Pressley 1995)
- the study, by both teachers and students, on a weekly and monthly basis, of progress, including levels of books the students can read, sight words learned, phonetic and structural analytic skills, information learned and fluency in writing (Calhoun 1999). Students study their progress and whether they are ready for exit because they are independent readers of grade-appropriate text.

The Read to Succeed curriculum requires about 90 minutes a day. For middle and high school students the 90-minute period replaces elective and exploratory subjects. Length of enrolment may vary considerably. The gap between their competence on enrolment and the level needed to manage grade-typical learning resources can be substantial. Eighth or ninth grade students may enter with the level of the average second or third grade student. In addition, most of the students arrive with well-developed phobias about reading and writing and, because of their lack of academic success, considerable resistance to instruction and well-developed skills for avoiding instruction of any sort. In several exploratory studies about half the students made considerable progress in a single semester, moving, for example, to the level of the level of the average fifth grade student. The other half responded equally well during the second semester (Showers et al. 1998). Thus, enrolment should be for an initial year with exit provided as adequate competence has been achieved. A rule of thumb is the level of average students at the end of sixth grade. When they reach that point, most appear to be able to handle middle and high school learning resources, provided that they apply themselves.

Mode of inquiry/data sources

In the Northern Lights school district, Second Chance is nested in a broader programme of initiatives, all of which are conducted from an action research frame of reference whereby the teachers and administrators in each initiative study implementation and student learning on a formative basis. The 20 schools of the district include populations of considerable variance in SES and ethnicity terms. As we began in 1999, both teacher opinion and provincial assessments indicated that the district had been typical of those in North America: about one third of the students become overage beginning readers.

The components of the programme require substantial staff development into research-based curricular and instructional patterns. Some of the components address needs of all students at every level while others address specific levels or students of particular needs:

- *Just Read.* A district-wide programme to increase student independent reading, particularly 'at home' reading (Joyce and Wolf 1996). The rationale is direct: students need to read widely to consolidate skills, to explore the world that lies within books and Just Read involves the entire school and neighbourhood community in an active action research effort to ensure that all students are reading independently.
- *Primary Curriculum (K-3).* The teachers are studying and beginning to implement strategies, particularly the picture – word inductive model (Calhoun 1999; Joyce and Calhoun 1996), that are designed to increase vocabulary, enhance phonetic and structural analysis and increase comprehension strategies. Kindergarten teachers are beginning to study how to teach their students to read (see Chapter 15). The first emphasis of the action research includes studying the acquisition of vocabulary and phonetic analysis skills. These teachers engage in from 10 to 15 days of staff development that includes demonstrations, the study of the literature on literacy and support by a cadre of teachers and administrators.

The present study involves 12 sections involving 300 students in the Northern Lights School District #69. The Second Chance teachers received 10 to 15 days of staff development, studied their implementation and the growth of their students by a variety of measures including standard tests (the Canadian Tests of Basic Skills or the Gates-McGinnitie battery administered on enrolment and at the end of the academic year 1999–2000). The 20 schools of the district include populations of considerable variance in SES and ethnicity.

In this report, standard tests are the primary source of data and are interpreted, first, in terms of the characteristics of the students and, second, in terms of their progress. Complete data were available for 250 students in the 12 sections. For each student, learning history indices were computed providing estimates of student progress compared with the 'average' student. Each of the 12 teachers of the sections studied the growth of each student, the progress of the students in their section and the progress of the Second Chance initiative as a whole. The study included the acquisition of sight vocabulary, phonetic and structural analysis skills and gain scores computed from the standard tests. The overall picture that emerged is the emphasis in this section.

Table 8.1 provides an example of the data that were accumulated in each section.

Table 8.1 Pre- and postest CTBS vocabulary and comprehension scores for 16 students.

Student number, gender and code	Grade	Length in months	Vocabulary (GLE)			Comprehension (GLE)		
Gender		(mos)	Initial	Final	Gain	Initial	Final	Gain
1. F	5	9	2.3	4.4	2.1	2.9	4.9	2.0
2. F	5	9	1.9	4.3	2.4	2.9	4.6	1.7
3. M	5	9	1.7	4.2	2.5	1.4	5.0	3.6
4. M	5	5	3.3	3.9	0.6	3.0	4.8	1.8
6. M	5	9	1.4	4.3	2.9	3.0	4.7	1.7
7. M	5	5	2.8	2.9	0.1	3.2	3.7	0.5
8. M	5	5	1.9	4.0	2.1	2.1	3.5	1.4
9. M	5	9	2.3	4.3	2.0	3.5	4.8	1.3
10.M	4/5	7	3.9	3.3	(0.6)	3.0	4.1	1.1
11.M	4/5	5	3.1	4.1	1.0	4.8	5.1	0.3
12.F	4/5	5	3.6	4.4	0.8	3.0	4.6	1.6
13.M	4/5	5	2.6	3.0	0.4	2.9	3.5	0.6
14.F	4/5	5	4.5	4.9	0.4	3.3	5.1	1.8
15.M	4/5	9	3.9	4.9	1.0	2.7	5.3	2.6
16.M	4/5	5	2.3	3.0	0.7	2.4	3.6	1.2

All these students made substantial gains on the vocabulary subtest, the comprehension subtest or both subtests of the Canada Tests of Basic Skills. In this class, there were just three females; thus, there is a big gender difference in enrolment, but no gender difference appears in effects. The mean gain on the vocabulary subtest was 1.2 and, on the comprehension subtest, 1.5. Gains relative to initial scores are particularly interesting. The initial scores for six students were in the average range of end-of-first-grade students (1.7–2.3). The average gain for this subgroup of students was 2.1. In their previous 4 or 5 years of schooling, the average gain for these six students had been around 0.25 per year and the prognosis that that level of gain would rise would normally be poor (Juel 1992).

Data like those in Table 8.1 were merged into the picture that follows.

Results/evidence

Characteristics of the students enrolled

Each school arranged to identify students and enrol them. The resulting sections of Read to Succeed reflected differences in the process undertaken in the schools, especially the priorities that emerged. In all schools, there were more overage beginning readers than could be served at any given time and the faculties and administrators had to make some tough decisions about whom to enrol. The 250 students are about 10 per cent of the district student body from fourth to twelfth grades. The overall Second Chance student body looks like this:

- *Gender*: two-thirds are males. Some sections were virtually all males (11 of 12, in one case) and a few were relatively even (eight of 14 were females in one case).
- *Coded as having special needs*: 70 per cent. Mostly codes 54 (mild to moderate learning disabilities), 30 per cent and 57 (communication problems), also 30 per cent.
- *Standard test scores on entry*: 46 per cent of the elementary grade students tested at or below the average for graduating second grade students. For those who were fifth grade students, the gain through their 4 or more years of schooling was about a quarter the gain of the average student (in GLE terms). A similar picture appeared for the entering middle-school students.

What was their progress?

Data such as those in Table 8.1 were organized and the following picture emerged.

- *Overall*: 56 per cent of the gain scores indicated progress of from one and a half times the gains of the average student to three times the gain of average students and 18 per cent more achieved gains equal to those of average students (approximately two to four times the rate of their previous progress).
- *Gender*: almost identical progress by males and females as a whole.
- *Elementary and middle school sections* made almost identical gains. Grade level of students within sections (some included students from two or three grade levels) was not a factor either. For example, seventh grade students in sections where there were also sixth and eighth grade students gained about as much as did seventh grade students in sections containing only seventh grade students.

- *Scores on entry* were not a factor. Gains were similar for students beginning at 2.0, 3.0, 4.0 and so on.
- *Special needs codes*: overall, progress of students with and without special needs codes was almost identical across all grades.
- *SES of students* was not a factor.

During this year, or half-year in one case, the student gains were twice the gain of average students for a year and eight times their own previous average annual gain. For most of these students, another year of this magnitude of gain would bring them to where they 'look like' average students, at least from a test score perspective. As it is, they have experienced a year of considerable growth and have reached a level in reading where, with effort, they can manage typical upper elementary grade academic tasks. As an aside, all these students were coded as having serious learning disabilities or communication disorders.

Most important is that research on curriculum for overage beginning readers appears to have reached the point at which we can design curriculums that can reach those students and provide them with an opportunity to grow at normal rates and better. In this case, a series of studies have been conducted and there are more to follow. Further studies will examine students whose response is slower and the academic progress of all the students in order to improve the curricular framework.

Part 3

Learning to study oneself

9 Learning through counselling

"The idea that you teach kids how to ask and answer questions, rather than just asking them questions, came as a revelation to me."

A teacher of 20 years, to Bruce Joyce, May 1995

From the personal family of models of learning and teaching, we have selected Carl Rogers' nondirective model to illustrate the philosophy of helping students learn about themselves and learn how to think about themselves and others in school and throughout their lives.

Scenario 1

One of the important uses of nondirective teaching occurs when a class becomes 'stale' and the teacher finds himself or herself just 'pushing' the students through exercises and subject matter. Jane Goring, a middle school teacher exhausted by the failure of more traditional attempts to cope with discipline problems and lack of interest on the part of her class, decided to experiment with student-centred teaching. She turned to nondirective approaches to help her students take more responsibility for their learning and to ensure that the subject matter would be related to their needs and learning styles. She has provided an account of that experience, from which excerpts are presented here.

> *5 March, we begin*
>
> A week ago I decided to initiate a new programme in my classroom, based on student-centred teaching – an unstructured or nondirective approach.
>
> I began by telling the class that we were going to try an 'experiment'. I explained that for one day I would let them do anything they wanted to do – they did not have to do anything if they did not want to.
>
> Many students started with art projects; some drew or painted for most of the day. Others read or did work in maths and other subjects. There was an air of excitement all day. Many were so interested in what they were doing that they did not want to go out at break!
>
> At the end of the day, I asked the class to evaluate the experiment. The comments were most interesting. Some were 'confused', distressed without the teacher telling them what to do, without specific assignments to complete.

The majority of the class thought the day was 'great', but some expressed concern over the noise level and the fact that a few students 'messed around' all day. Most felt that they had accomplished as much work as we usually do and they enjoyed being able to work at a task until it was completed, without the pressure of a time limit. They liked doing things without being 'forced' to do them and liked deciding what to do.

They begged to continue the 'experiment', so it was decided to do so, for two more days. We could then re-evaluate the plan.

The next morning, I implemented the idea of a 'work contract'. I gave them worksheets listing all our subjects with suggestions for activities or accomplishments under each. There was a space provided for their 'plans' in each area and for comments on completion.

Each child was to write his or her contract for the day – choosing the areas in which to work and planning specifically what to do. On completion of any exercise, drill, review, etc., the student was to check and correct his or her own work, using the teacher's manual. The work was to be kept in a folder with the contract.

I met with each child to discuss his or her plans. Some completed theirs in a very short time; we discussed as a group what this might mean and what to do about it. It was suggested that the plan might not be challenging enough, that an adjustment should be made – perhaps going on or adding another idea to the day's plan.

Resource materials were provided, suggestions made and drill materials made available to use when needed.

I found I had much more time, so I worked, talked and spent the time with individuals and groups. At the end of the third day, I evaluated the work folder with each child. To solve the problem of assessment, I had each child tell me what he or she had learned.

12 March, progress report

Our 'experiment' has, in fact, become our programme – with some adjustments.

Some children continued to be frustrated and felt insecure without teacher direction. Discipline also continued to be a problem with some; and I began to realize that, although some of the children may need the programme more than others, I was expecting too much from them, too soon – they were not ready to assume self-direction yet. Perhaps a gradual weaning from the spoon-fed procedures was necessary.

I regrouped the class – creating two groups. The larger group is the nondirected. The smallest is teacher directed, made up of children who wanted to return to the former teacher-directed method and those who, for varied reasons, were unable to function in the self-directed situation. I would have waited longer to see what would happen, but the situation for some disintegrated a little more each day – penalizing the whole class. The disrupting factor kept everyone upset and limited those who wanted to study and work. So it seemed to me best for the group as a whole, as well as the programme, to modify the plan.

Those who continued the 'experiment' have forged ahead. I showed them how to design or 'programme' their work, using their texts as a basic guide. They have learned that they can teach themselves (and each other) and that I am available when a step is not clear or advice is needed.

At the end of each week, they evaluate themselves in each area – in terms of work accomplished, accuracy, progress toward long-term goals, etc. We have learned that the number of errors is not a criterion of failure or success, for errors can and should be part of the learning process. We also discussed the fact that consistently perfect scores may mean that the work is not challenging enough and perhaps we should move on.

After self-evaluation, each child brings the evaluation sheet and work folder to discuss with me.

Some of the members of the group working with me are most anxious to become 'independent' students. We evaluate together each week their progress toward that goal.

Some students (there were two or three) who originally wanted to return to the teacher-directed programme are now anticipating going back into the self-directed programme. (I sense that it has been as difficult for them to readjust to the old programme as it would be for me to do so.)

Let us now look at the nondirective model being used with an individual student.

Scenario 2

Ray Bolam, a 26-year-old secondary school English teacher in Sheffield, is very concerned about Sue Fortnay, one of his students. Sue is a compulsive worker who does an excellent job with literature assignments and writes excellent short stories. She is, however, reluctant to share those stories with other members of the class and declines to participate in any activities in the performing arts.

Mr Bolam recognizes that the issue cannot be forced, but he wants Sue to understand why she is reluctant to allow any public display of her talents. She will make her own decisions about participation that involves sharing her ideas.

One afternoon she asks him to read some of her pieces and give her his opinion:

[*Sue*] Mr Bolam, could you take a look at these for me?

[*Bolam*] Certainly, Sue. Another short story?

[*Sue*] No, some poems I've been working on. I don't think they're very good, but I'd like you to tell me what you think.

[*Bolam*] When did you write them?

[*Sue*] One Sunday afternoon a couple of weeks ago.

[*Bolam*] Do you remember what started you thinking that you wanted to write a poem?

[*Sue*] I was feeling sort of sad and I remembered last month when we tried to read *The Waste Land* and it seemed to be trying to say a lot of things that we couldn't say in the usual way. I liked the beginning lines, 'April is the cruellest month, breeding lilacs out of the dead land'.

[*Bolam*] And this is what you wrote down?

[*Sue*] Yes. It's the first time I've ever tried writing anything like this.

[*Bolam* reads for a few minutes, then looks up] Sue, these are really good.

[*Sue*] What makes a poem good, Mr Bolam?

[*Bolam*] Well, there are a variety of ways to judge poetry. Some methods are technical and have to do with the quality of expression and the way one uses metaphors and analogies and other literary devices. Others are subjective and involve the quality of expression, the real beauty of the words themselves.

[*Sue*] I felt very good when I was writing them, but when I read them over, they sound stupid to me.

[*Bolam*] What do you mean?

[*Sue*] Oh, I don't know. I guess the main thing is that I feel ashamed if anybody else sees them.

[*Bolam*] Ashamed?

[*Sue*] I really don't know. I just know that if these were to be read aloud, say to my class, I would be so embarrassed.

[*Bolam*] You really feel that the class would laugh at these?

[*Sue*] Oh yeah, they wouldn't understand.

[*Bolam*] How about your short stories? How do you feel about them?

[*Sue*] You know I don't want *anybody* to see what I write.

[*Bolam*] You really feel that you want to put them away somewhere so nobody can see them?

[*Sue*] Yes, I really think so. I don't know exactly why, but I'm pretty sure that no one in my class would understand them.

[*Bolam*] Can you think of anybody else that might understand them?

[*Sue*] I don't know. I suppose there are people out there who might, but nobody around here, probably.

[*Bolam*] How about your parents?

[*Sue*] Oh, they like everything I write.

[*Bolam*] Well, that makes three of us. Can you think of anybody else?

[*Sue*] I guess I think adults would, but I'm not really so sure about other people my age.

[*Bolam*] Are people your age somehow different from adults in this respect?

[*Sue*] Well, they just don't seem to be interested in these kinds of things. I feel they put down anybody who tries to write anything.

[*Bolam*] Do you think they feel this way about the authors we read in class?

[*Sue*] Well, sometimes they do, but I guess a lot of the time they really enjoy the stories.

[*Bolam*] Well then, why do you think they wouldn't like what you write?

[*Sue*] I guess I don't really know, Mr Bolam. I guess I'm really afraid, but I can't put my finger on it.

[*Bolam*] Something holds you back.

[*Sue*] In a lot of ways, I really would like to find out whether anybody would appreciate what I write. I just don't know how to go about it.

[*Bolam*] How would you feel if I were to read one of your short stories but not tell them who wrote it?

[*Sue*] Would you promise?

[*Bolam*] Of course I would. Then we could talk about how everybody reacted. You would know that they didn't know who had written it.

[*Sue*] I don't know, but it sounds interesting.

[*Bolam*] Depending on what happened, we could cook up some kind of strategy about what to do next.

[*Sue*] Well, I guess I don't have much to lose.

[*Bolam*] I hope we're always where you don't have anything to lose, Sue; but there's always a risk in telling about ourselves.

[*Sue*] What do you mean, telling about ourselves?

[*Bolam*] I have to go now – but let me pick one of your stories and read it next week, and then let's get together on Wednesday and talk about what happened.

[*Sue*] OK, and you promise not to tell?

[*Bolam*] I promise. I'll see you next Wednesday after school.

[*Sue*] OK. Thanks a lot, Mr Bolam. Have a good weekend.

The nondirective model of learning and teaching

Both Jane Goring and Ray Bolam were using the nondirective model of learning and teaching based on the work of psychologist and counsellor Carl Rogers (1961, 1982) and other advocates of nondirective counselling. Rogers believed that positive human relationships enable people to grow; instruction therefore, should be based on concepts of human relations in contrast to concepts of subject matter. Basically, he extended to education his view of therapy as a mode of learning.

For almost five decades, Carl Rogers was the acknowledged spokesperson for models in which the teacher plays the role of counsellor. Developed from counselling theory, the nondirective model emphasizes a partnership between students and teacher. The teacher endeavours to help the students understand how to play major roles in directing their own education – for example, by behaving in such a way as to clarify goals and participate in developing avenues for reaching those goals. The teacher provides information about how much progress is being made and helps the students solve problems. The nondirective teacher has to build the partnerships that are required and provide the help needed as students try to work out their problems.

As with other models in the personal family, the nondirective model has the following purposes:

- to lead the student toward greater mental and emotional health by developing self-confidence, forming a realistic sense of self and building empathetic reactions to others
- to increase the proportion of education that emanates from the needs and aspirations of the student – that is, taking each student as a partner in determining what he or she will learn and how he or she will learn it
- to develop specific kinds of qualitative thinking, such as creativity and personal expression.

Rogerian teaching is an emergent, 'rolling' model rather than a linear one. It advocates the following of principles rather than scripts when working with students, and the principles create the structure by guiding our interactions. The model can be used with any other model of teaching or to counsel a group or an individual.

When used in the context of another model, Rogerian principles can guide our behaviour as we help students reach out to learn and reach out to one another. Thus in any teaching/learning encounter we can behave so as to:

- radiate warmth and confidence to the students
- radiate empathy and understanding
- help the students understand how their stance toward tasks and others can draw them toward self-actualization.

When counselling, we add the dimensions of:

- helping the students clarify a general or specific problem

- helping the students take responsibility for changing their behaviour so as to solve the problem
- helping the students experiment and reflect on the results of their experimentation
- helping them develop empathy toward others in their environment.

Phases of the model

Despite the fluidity of the nondirective strategy, Rogers points out that the nondirective interview has a sequence and that sequence is important when we are helping the students to take charge of the inquiry into their behaviour.

In *phase 1*, the helping situation is defined. This includes structuring remarks by the counsellor that define the student's freedom to express feelings, an agreement on the general focus of the interview, an initial problem statement, some discussion of the relationship if it is to be ongoing and the establishment of procedures for meeting. Phase 1 generally occurs during the initial session on a problem. However, some structuring or definition by the teacher may be necessary for some time, even if this consists only of occasional summarizing moves that redefine the problem and reflect progress. Naturally, these structuring and definitional comments vary considerably with the type of interview, the specific problem and the student.

In *phase 2*, the student is encouraged by the teacher's acceptance and clarification to express negative and positive feelings to state and explore the problem.

In *phase 3*, the student gradually develops insight: he or she perceives new meaning in his or her experiences, sees new relationships of cause and effect and understands the meaning of his or her previous behaviour. In most situations, the student seems to alternate between exploring the problem itself and developing new insight into his or her feelings. Both activities are necessary for progress. Discussion of the problem without exploration of feelings would indicate that the student him- or herself was being avoided.

In *phase 4*, the student moves toward planning and decision making with respect to the problem. The role of the teacher is to clarify the alternatives.

In *phase 5*, the student reports the actions he or she has taken, develops further insight and plans increasingly more integrated and positive actions.

These five phases could occur in one session or, more likely, over a series of encounters. In the latter case, phases 1 and 2 could occur in the first few discussions, phases 3 and 4 in the next and phase 5 in the last interview. Or, if the encounter consists of a voluntary meeting with a student who has an immediate problem, phases 1 through 4 could occur in only one meeting, with the student returning briefly to report his or her actions and insights. Contrariwise, the sessions involved in negotiating academic contracts are sustained for a period of time and the context of each meeting generally involves some kind of planning and decision making, although several sessions devoted entirely to exploring a problem might occur.

Research

Personal models are very difficult to research, because, by their nature, the 'treatments' change as the students become more able to take charge of their own development. So, we don't have a plan where a carefully designed 'X' is used with the student or client and relentlessly pursued. No, conditions change.

Over the years, the nondirective model has been used with all types of student and across all subjects and teaching roles. Although it is designed to promote self-understanding and independence, it has fared well as a contributor to a wide range of academic objectives.

While enhancing the learner as a person is a worthwhile educational goal in its own right, a major thesis of the nondirective model of teaching is that better developed, more affirmative, self-actualizing learners have increased learning capabilities. This thesis is supported by a number of studies indicating that teachers who incorporate personal models into their repertoires increase achievement among their students (Roebuck et al. 1976).

A major review of research from the late 1940s to the present (Cornelius-White 2007) displays more than a thousand studies with, altogether, more than 350,000 students and, among the studies, 1,400 findings. The review examined cognitive, affective and behavioural effects. The reviewers believe that, looking over the whole of this long-term set of inquiries which employed a large number of designs, the result is a remarkably consistent, modest effect. Personal inquiry is not a sharp-edged intervention that drives change, but a soft intervention (the term nondirective continues to capture the essence) whose effects accumulate by degrees over a period of weeks or months. However, in the studies that used other interventions in curriculum and instruction as the control, the effect sizes averaged a positive 0.30. (See Chapter 11 for a discussion of the concept of effect size and its use as a statistic.) Many sharp-edged interventions get no larger effects.

Reflections

Since the activities and content that comprise each phase are not prescribed but are determined by the student as he or she interacts with the teacher and other students, the nondirective teaching model depends largely on its nurturant effects rather than its immediate instructional effects. Its instructional effects are primarily dependent on its success in nurturing more effective self-development. Thus this model can be thought of as entirely nurturant in character, dependent for effects on experiencing the nondirective learning environment rather than on developing specific academic content and skills.

From birth, we are acted on by the world. Our social environment gives us our language, teaches us how to behave and provides love to us. But our individual selves configure themselves relentlessly and create their own interior environments. Within those worlds each of us creates our identity and our personalities have remarkable continuity from early in life (White 1986). Yet, while much within out interior world remains stable, we have great capacity to change. We can adapt to a wide range of climates and physical environments. We are incomplete without others and can love and receive love, generating perhaps the greatest growth of all.

Paradoxically, we also have the capacity to hold tight to behaviour that doesn't work – as if to force the world to yield and make our worst features productive. We are the greatest! And we can be mulish!

Personal models of teaching share several purposes, all depending on helping the student to inquiry into his/her behaviour and to develop empathetic engagement with others. The first is to lead the student toward greater mental and emotional health by developing self-confidence and a realistic sense of self and by building empathetic reactions to others. The second is to increase the proportion of education that emanates from the needs and aspirations of the students themselves, taking each student as a partner in determining what he or she will learn and how he or she will learn it. The third is to develop specific kinds of qualitative thinking, such as creativity and personal expression.

In addition to the belief that enhancing the learner as a person is a worthwhile educational goal in its own right, a major thesis of this family of models is that better developed, more affirmative, self-actualizing learners have increased learning capabilities. Thus, personal models will increase academic achievement by tending the psyches of the learners.

Summary in motion: final scenarios

The hard part of figuring out how to teach is learning when to keep your mouth closed, which is most of the time.

Carl Rogers, to a seminar at Columbia University, about 1960

Scenario: real fear and tension

We are in a Department of Defense dependents school (DODDS) in Germany, in Charley Wilson's fifth grade class of the children of soldiers. Many of the parents have just been sent to Afghanistan to secure an airfield against attacking forces. Charley has decided that the best course of action is to busy his students in academic study and he is ready to begin a unit on writing that begins with a set of film clips that the students will write about.

However, as he readies the VCR and turns to the class, he can see unusual stress on the students' faces. He asks, 'What's up?' There is no response. He says: 'Are you worried?'

One student responds strongly: 'We're worried sick.' The others nod.

'OK. Now, shall we deal with it? Do you want to talk about it?'

'I don't know what to say. I'm just frozen', says Pamela. More nodding.

'What does frozen feel like?'

'It's like I'm hardly alive. I'm hiding inside a cave.'

'That's a good way to put it', says Josh. 'It's like I'm somewhere else, trying to freeze out what's happening.'

'It's like if you let your fear in – really in – you won't be able to stand it. You have to hide and keep it away,' says Nancy.

The students are looking directly at Charley, avoiding one anothers' eyes. Charley keeps the discussion going, primarily eliciting comments like these here.

'You know what? We all fear', Charley says. Again, everyone nods. 'Our fear is a good thing. It's not crazy. There's real danger out there.' The students begin to look at one another now, and nod. They are miserable.

'The problem is that we have to support those mothers and fathers and keep ourselves going when we are scared and anxious.' More nods and eye contact with Charley. 'So, let's directly face how we are going to do that.'

Charley is beginning an inquiry into feelings and the very immediate problem of how these children will carry on and help their parents deal with a life-threatening danger.

Scenario: the third day of a Read to Succeed class

'You expect me to read to myself for 20 minutes every day in this class?'

'Absolutely. You've got to learn to read better and you won't unless you read more.'

'Who says so.'

'Well, who is talking to you right now, Tom?'

'I can read all right. Why do I have to be in this class?'

'I'd like you to read something to me, now.' [Hands the student an open book.] 'Begin at the top of the page on the left.'

'What's this word?'

'Do you mean the first word, Tom?'

'Yes.'

'Is that the heading of the page?'

'Yes, Miss Tamron.'

'The word that probably tells us what the page is about?'

'Yes. Come on, what is it?'

'Listen carefully, Tom. That word is addition. Kids in first grade have to learn to read that word at sight. You are in the sixth grade. What does that tell you?'

'I don't like to read.'

'You may, when you learn how.'

In this rather abrupt session, Miss Tamron is trying to get Tom to face himself and what he has to do. For years, Tom has resisted teachers who have tried to teach him to read. The passage illustrates that nondirective doesn't mean 'wimpy.'

Reflections

The nondirective atmosphere has four qualities. First, the teacher shows warmth and responsiveness, expressing genuine interest in the student and accepting him or her as a person. Second, it is characterized by permissiveness in regard to the expression of feeling; the teacher does not judge or moralize. Because of the importance of emotions, much content is discussed that would normally be guarded against in more customary student relationships with teachers or advisers. Third, the student is free to express feelings symbolically but is not free to control the teacher or to carry impulses into action. Fourth, the relationship is free from any type of pressure or coercion. The teacher avoids showing personal bias or reacting in a personally critical manner to the student. Every learning task is viewed as an opportunity to help the student grow as a person.

10   Learning to study values

"The analysis of values is what's important. Playing the roles lets the values become visible if the analysis is right. Understanding that what you do is as living-out of your values starts the inquiry."

Fannie Shaftel to a group of Palo Alto teachers, May 1969

Role playing is another way of building a learning community by teaching students another way of learning. In role play, students explore human relations problems by enacting problem situations and then focusing on the values that are revealed. Together, students can explore feelings, attitudes and problem-solving strategies as well as values.

Scenario 1

We are in the Year 7 class of a middle school in the East End of London. The students have returned to the classroom from a break and are complaining excitedly to one another. Mr Williams, the teacher, asks what the matter is and they all start joining in at once, discussing a series of difficulties throughout the break. Apparently two of the students began to squabble about who was to take the sports equipment outside. Then all the students argued about what game to play. Next there was a dispute about choosing sides for the games. This included a dispute over whether the girls should be included with the boys or whether they should play separately. The class finally began to play volleyball, but very shortly there was a dispute over a line call and the game was never completed.

   At first Mr Williams displays his displeasure toward the class. He is angry, not simply over the incidents, but because these arguments have been going on since the beginning of the year. At last he says: 'OK, we really have to face this problem. You must be as tired of it as I am and you really are not acting maturely. So we are going to use a technique that we have been using to discuss family problems to approach our own problems right here in this classroom: we're going to use role playing. Now, I want you to divide into groups and try to identify the types of problems that we've been having. Just take today, for example and outline the problem situations that got us into this fix.'

   The students begin with the argument over taking the sports equipment outside and then outline other arguments. Each is a typical situation that people face all the time and that they must learn to take a stand on. After the separate groups of students have listed their problems, Mr Williams appoints one of the students to lead a discussion in which each group reports the kinds of problem situation that have come up; the groups agree on half a dozen problems that have consistently bothered the class.

The students then classify the problems according to type. One type concerns the division of labour. A second type deals with deciding principles for selecting teams. A third type focuses on resolving disputes over the particulars of games, such as whether balls have been hit out of bounds, whether players are out or safe and so on. Mr Williams then assigns one type of problem to each group and asks the groups to describe situations in which the problems come up. When they have done this, the class votes on which problem to start with. The first problem they select is disputes over rules; the actual problem situation they select is the volleyball game in which the dispute over a line call occurred.

The students talk about how the problem situation develops. It begins when a ball is hit close to the boundary line. One team believes it is in and the other believes it is out of bounds. The students then argue with one another and the argument goes on so that the game cannot continue.

Several students are selected to enact the situation. Others gather around and are assigned to observe particular aspects of the role playing that follows. Some students are to look for the particulars of how the argument develops. Some are to study one role player and others another, to determine how they handle the situation.

The enactment is spirited. The students select as role players those who have been on opposite sides during the game and they become as involved in the argument during the role playing as they were during the actual situation. Finally, they are standing in the middle of the room shouting at one another. At this point, Mr Williams calls 'Time!' and asks the students to describe what has gone on.

Everyone is eager to talk. The discussion gradually focuses on how the attitude of the participants prevented any solution of the problem. No one was listening to the other person and no one was dealing with the problem of how to resolve honest disputes. Mr Williams asks the students to suggest other ways in which people could behave in this kind of conflict. Some students suggest giving in gracefully. But others object that, if someone believes he or she is right, that is not an easy thing to do. Finally, the students identify an important question to focus on: 'How can we develop a policy about who should make calls and how should others feel about those calls?' They decide to re-enact the scene by having all the participants assume that the offensive team should make the calls only when they see clear evidence that a ball is out and the other team has not seen the evidence.

The enactment takes place. This time the players attempt to follow the policy that the defensive team has the right to make the call, but the offensive team has the right to object to a call. Once again, the enactment results in a shouting match; however, after it is over, the students who have watched the enactment point out that the role players have not behaved as if there is a resolution to the situation. They recognize that if there are to be games, there has to be agreement about who can make calls and a certain amount of trust on both sides.

They decide to try a third enactment, this time with two new role players inserted as dispute referees. The introduction of referees completely changes the third enactment. The referees insist that the other players pay attention to them, which the players do not want to do. In discussing this enactment, the students point out that there has to be a system to ensure reasonable order and the resolution of disputes. The students also agree that as things stand, they probably are unable to resolve disputes without including a referee of some sort, but that no referees will be effective unless the students agree to accept the referees' decisions as final. They finally decide that, in future games, two students will be referees. Those students will be chosen by lottery prior to the game; their function will be to arbitrate and to make all calls relevant to the rules of the game and their decisions will be final. The students agree that they will see how that system works.

The next day Mr Williams opens up the second set of issues and the students repeat this process. The exploration of other areas of dispute continues over the next few weeks. At first, many of the notions that are clarified are simply practical ones about how to solve specific problems. Gradually, however, Mr Williams directs the discussion to a consideration of the basic values governing individual behaviour. The students begin to see the problems of communal living; and they develop policies for governing their own behaviour, both as individuals and as members of a group. They also begin to develop skills in negotiating. The students who were locked in conflict gradually learn that if they behave in a slightly different way, others may also modify their behaviour and problems become easier to solve.

Role playing as a model of learning and teaching

Role playing has roots in both the personal and social dimensions of education, because it attempts both to help individuals find personal meaning within their social worlds and to resolve personal dilemmas with the assistance of the social group. In the social dimension, it allows individuals to work together in analysing social situations, especially interpersonal problems, and in developing decent and democratic ways of coping with these situations. The version we explore here was formulated by Fannie and George Shaftel (1967). We have also incorporated ideas from the work of Mark Chesler and Robert Fox (1966).

On its simplest level, role playing is dealing with problems through action: a problem is delineated, acted out and discussed. Some students are role players, others observers. A person puts himself or herself in the position of another person or category of people and then tries to interact with others who are also playing roles. As empathy, sympathy, anger and affection are all generated during the interaction, role playing, if done well, becomes a part of life. This emotional content, as well as the words and the actions, becomes part of the later analysis. When the acting out is finished, even the observers are involved enough to want to know why each person reached his or her decision, what the sources of resistance were and whether there were other ways to approach this situation.

The essence of role playing is the involvement of participants and observers in a real problem situation and the desire for resolution and understanding that this involvement engenders. The role-playing process provides a live sample of human behaviour that serves as a vehicle for students to:

- explore their feelings
- gain insight into their attitudes, values and perceptions
- develop their problem-solving skills and attitudes
- explore subject matter in varied ways.

These goals reflect several assumptions about the learning process in role playing. First, role playing implicitly advocates an experience-based learning situation in which the 'here and now' becomes the content of instruction. The model assumes that it is possible to create authentic analogies to real-life problem situations and that through these recreations students can 'sample' life. Thus the enactment elicits genuine, typical emotional responses and behaviours from the students.

A related assumption is that role playing can draw out students' feelings, which they can recognize and perhaps release. The Shaftels' version of role playing emphasizes the intellectual content as much as the emotional content; analysis and discussion of the enactment are as important as the role playing itself. We, as educators, are concerned that students recognize and understand their feelings and see how their feelings influence their behaviour.

Another assumption is that emotions and ideas can be brought to consciousness and enhanced by the group. The collective reactions of the peer group can bring out new ideas and provide directions for growth and change. The model de-emphasizes the traditional role of teacher and encourages listening and learning from one's peers.

And, finally, that covert psychological processes involving one's own attitudes, values and belief system can be brought to consciousness by combining spontaneous enactment with analysis. Furthermore, individuals can gain some measure of control over their belief systems if they recognize their values and attitudes and test them against the views of others. Such analysis can help them evaluate their attitudes and values and the consequences of their beliefs, so that they can allow themselves to grow.

The concept of role

Each individual has a unique manner of relating to people, situations and objects. One person may feel that most people are dishonest and cannot be trusted; someone else may feel that everyone is interesting and may look forward to meeting new people. People also evaluate and behave in consistent ways toward themselves, seeing themselves as powerful and smart or perhaps afraid and not very able. These feelings about people and situations and about themselves influence people's behaviour and determine how they will respond in various situations. Some people respond with aggressive and hostile behaviour, playing the part of a bully. Others withdraw and remain alone, playing the part of a shy or sulking person.

These parts people play are called *roles*. A role is a 'patterned sequence of feelings, words, and actions ... It is a unique and accustomed manner of relating to others' (Chesler and Fox 1966: 5, 8). Unless people are looking for them, it is sometimes hard to perceive consistencies and patterns in behaviour. But they are usually there. Terms such as *friendly, bully, snob, know-it-all* and *grouch* are convenient for describing characteristic responses and roles.

The roles individuals play are determined by several factors over many years. The kind of people someone meets determine his or her general feelings about people. How those people act toward the individual and how the individuals perceive their feelings toward them influence their feelings about themselves. The rules of one's particular culture and institutions help determine which roles a person assumes and how he or she plays them. People may not be happy with the roles they have assumed. And they may misperceive the attitudes and feelings of others because they do not recognize *their* role and *why* they play it. Two people can share the same feelings but behave in very different ways. They can desire the same goals, but if one person's behaviour is misperceived by others, he or she may not attain that goal.

Consequently, to gain a clear understanding of oneself and of others, it is extremely important that a person be aware of roles and how they are played. To do this, each person must be able to put himself or herself in another's place and to experience as much as possible that person's thoughts and feelings. If someone is able to empathize, he or she can accurately interpret social events and interactions. Role playing is a vehicle that forces people to take the roles of others.

The concept of role is one of the central theoretical underpinnings of the role-playing model. It is also a major goal. To learn to analyse their values, students need to recognize different roles and to think of their own and others' behaviour in terms of roles.

Phases of the model

The Shaftels outline a role-playing episode in nine steps that build on and feed one another:

1 Warm up the group.
2 Select participants.
3 Set the stage.
4 Prepare observers.
5 Enact.
6 Discuss and evaluate.
7 Re-enact.
8 Discuss and evaluate.
9 Share experiences and generalize.

The episode begins with a scenario of a problem or experience with a problem (as in Scenario 1). It proceeds to an analysis of the nature of the encounters in which the problem emerges. Then enactments with observations are followed by analyses of the value positions that are elicited through the enactment. Successive enactments and analyses gradually surface the value positions and lead the students toward conceptual control.

Reflections

Role playing is designed specifically to foster:

1   the analysis of personal values and behaviour
2   the development of strategies for solving interpersonal (and personal) problems
3   the development of empathy toward others.

Part 4

Sources of developed models of learning

11 An inquiry into learning and teaching

"Last September, a hundred years ago, I thought teaching was one job with a few variations. I had an image of the one kind of teaching I could do well with the one kind of student I could see myself teaching well. It turned out that it is 20 jobs to do with 20 different personalities."

A beginning teacher to Bruce Joyce, December 1995

Think of Chapters 11 and 12 as a sourcebook of models of learning and the models of teaching that we use to increase the learning repertoire of our students.

Learning experiences are composed of content, process and social climate. As learners, we create for and with our children opportunities to explore and build important areas of knowledge, develop powerful tools for learning and live in humanizing social conditions.

As we saw in the preceding chapters and their scenarios, our toolbox contains models for learning that simultaneously define the nature of the content, the learning strategies and the arrangements for social interaction that create the learning environments of our students.

We can't do everything simultaneously, thus selection of models becomes very important. Through selection of particular models, content can become conceptual rather than particular, the process can become constructive inquiry rather than passive reception and the social climate can become expansive not restrictive.

Here we introduce some of the array of models of learning that have been developed, polished and studied during the modern era of educational research. We hope that teachers and heads will inquire into them, because they will have the pleasure we have had in finding more ways of providing our students with more ways of teaching. When students learn these well, some accelerate rates of learning, sometimes substantially, and also bring within the reach of students types of conceptual control and modes of inquiry that have been almost impossible to generate through many of the most common methods of teaching, such as the 'recitation' or 'chalk and talk'.

The most powerful models adapt to a wide spectrum of curriculum areas and types of learner. They work when teaching phonics and physics. They help both the 'gifted' and those most 'at risk' of failure. They do not tolerate socioeconomic or gender differences as inhibitors of learning but, instead, capitalize on them. Their effects are enhanced by variety in cultural and linguistic background.

Each model is an inquiry into teaching and learning: this is the basis for much of their strength. Rather than being formulas to be followed slavishly, each model brings us into the study of how our students learn and makes us reflective action researchers in our classrooms, reshaping environments for learning and preparing to select new experiences for our students.

We are grateful to the great teacher–researchers who give us this rich professional heritage. In the search for an increasing range of teaching strategies, they both exercised their splendid imaginations and followed their ideas with a tenacious pursuit of knowledge.

Thinking about the roles that make up teaching can make you dizzy. Just for starters, these roles include helping students grow in understanding, knowledge, self-awareness, moral development and the ability to relate to others. Simultaneously, we are managers of learning, curriculum designers, facilitators, counsellors, evaluators and, reluctantly, disciplinarians. To the best of our ability, we modulate across roles according to individual and group needs as we select and create learning experiences for all our students.

The key to managing those roles well is teaching the students how to learn in a variety of ways.

Consider these four teachers at work on the first day of school.

Scenario 1: Year 1

In a Year 1 class, the children are gathered around a table on which there is a candle and a jar. The teacher, Jackie Wiseman, lights the candle and, after it has burned brightly for a minute or two, places the jar carefully over the candle. It grows dim, flickers and goes out. Then she produces another candle and a larger jar and the exercise is repeated. The candle goes out, but more slowly. Jackie produces two more candles and jars of different sizes and the children light the candles, place the jars over them and the flames slowly go out. 'Now we're going to develop some ideas about what has just happened', she says. 'I want you to ask me questions about those candles and jars and what you just observed.' The children begin. She gently helps them rephrase their questions or plan experiments. When one asks: 'Would the candles burn longer with an even bigger jar?' Jackie responds: 'How might we find out?' Periodically, she will ask them to dictate to her what they know and the questions they have. Then she writes what they say on large sheets of paper. Their own words will be the content of their first study of reading.

Scenario 2: Year 1

Next door, the children are seated in pairs. In front of them is a pile of small objects. Each pair of children also has a magnet. Their teacher, Jan Fisher, smiles at them and explains that the 'U-shaped' object is called a magnet. 'We're going to find out something about this thing we call a magnet. We'll begin by finding out what it does when it's held close to different things. So I want you to explore with your magnet. Find out what happens when you bring it close to or touch the things in front of you with it. And sort the other objects according to what happens.' Like Jackie, Jan will take notes on the categories they form and use those to begin their study of written vocabulary.

Commentary: scenarios 1 and 2

Jackie is beginning her year with the model of teaching we call 'inquiry training'. The model begins by having the students encounter what will be, to them, a puzzling situation. Then by asking questions and conducting experiments, they build ideas and test them. Jackie will study their inquiry and plan the next series of activities to build a community that can work together to explore their world.

Jan has begun with concept formation. As we saw in Chapter 3, the model begins by presenting the children with information or having them collect information and engage in classifying. As the children develop categories, in this case, concerning the response of objects to what the kids will eventually learn to call a magnetic field, they will build hypotheses to test. Jan will study how they think, what they see and don't see and help them learn to tackle other topics and questions as a community of inductive thinkers. She will proceed by giving them batteries, large nails and wire and showing them how to build simple electromagnets.

Scenario 3: tenth grade

Mariam True's tenth grade social studies class begins with a videotape taken in a California courtroom, where litigation is being conducted over whether a mother can prevent a father and their 12-year-old son from having time together. The parents are divorced and have joint custody of their son, who lives with the mother.

The tape presents the opening arguments in the case. Mariam then asks the students to generate, individually, the issues as they see them and request further information about the situation. She then asks them to share the issues and questions they see; she requests each student to accumulate the ideas and questions that all the students share under headings of 'issues' and 'questions'. They find it necessary to develop another category, called 'positions and values', because many of the students articulated positions during the sharing exercise.

The inquiry will continue by watching more segments of the tape and analysing several abstracts of similar cases that Mariam has collected for them. One such case is their first homework assignment. Gradually, through the week, Mariam leads the students to develop sets of policy statements and identify the values that underlie the various possible policies. As the study proceeds, she will be studying how well the students are able to clarify facts, distinguish value positions from one another and discuss differences between seemingly opposing values and policy positions. She, too, is beginning the development of a learning inquiry and is herself an inquirer into her students and their learning.

Scenario 4: Year 9

Now let's move to Gill Murray's English class, which opens with a scene from the film *Kes*. The students share their reactions to the setting, the actions and the characters who are introduced in the scene. Among the students a variety of different views are expressed and when the students want to defend their interpretations or argue against the ideas of others, Gill announces that, for the time being, she wants to preserve their differences so that they can inquire into them. She then passes out copies of the novel of the same name by the author Barry Hines and asks them to begin reading it. During the week she will lead them to develop an inquiry into the social issues presented by the book and film and, simultaneously, by comparing the film with the book, to study the devices used by the author and by the filmmakers. She will watch closely to determine what issues and devices they see and don't see as she builds her community of learners.

Keeping these four teachers and classrooms in mind, let's return to the discussion of our work. As we teach, we try to find out what learning has taken place in our classrooms and what readiness there is for new learning. But teachers cannot crawl inside students' heads and look around – we have to infer what is inside from what we can see and hear. Our educated guesses are part of the substance of our profession as we try to construct in *our* minds the pictures of what our students are experiencing. The never ending cycles of arranging environments, providing tasks and building pictures of the minds of the students makes the character of teaching. This inquiry into mind and environment never completes itself, for the results of these inquiries tell us what next to say and do with our students.

The inquiry process that guides the creation of learning experiences is exactly the same in the secondary phase of education and in the university as it is with young children. The maths teacher and the professor of physics arrange environments, provide tasks and try to learn what is going on in the minds of their students, just as does the teacher who first introduces reading and writing to her students.

The challenge of designing learning experiences is the central substance of the study of teaching. The quest for ways to help people learn more efficiently and the design of environments that make this learning possible guide the research that has spawned the range of models we use to design learning experiences. These models are the products of teacher–researchers who have beaten a path for us and given us a head start in our personal and collaborative inquiries.

Currently we operate on several theses about the product of these inquiries. The first thesis is that *there exists a considerable array of alternative approaches to learning*. Many of these are practical and implementable in classrooms and schools where persons have the combination of will and skill. Further, these models of teaching are sufficiently different from one another that various kinds of outcomes result when they are used (Joyce et al. 2008). Thus the second thesis is that *methods make a difference in what is learned as well as how it is learned*. Particular methods boost certain outcomes and diminish others, but rarely do they guarantee some while obliterating the rest. The third thesis is that *students are a powerful part of the learning experience being created and students react differently to any given way of learning*. Combinations of personality, aptitudes, interpersonal skills and previous achievement contribute to configurations of learning styles so that no two people react in exactly the same way to any approach. *And* learning how to learn is a major part of student capacity.

Possibly the most important long-term outcome of teaching may be the students' increased capabilities to learn more easily and effectively in the future, both because of the knowledge and skill they have acquired and because they have mastered learning processes.

Let's look now at the nurturant relationship between classrooms and schools as learning communities and at the symbiotic relationship between individual and group learning.

Settings for learning: schools, classes, groups and individuals

We learn in human *settings* – assemblages of children and adults created for the purpose of learning. The fact of assembly is more important than the place we usually call school, as is apparent today when people can easily relate to one another electronically. Because we can communicate so effectively through media, we can 'assemble' without being in close physical proximity.

However, the familiar schoolhouse has great importance, for within it and in cooperation with our surrounding community, staff and students generate social climates that influence the energy that is focused on education and the substance and process of that education. Some schools are not only more *effective* than others in drawing the students together to learn (see, for example, Levine and Lezotte 1990; Mortimore et al. 1988; Rutter et al. 1979), they also pull the students toward specific *kinds* of inquiry. The social climate of great schools energizes all their students in particular ways: for example the Bronx School of Science, Cranmore, in the USA, or Summerhill in England.

In the USA in the 1930s, the schools that belonged to the Progressive Education Association developed social climates and curriculums that helped the entire student body learn to cooperate, to pursue academic inquiry and to develop self-reliance. In Lawrence Kohlberg's (1981) work with *Just Schools*, the exploration of morality came to be a hallmark and democratic process (with the continuing exploration of social values) became normative.

In England, the work of Henry Morris in the 1940s (through the establishing of community colleges in Cambridgeshire) typified a commitment to a particular style of educational and community ethos. Similarly, the work of Sir Alec Clegg in the West Riding of Yorkshire during the 1960s and 1970s exemplified how a coherent educational philosophy can influence not only the structure and curriculum of schooling but also the regeneration of communities.

Today we can use our knowledge and skill to design the social climates and curriculums of schools, fostering independence, rigorous inquiry, collaboration, the development of social values and self-esteem. Because social climate can be so powerful, its design has considerable importance and should not be left to chance. Again, the educational environment is part *what* we teach, part *how* we teach, and part the *kind of place we make*.

12 Sources: families of models of learning and teaching

"At first, when people create or find a new model of learning or teaching that works for some purpose, they're so thrilled they try to use it for everything. Our job is to provide some order – finding out what each model can do and building categories to help folks find the tools they need."

Bruce Joyce, again and again in staff meetings from 1965 to the present day

Among us, we have been searching continuously for promising approaches to learning and teaching since the late 1950s. The hunt has many facets. We visit schools (about 50 in the last year alone) and classrooms (about 300 last year), interview teachers, study research on teaching and learning and look at people in teaching roles outside of schools, such as therapists and trainers in industrial, military and athletic or outdoor settings.

We have found models of teaching and learning in abundance. There are simple procedures that students can easily respond to; there are complex strategies that students acquire gradually through patient and skilful instruction. Some aim at specific objectives, while others are broadly useful. Some are quite formal, while others are casual and emergent. Among them, they address a great variety of objectives in the personal, social and academic domains – our major responsibilities as teachers.

There was a considerable commitment to curriculum development in England from the late 1950s until the 1970s. The work of the Schools Council, and the Nuffield Foundation in particular, was highly influential in not only introducing a range of new curriculums into the English educational system, but also in establishing a distinctive style of curriculum research and development that focused on the teacher (Rudduck and Hopkins 1985; Stenhouse 1975, 1980). Many of these curriculum projects highlighted the importance of integrating teaching strategies and the learning needs of students into the design of curriculum materials (Hopkins 1987).

In the United States during this period, research sponsored by foundations, the Federal government and school districts refined longstanding models of teaching and developed new ones to a degree not seen before or since. Some of the research was concentrated on specific curriculum areas, especially English, humanities, science and mathematics.

During the same period, research on effective teachers and schools shed light on their practices. During the last 20 years, research on mnemonics and cooperative learning has redeveloped and refined models in those areas and research on training has clarified how people acquire skills and apply (transfer) them to solve problems. Recent work on how students construct knowledge is enriching those models, as is research on how students develop the 'metacognitions' that enable them consciously to improve their strategies for learning.

These models can be used by individual teachers and by staff as instructional strategies; as guides when planning lessons, units, courses and curricula or when designing classroom activities and instructional materials.

To bring order into the study of the growing storehouse of models, we have grouped them into four families based on the types of learning they promote and on their orientation toward people and how they learn: the information processing family, the social family, the personal family and the behavioural systems family.

Criteria of practicability were used to select the models from each family that would have considerable utility in instructional settings. Thus the models we draw on have long histories of practice behind them: they have been refined through experience so that they can be used comfortably and efficiently in classrooms and other educational settings. Furthermore, they are adaptable: they can be adjusted to the learning styles of students and to the requirements of subject matter. They have lifetime utility: most are useful across the primary and secondary levels, as well as in university and are learning tools for life. And finally, there is evidence that they work in enhancing students' ability to learn: all of them are backed by some amount of formal research that tests their theories and their abilities to affect learning. The amount of related research varies from model to model. Some are backed by a few studies while others have a history of literally hundreds of items of research.

Information processing family of models

Information processing models emphasize ways of enhancing the human being's innate drive to make sense of the world by acquiring and organizing data, sensing problems and generating solutions to them and developing concepts and language for conveying them. Some models in this family provide the learner with information and concepts; some emphasize concept formation and hypothesis testing by the learner; and still others generate creative thinking. A few are designed to enhance general intellectual ability. Many information processing models are useful for studying the self and society and thus for achieving the personal and social goals of education.

Table 12.1 displays the developers and redevelopers of seven information processing models. The literature section of the book includes the primary works of the developers.

The information processing models help students learn how to construct knowledge. They focus directly on intellectual capability. As the term implies, these models help students operate on information obtained either from direct experience

Table 12.1 Information processing models

Model	Developer (redeveloper)	Purpose
Inductive thinking (classification)	Hilda Taba (Bruce Joyce)	Development of classification skills, hypothesis building and testing and understanding of how to build conceptual understanding of content areas
Concept attainment	Jerome Bruner Fred Lighthall (Bruce Joyce)	Learning concepts and studying strategies for attaining and applying them. Building and testing hypotheses
Scientific inquiry	Joseph Schwab and many others	Learning the research system of the academic disciplines – how knowledge is produced and organized
Inquiry training	Richard Suchman (Howard Jones)	Causal reasoning and understanding of how to collect information, build concepts and build and test hypotheses
Cognitive growth	Jean Piaget Irving Sigel Constance Kamii Edmund Sullivan	Increase general intellectual development and adjust instruction to facilitate intellectual growth
Advance organizers	David Ausubel and many others	Designed to increase ability to absorb information and organize it, especially in learning from lectures and readings
Mnemonics	Michael Pressley Joel Levin (and associated scholars)	Increase ability to acquire information, concepts, conceptual systems and metacognitive control of information processing capability
Picture–word inductive	Emily Calhoun	Learning to read and write, inquiry into language

or from mediated sources so that they develop conceptual control over the areas they study. The emphases of the various information processing models are somewhat different, however, in the sense that each one has been designed to enhance particular kinds of thinking.

In Chapters 3 to 6, we share four models from the information processing family: in Chapter 3 the *inductive thinking model* induces students to learn to collect and classify information and to build and test hypotheses. Classification, which is one phase of this model, is probably the basic higher order 'thinking skill' and is certainly a necessary skill for mastering large amounts of information.

In Chapter 4, the *concept attainment model* both helps students learn concepts and also to study how they think. Simultaneously, it leads students to develop concepts and to obtain conceptual control (metacognitive understanding) over their thinking strategies.

In Chapter 5, *synectics* teaches metaphoric thinking – ways of consciously 'breaking' set ideas and generating new ones.

Chapter 6 opens inquiry into the picture–word inductive model, which helps students learn how to learn to read and write and inquire into the content of the core curriculum areas.

As we saw in Chapters 8 and 11, and will in Chapters 13 and 15, these models may be combined in many ways as curriculums are prepared.

The academic curriculum of our schools requires the acquisition and use of massive amounts of information. The information processing family of models provides students with learning strategies to use in gathering, organizing, summarizing and applying this information, forming and testing hypotheses, making generalizations, and developing concepts that define the content of the disciplines, i.e. how language, mathematics, science and social science work.

Social family of models: building the learning community

When we work together, we generate collective energy that we call 'synergy'. The social models of teaching are constructed to take advantage of this phenomenon by building learning communities. Essentially, 'classroom management' is a matter of developing cooperative relationships in the classroom. The development of positive school cultures is a process of developing integrative and productive ways of interacting and norms that support vigorous learning activity.

Table 12.2 identifies several social models, the persons who have developed and redeveloped them and their basic purposes.

Table 12.2 Social models

Model	Developer (redeveloper)	Purpose
Group investigation	John Dewey Herbert Thelen Shlomo Sharan Rachel Hertz-Lazarowitz	Development of skills for participation in democratic process. Simultaneously emphasizes social development, academic skills and personal understanding
Social inquiry	Byron Massialas Benjamin Cox	Social problem solving through collective academic study and logical reasoning
Jurisprudential inquiry	James Shaver Donald Oliver	Analysis of policy issues through a jurisprudential framework. Collection of data, analysis of value questions and positions, study of personal beliefs
Laboratory method	National Training Laboratory (many contributors)	Understanding of group dynamics, leadership, understanding of personal styles
Role playing	Fannie Shaftel	Study of values and their role in social interaction. Personal understanding of values and behaviour

Model	Developer (redeveloper)	Purpose
Positive interdependence	David Johnson Roger Johnson Elizabeth Cohen	Development of interdependent strategies of social interaction. Understanding of self–other relationships and emotions
Structured social inquiry	Robert Slavin and colleagues	Academic inquiry and social and personal development. Cooperative strategies for approaching academic study

The social family of models helps students learn how to sharpen their own cognitions through interactions with others, how to work productively with individuals who represent a range of personalities and how to work as a member of a group. In terms of cognitive and academic growth, the models help students use the perspectives of other persons, both individual and group perspectives, to clarify and expand their own thinking and conceptualization of ideas.

As with the information processing family, the emphases of the various models in the social family are somewhat different, in the sense that each one has been designed to enhance particular kinds of thinking and modes of interaction. Among the developed spectrum of models in the social family, we will look briefly at two models: group investigation (a complex form of cooperative learning) and role playing.

Chapter 7 looks at *group investigation* as a direct route to the development of the community of learners. All the simpler forms of cooperative learning are preparation for the rigorous, active and integrative collective action required in group investigation. John Dewey (1916) developed the idea – extended and refined by a great many teachers and theorists and shaped into powerful definition by Herbert Thelen (1960) – that education in a democratic society should teach democratic process directly. A substantial part of the students' education should be by cooperative inquiry into important social and academic problems. Essentially, the group investigation model provides a social organization within which many other models can be used.

Group investigation has been used in all subject areas, with children of all ages and even as the core social model for entire schools. The model is designed to lead students to define problems, to explore various perspectives on the problems and to study together to master information, ideas and skills – while simultaneously developing their social competence. The teacher's primary role in this model is to help organize the group process and discipline it, to help the students find and organize information and to ensure that there is a vigorous level of activity and discourse.

As the term *social* implies, these models help students learn to identify multiple facets of a situation or problem, to understand the reasoning underpinning positions different from their own and to form disciplined cases and reasoned arguments to support their positions. The interactive mode required by these models also means that students simultaneously practise the complex processes of accessing needed information, gathering information and using their social skills. These models require intense use of listening comprehension skills, of on-your-feet organization of information, of the ability to formulate and ask questions in such a fashion that the information sought will be forthcoming and of being able to put it all together to resolve tough issues or negotiate new solutions. *Thus students are also practising many of the skills that they will need to participate fully as family members, as citizens and as successful workers.*

Personal family of models

The personal models of learning begin from the perspective of the selfhood of the individual. They attempt to shape education so that we come to understand ourselves better, take responsibility for our education and learn to reach beyond our current development to become stronger, more sensitive and more creative in our search for high-quality lives. The cluster of personal models pays great attention to the individual perspective and seeks to encourage productive independence, so that people become increasingly self-aware and responsible for their own destinies. Table 12.3 displays the models and their developers.

Table 12.3 Personal models

Model	Developer	Purpose
Nondirective teaching	Carl Rogers	Building capacity for personal development, self-understanding, autonomy and esteem of self
Awareness training	Fritz Perls	Increasing self-understanding, self-esteem and capacity for exploration. Development of interpersonal sensitivity and empathy
Classroom meeting	William Glasser	Development of self-understanding and responsibility to self and others
Self-actualization	Abraham Maslow	Development of personal understanding and capacity for development
Conceptual systems	David Hunt	Increasing personal complexity and flexibility in processing information and interacting with others

As we saw in Chapter 9, personal models of learning emphasize the unique character of each human being and the struggle to develop as an integrated, confident and competent personality. The goal is to help each person 'own' his/her development and to achieve a sense of self-worth and personal harmony. The models that comprise this family seek to develop and integrate the emotional and intellectual aspects of personality.

Behavioural systems family of models

A common theoretical base – most commonly called social learning theory, but also known as behaviour modification, behaviour therapy and cybernetics – guides the design of the models in this family. The stance taken is that human beings are self-correcting communication systems that modify behaviour in response to information about how successfully tasks are navigated. For example, imagine a human being who is climbing (the task) an unfamiliar staircase in the dark. The first few steps are tentative as the foot reaches for the treads. If the stride is too high, feedback is received as the foot encounters air and has to descend to make contact with the surface. If a step is too low, feedback results as the foot hits the riser. Gradually behaviour is adjusted in accordance with the feedback until progress up the stairs is relatively comfortable.

Capitalizing on knowledge about how people respond to tasks and feedback, psychologists (see, especially, Skinner 1953) have learned how to organize task and feedback structures to make it easy for human beings' self-correcting capability to function. The result includes programmes for reducing phobias, for learning to read and compute, for developing social and athletic skills, for replacing anxiety with relaxation and for learning the complexities of intellectual, social and physical skills necessary to pilot an aeroplane or a space shuttle. Because these models concentrate on observable behaviour and clearly defined tasks, and on methods for communicating progress to the student, this family of teaching models has a very large foundation of research. Table 12.4 displays six models and their developers.

Table 12.4 Behavioural and cybernetic models

Model	Developer	Purpose
Social learning	Albert Bandura Carl Thoresen Wes Becker	Management of behaviour. Learning new patterns of behaviour, reducing phobic and other dysfunctional patterns, learning self-control
Mastery learning	Benjamin Bloom James Block	Mastery of academic skills and content of all types
Programmed learning	B. F. Skinner	Mastery of skills, concepts, factual information
Simulation	Many developers. Carl Smith and Mary Foltz Smith provide guidance through 1960s when design had matured	Mastery of complex skills and concepts in a wide range of areas of study
Direct teaching	Thomas Good Jere Brophy Wes Becker Siegfried Englemann Carl Bereiter	Mastery of academic content and skills in a wide range of areas of study
Anxiety reduction	David Rinn| Joseph Wolpe John Masters	Control over aversive reactions. Applications in treatment and self-treatment of avoidance and dysfunctional patterns of response

Overall, behavioural techniques are amenable to learners of all ages and to an impressive range of educational goals. In Chapter 10, we look more closely at one member of this family. We explore the principles of simulation, share examples of various kinds of simulations and relate the framework of the behaviourists to daily classroom management.

The behavioural systems family, based on the work of B. F. Skinner and the cybernetic training psychologists (Smith and Smith 1966), has the largest research literature of the four families. Studies range from programmed instruction to simulations and include training models (Joyce and Showers 1983) and methods derived directly from therapy (Wolpe and Lazarus 1966).

There is a great deal of research on the application of social learning theory to instruction (Becker and Gersten 1982), training (Smith and Smith 1966) and simulations (Boocock and Schild 1968). The behavioural technologists have demonstrated that they can design programmes for both specific and general goals (Becker and Gersten 1982) and also that the effective application of those techniques requires extensive cognitive activity and precise interactive skills (Spaulding 1970).

The concept of effect size

We use the concept of 'effect size' (Glass 1982) to describe the magnitude of gains from any given change in educational practice and thus to predict what we can hope to accomplish by using that practice.

To introduce the idea, let us consider a study conducted by Dr Bharati Baveja (1988) with one of the authors in the Motilal Nehru School of Sports about 30 miles northwest of New Delhi, India (see the scenario in Chapter 3). Dr Baveja designed her study to test the effectiveness of an inductive approach to a botany unit compared with an intensive tutorial treatment. All of the students were given a test at the beginning of the unit to assess their knowledge before instruction began and were divided into two groups equated on the basis of achievement. The control group studied the material with the aid of tutoring and lectures on the material – the standard treatment in Indian schools for courses of this type. The experimental group worked in pairs and were led through inductive and concept attainment exercises emphasizing classification of plants.

Figure 12.1 shows the distribution of scores for the experimental and control groups on the posttest which, like the pretest, contained items dealing with the information pertaining to the unit.

The difference between the experimental and control groups was a little above a standard deviation. The difference, computed in terms of standard deviations, is the *effect size of the inductive treatment*. What that means is that the experimental group average score was where the 80th percentile score was for the control group. The difference increased when a delayed recall test was given 10 months later, indicating that the information acquired with the concept-oriented strategies was retained somewhat better than information gained via the control treatment.

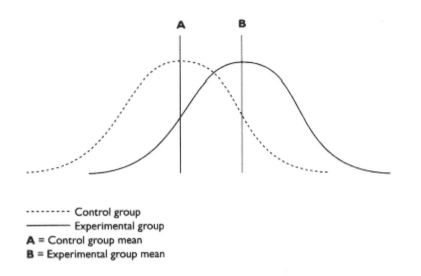

-------- Control group
————— Experimental group
A = Control group mean
B = Experimental group mean

Figure 12.1 Compared distributions for experimental and control groups (from Baveja 1988)

Calculations like these enable us to compare the magnitude of the potential effects of the innovations (teaching skills and strategies, curricula and technologies) that we might use in an effort to affect student learning. We can also determine whether the treatment has different effects for all kinds of student or just for some. In the Baveja (1988) study the experimental treatment was apparently effective for the whole population. The lowest score in the experimental group distribution was about where the 30th percentile score was for the control group; about 30 per cent of the students exceeded the highest score obtained in the control.

Although substantial in its own right, learning and retention of information was modest when we consider the effect on the students' ability to identify plants and their characteristics, which was measured on a separate test. The scores by students from the experimental group were *eight* times higher than the scores for the control group. Dr Baveja's inquiry confirmed her hypothesis that the students, using the inductive model, were able to apply the information and concepts from the unit much more effectively than were the students from the tutorial treatment.

Further inquiry into effect size

Let's work through some concepts that are useful in describing distributions of scores to deepen our understanding a little. We describe distributions of scores in terms of the *central tendencies*, which refer to the clustering of scores around the middle of the distribution, and *variance*, or their dispersion. Concepts describing central tendency include the *average* or arithmetic mean, which is computed by summing the scores and dividing by the number of scores and the median or middle score (half of the others are above and half below the median score) and the *mode*, which is the most frequent score (graphically, the highest point in the distribution). In Figure 12.2 the median, the average and the mode are all in the same place, because the distribution is completely symmetrical.

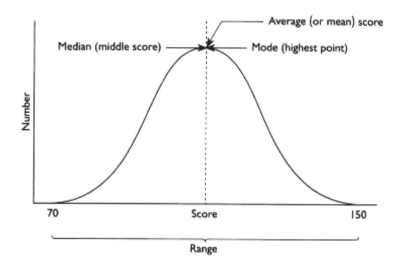

Figure 12.2 A sample normal distribution

Dispersion is described in terms of the *range* (the distance between the highest and lowest scores), the rank, which is frequently described as the *percentile* (the 20th score from the top in a 100-person distribution is at the 80th percentile because 20 per cent of the scores are above and 80 per cent are below it) and the *standard deviation*, which describes how widely or narrowly scores are distributed. In Figure 12.3, the range is from 70 (the lowest score) to 150 (the highest score). The 50th percentile score is at the middle (in this case corresponding with the average, the mode and the median). The standard deviations are marked off by the vertical lines labelled +1 SD, +2 SD and so on. Note that the percentile rank of the score one standard deviation above the mean is 84 (84 per cent of the scores are below that point); the rank two standard deviations above the mean is 97; and three standard deviations above the mean is 99.

When the mean, median and mode coincide as in these distributions and the distribution of scores is as symmetrical as the ones depicted in these figures, the distribution is referred to as *normal*. This concept is very useful in statistical operations, although many actual distributions are not symmetrical, as we will see.

However, to explain the concept of effect size, we will use symmetrical, 'normal' distributions before illustrating how the concept works with differently shaped distributions. Figure 12.4 compares the posttest scores of the low SES students in Chapter 7 between the 'whole class' and 'group investigation' treatments. The average score of the 'group investigation' treatment corresponds to about the 92nd percentile of the distribution of the 'whole class' students. The effect size is computed by

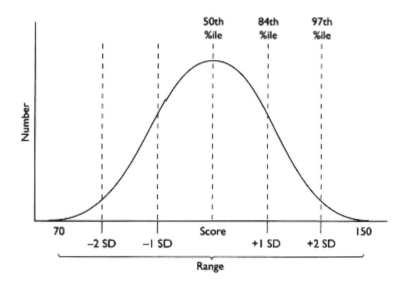

Figure 12.3 A sample normal distribution with standard deviations

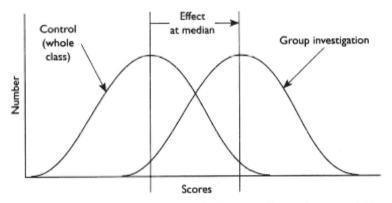

Figure 12.4 A sample depiction of effect size (from Sharan and Shachar 1988)

dividing the difference between the two means by the standard deviation of the 'control' or 'whole class' group. The effect size in this case is 1.6 standard deviations using the formula:

$$E = \text{average of experimental group} - \frac{\text{average of control}}{\text{standard deviation of control}}$$

Figures like these provide an idea about the relative effects we can expect if we teach students with each model of teaching compared with using the normative patterns of curriculum and instruction. We create each figure from an analysis of the research base that is currently available and will usually build the figure to depict the average effects from large numbers of studies.

When using the research base to decide when to use a given model of teaching, it is important to realize that size of effects is not the only consideration. We have to consider the nature of the objectives and the uses of the model. For example, in Spaulding's (1970) study, the effect size on ability measures was just 0.5 or about a half standard deviation (see Figure 12.5).

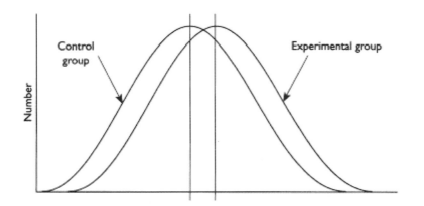

Figure 12.5 A sample effect size: ability scores (from Spaulding 1970)

However, ability is a very powerful attribute and a model or combination of models that can increase ability will have an effect on everything the student does for years to come, by increasing learning through those years. The simplest cooperative learning procedures have relatively modest effect sizes, affecting feelings about self as a learner, social skills and academic learning *and they are easy to use and have wide applications*. Thus their modest effect can be felt more regularly and broadly than some models that have more dramatic effect sizes with respect to a given objective.

Some models can help us virtually eliminate dispersion in a distribution. For example, a colleague of ours used mnemonic devices to teach his fourth grade students the names of the states and their capitals. *All* his students learned *all* of them and remembered them throughout the year. Thus the distribution of his class members' scores on tests of their ability to supply all the names on a blank map had no range at all. The average score was the top possible score. There were no percentile ranks because the students' scores were all tied at the top. For some objectives – a basic reading vocabulary and computation skills, for example – we want, in fact, to have a very high degree of success for all our students because anything less is terribly disadvantaging for them – and for their society.

You may find the results of the research on some of the behavioral techniques surprising. For example, an analysis by White (1986) examined the results of studies on the application of the DISTAR version of social learning theory to special education. The average effect sizes for mathematics and reading ranged from about one-half to one standard deviation. The effects for moderately and severely handi-capped students were similar. Perhaps most importantly, there were a few studies in which the effects on aptitude (measures of intellectual ability) were included; and where the DISTAR programme was implemented for several years, the effect sizes were 1.0 or above, representing an increase of about 10 points in the standard IQ ratio.

Although high effect sizes make a treatment attractive, size alone is not the only consideration when choosing among alternatives. Modest effect sizes that affect many persons can have a large payoff for the population. A comparison with medicine is worthwhile. Suppose a dread disease is affecting a population and we possess a vaccine that will reduce the chances of contracting the disease by only 10 per cent. If 1 million persons might become infected without the vaccine but 900,000 if it is used, the modest effect of the vaccine might save 100,000 lives. In education, some estimates suggest that during the first year of school in the USA about 1 million children each year (about 30 per cent) make little progress toward learning to read. We also know that lack of success in reading instruction is, in fact, a dread educational disease, since for each year that initial instruction is unsuccessful the probability that the student will respond to instruction later is greatly lowered. Would a modestly effective treatment, say one that reduced the lack of success in the first year for 50,000 children (5 per cent) be worthwhile? We think so. Also several such treatments might be cumulative. Of course we prefer a high-effect treatment, but one is not always available. Even when it is, it might not reach some students and we might need to resort to a less powerful choice for those students.

Also there are different types of effect that need to be considered. Attitudes, values, concepts, intellectual development, skills and information are just a few. Keeping to the example of early reading, two treatments might be approximately equal in terms of learning to read in the short run, but one might affect attitudes positively and leave the students feeling confident and ready to try again. Similarly, two social studies programmes might achieve similar amounts of information and concepts, but one might excel in attitudes toward citizenship.

In the most dramatic instances, when the effect size reaches five or six standard deviations, the lowest scoring student in the experimental treatment exceeds the highest scoring student in the control treatment! This is a rare event, of course, but when it does occur, it gives us great hope about the potential of educational practice. Again, as we describe some practices and the effects that can be expected from them, we should not concentrate on magnitude of effects alone. Self-instructional programmes that are no more effective than traditional teaching can be very useful because they enable students to learn by themselves. Broadcast television, because of its potential to reach so many children, can make a big difference even though it is modestly effective in comparison with standard instruction. *Sesame Street* is a well-known example (Ball and Bogatz 1970). It is not dramatically more effective than early reading instruction that does not include it, but *Sesame Street* produces positive attitudes and augments the teaching of reading handsomely, enabling a certain percentage of students virtually to teach themselves. In fact, distance education and media-based instruction (learning from television, computer-assisted instruction and packages of multimedia materials) need not be more effective to be very useful. For example, in a secondary school that does not offer a given foreign language, a student who can learn that language by self-study assisted by television, computer programs and similar packages can be greatly benefited. The Open University, which operates as a distance education agency augmented by tutorial centres, has virtually doubled the number of university graduates in the UK. The performance of its students on academic tests compares favourably with the performance of 'regular' university students.

Some procedures can interact productively with others. One-to-one tutoring has a very large effect size (Bloom 1984) and might interact productively with some teaching strategies. Or, as is evidently the case within the 'Success for All' (Slavin et al. 1990; Slavin 1991) and 'Reading Recovery' (Pinnell 1989) programmes, it is incorporated within a curriculum management system that enables short periods of tutoring to pay off wonderfully. By way of contrast, 'tracking' or 'streaming' hurts the effectiveness of any procedure (Oakes 1986).

Simply learning the size of effects of a year's instruction can be very informative, as we learned from the National Assessment of Writing Progress (Applebee et al. 1990), which discovered that the effect size of instruction in writing nationally is such that the average eighth grade student is about at the 62nd percentile of the fourth grade distribution! Schools may want to learn how much better they can do than that!

Measures of learning can be of many kinds. School grades are of great importance, as are measures of conduct such as counts of referrals and suspensions. In fact, staff development programmes want to give close attention to those measures as well as simple measures, such as how many books students read. Content analyses of student work are very important, as in the study of quality of writing. Curriculum relevant tests (those that measure the content of a unit or course) are important. Finally, the traditional standardized tests can be submitted to an analysis that produces estimates of effect size.

Educational research is in its infancy. The state of the art is not such that any specific curricular or instructional models can solve all the problems of student learning. We hope that the readers of this book will not just use it as a source of teaching and learning strategies, but will learn how to add to the knowledge base. There are millions of teachers at work today. If only 1 per cent conducted and reported one study each year, there would be tens of thousands of new studies every year, a knowledge increment many times larger than the entire current research base. But aside from contributing to the larger knowledge base, teachers in any school can, by studying their teaching, share ideas that can help everyone in the school to become more effective.

Students will change as their repertoire of learning strategies increases. As they become a more powerful learning community, they will be able to accomplish more and more types of learning more effectively. In a very real sense, increasing aptitude to learn is a purpose that pervades our other objectives.

Debates about educational method have seemed to imply that schools and teachers should choose one approach over another. However, it is far more likely that, for optimum opportunity to learn, students need a range of models of learning.

13 Conditions of learning: integrating models of learning and teaching

"Mental growth is in considerable measure dependent upon growth from the outside in – a mastering of techniques that are embodied in the culture and that are passed on in a contingent dialogue by agents of the culture … I suspect that much of growth starts out by our turning around on our own traces and recoding new forms of what we have been doing or seeing, then going on to new modes of organisation with the new products that have been formed by these recodings … And it is for this reason that I think a theory of development must be linked to a theory of knowledge and to a theory of instruction, or be doomed to triviality."

Jerome Bruner (1966: 21)

Planning curriculums, courses, units and lessons is a sine qua non of good teaching. In this chapter, we study planning with a master and then try to apply his framework to the problem of planning for learning and teaching.

One of the most important books on learning and teaching is Robert N. Gagné's *Conditions of Learning* (1965). Gagné gives us a careful analysis of the important variables in learning and how to organize teaching to take these variables into account. His picture of the 'varieties of chance called learning' enables us to classify and specify learning objectives and the relationships *between* various kinds of learning performances.

Varities of performance

Gagné identifies six varieties of performance that represent different classes or types of learning:

1 specific responding
2 chaining
3 multiple discrimination
4 classifying

5 rule using
6 problem solving.

Specific responding is making a specific response to a particular stimulus. An example occurs when a Year 1 teacher holds up a card (the stimulus) on which the word *dog* is printed and the children say 'dog' (the response). Specific responding is an extremely important type of learning and is the way we have acquired much of the information we possess. In order for the pupil to learn to make correct, specific responses, we must assume he or she has the ability to make connections between things. In the previous example, the printed word *dog* is associated, or connected, with the verbal statement 'dog'.

Chaining is making a series of responses that are linked together. Gagné uses the example of unlocking a door with a key and of translating from one language to another. Unlocking a door requires us to use a number of specific responses (selecting a key, inserting it, turning it) in an order that will get the job done. When one takes the English words 'How are you?' and translates them to the Spanish (¿Cómo está usted?), one is chaining by taking a series of specific responses and linking them into a phrase.

Multiple discrimination is involved in learning a variety of specific responses and chains and in learning how to sort them out appropriately. For example, one learns to associate colours with their names under very similar conditions, but then has to sort out the colours and apply them to varieties of objects under different conditions, choosing the right responses and chains. Similarly, when learning a language, one develops a storehouse of words and phrases. When spoken to, one has to sort out the reply, adjusting for gender, number, tense and so forth. Multiple discrimination, then, involves learning to handle previously learned chains of various sorts.

Classifying is assigning objects to classes denoting similar functions. Learning to distinguish plants from animals or cars from bicycles involves classifying. The result of this process is *concepts*, ideas that compare and contrast things and events or describe causal relations among them.

Rule using is the ability to act on a concept that implies action. For example, in spelling we learn varieties of concepts that describe how words are spelled. Then we apply those concepts in rule form in the act of spelling itself. For example, one learns that in consonant-vowel words ending in *t*, such as *sit*, the consonant is doubled when *ing* is added. This becomes a rule (double the *t*) that one usually follows in spelling such words.

Finally, *problem solving* is the application of several rules to a problem not encountered before by the learner. Problem solving involves selecting the correct rules and applying them in combination. For example, a child learns several rules about balancing on a seesaw and then applies them when moving a heavy object with a lever.

Facilitating the six varities of learning

Gagné believes that these six types of learning form an ascending hierarchy: thus, before one can chain, one has to learn specific responses; multiple discrimination requires prior learning of several chains; classifying builds on multiple discrimination; rules for action are forms of concepts learned through classification and the establishment of causal relations; and problem solving requires previously learned rules.

Certain conditions are necessary for the development of each class of learning. The task of the teacher is to create these conditions in the classroom. One way of doing this is by using the appropriate model of teaching. Let's look now at the integration of Gagné's classes with the models of learning and teaching:

- To facilitate *specific responding*, a stimulus is presented to the student under conditions that will bring about his or her attention and induce a response closely related in time to the presentation of the stimulus. The response is then reinforced. Thus the teacher may hold up the word *dog*, say 'dog', ask the children to say 'dog' and then smile and say 'good'. A teacher who does this repeatedly increases the probability that pupils will learn to recognize words and be able to emit the sounds associated with the letters. The mnemonic and simulations models are approaches that facilitate specific responding. So too are the first phases of the inductive and concept attainment models and the data-gathering activities in group investigations.

- To facilitate the acquisition of *chaining*, a sequence of cues is offered and appropriate responses are induced. A language teacher may say 'How are you?', followed by '¿Cómo está usted?', inviting the students to say 'How are you?' and '¿Cómo está usted?'; the teacher may thus provide sufficient repetition that the students will acquire the chain and achieve fluency. The mnemonics and inductive thinking models are appropriate to helping build chains.

- To facilitate *multiple discrimination*, practice with correct and incorrect stimuli is needed so that the students can learn to discriminate. For example, suppose the students are learning the Spanish expressions for 'How are you?', 'Good morning' and 'Hello'; they must learn to discriminate which one to use in a given situation. The teacher provides sets of correct and incorrect stimuli until the students learn the appropriate discrimination. Inductive reasoning and concept attainment models are useful in this process.

- *Classification* is taught by presenting varieties of exemplars and concepts so that the students can gradually learn bases for distinguishing them. Inductive thinking and concept attainment are appropriate.

- *Rule using* is facilitated by inducing the students to recall a concept and then apply it to a variety of specific applications. In the earlier spelling example, pupils recall the rule about doubling the final consonant when adding *ing* and are presented with examples they can practise. Simulations and the application phases of concept attainment and inductive thinking help students move from the identification of concepts to their application.

- *Problem solving* is largely done by the students themselves, because problem situations are unique. It can be facilitated by providing sets of problems that the students can attempt to tackle, especially when the teacher knows that the students have acquired the rules needed to solve the problem.

Group investigation, role playing, synectics, simulation and nondirective teaching models can be used for developing problem solving.

Functions of teaching

Gagné emphasizes that *it is the learner's activity that results in the learning*. It is the teacher's responsibility to provide conditions that will increase the probability of student learning. Practice is extremely important so that the learner makes the necessary connections, but it is the learner who makes the connections, even when they are pointed out to him or her. *The teacher cannot substitute his or her own activity for that of the student*. We agree completely with Gagné on this point.

Teachers help students learn to use the different classes of learning by incorporating the following seven functions into their lessons and curriculum units:

1   informing the learner of the objectives
2   presenting stimuli
3   increasing learners' attention
4   helping the learner recall what he or she has previously learned
5   providing conditions that will evoke performance
6   determining sequences of learning
7   prompting and guiding the learning.

Also the teacher continuously encourages the student to generalize what he or she is learning so that the new skills and knowledge will be transformed into other situations.

Informing the learner of the performance expected is critical for providing him or her with a definite goal. For example, the teacher might say 'Today we're going to try to learn about three prime ministers. We'll learn their names, when they lived and what they are most known for.' The teacher then presents the pictures of Benjamin Disraeli, Winston Churchill and Margaret Thatcher. Their names are printed under the pictures. Pointing to the pictures and names and saying the names will draw the students' attention.

To recall previous learning, the teacher may say: 'Do you remember that we discussed how our country has changed in various ways? Can you tell me what some of these changes were?' The students can reach into their memories and stimulate themselves with material that will later be connected to the prime ministers. To induce performance, the teacher may ask the students to name the three prime ministers and then read printed material describing the life of each. Then the teacher can ask them to tell him or her what they have learned.

A variety of sequences can be used, depending on the type of learning and the subject matter in question. Generally, however, presenting a stimulus, evoking attention, helping the learner understand the objectives, inducing performance and then helping the learner to generalize are major sequential teaching tasks that follow each other naturally.

Gagné's paradigm reminds us of a variety of important general principles of teaching: informing the learner of the levels of objectives being sought, encouraging generalization and pushing for application of what is learned.

Gagné emphasizes that we cannot control learning, but we can increase the probability that certain kinds of learning behaviour will occur. We can present stimuli in close connection and ask the student to perform, but it is the student who makes the connection between the printed and spoken word. Our careful design of lessons increases the probability of student learning and makes the learning process more sure, more predictable and more efficient. 'But, the individual nervous system [of each learner] must still make its own individual contribution. The nature of that contribution is, of course, what defines the need for the study of individual differences' (Gagné 1965: 291–313).

From this point of view, a model of learning and teaching brings structures to the student that change the probability that he or she will learn certain things. The phases of the models present tasks to the student; the instructional moves of the teacher pull the student toward certain responses; and the social system generates a need for particular kinds of interaction with others. The net effect is to make it more likely that various kinds of learning will take place. In Table 13.1, the models of learning and teaching shared in this book are paired with the six classes of learning/varieties of performance that Gagné has identified.

Table 13.1 Models especially appropriate for varieties of performance

Types of performance	Models of learning – tools for teaching				
Specific responding	Mnemonic	Simulations	Phase 1 inductive thinking	Phase 1 of concept attainment	Group investigation (data-gathering activities)
Chaining	Mnemonic	Inductive thinking			
Multiple discrimination	Inductive thinking	Concept attainment			
Classifying	Inductive thinking	Concept attainment			
Rule using	Simulations	Concept attainment	Inductive thinking (application phase)		
Problem solving	Group investigation	Role playing	Synectics	Simulations	Nondirective

Gagné's hierarchy is useful in helping us select models appropriate for varieties of curriculum objectives. It also reminds us of the multiple types of learning promoted by individual models and the attention that must be given to the varieties of performance as the students engage in the study of any important topic. For example, students using inductive thinking to explore a problem in international relations, such as the balance of payments, will gather data (specific responding and chaining), organize it (multiple discrimination and classifying) and develop principles (rule using) to explore solutions to problems (problem solving).

Planning for teaching

Let's see what happens when we put Gagné's hierarchy to work. Let's design a global education curriculum that we can use from primary school all the way through secondary school. Such a complex curriculum will give us the opportunity to consider quite a range of models and, almost certainly, we will want to use several of them to design the instructional aspects of such a curriculum. We'll begin with a somewhat arbitrary statement of our overall objectives: to ensure that the students have a working knowledge of human geography, can think about some of the critical issues facing the peoples of the world and are prepared to interact productively with people from cultures other than theirs. Our rationale is that the global perspective is essential for personal understanding, for the guidance of our country, for the betterment of the world and for economic competence. At one level, we want our students to leave secondary school with the learning that will enable them to spin a globe, put a finger down on a land mass and know considerable information about the country it lights on. At another level, we want them to have considerable knowledge of several representative cultures and to be able to think of the world and our country in terms of cultural history and cultural comparison. At yet another level, we want them to have experience thinking about and generating solutions to important global problems.

A secondary overall objective is to use the study of the globe to further the English curriculum, especially the reading and writing of expository prose. Other objectives will appear as we think through our curriculum design and consider the classes of learning developed through the various models of teaching.

Clarifying curriculum objectives

Now, let's think about the classes of learning and the teaching task that form part of our daily lessons and our longer curriculum units or schemes of work and about the use of these in clarifying our curriculum objectives into content and skills and in selecting the most efficient model of teaching.

Specific responding

We want our students to recognize basic information about different countries: their names, where they are and demographic information such as indicators of wealth (gross national product), indicators of population (size, fertility rates), of health (healthcare facilities, longevity) and culture (linguistic data, religious heritage, cultural groups). For this, we might use mnemonics and the inductive model, teaching the names of the countries and asking students to classify the countries with respect to basic demographic information.

Chaining

We might ask the students to collect information about the kind of life that is lived within these countries and to begin to develop pictures of how the demographic information might relate to quality of life. For this class of learning, we might continue to use mnemonics and the inductive model.

Multiple discrimination.

We might ask the students to develop matrices that allow the countries to be classified on multiple variables, such as how types of government are related to the rights of women. For this class of learning, we might use both the inductive model and the concept attainment model.

Classifying

We might ask the students to develop typologies of countries and to generate maps that permit sets of variables to be used to generate pictures that lead to correlations, such as whether educational levels, industrial capacity, commercial activity and family structures are associated with one another. For this class of learning, we would surely use the inductive model of teaching.

Rule using

We might ask the students to create predictions about how the countries can be expected to respond to various types of conditions, such as population growth, ecological crises and natural disasters. For this class of learning, the application phases of concept attainment and the inductive model and the simulation model would be highly efficient.

Problem solving

We might present the students with sets of problems that can only be dealt with from an international perspective, such as cooperation to solve ecological problems and conflicts of various sorts (e.g. fishing rights, deforestation, nuclear testing, protection of the ozone layer). We might ask students to use the group investigation model to analyse the positions that underlie decisions about international cooperation. We might also ask them to categorize changes that are currently affecting the international situation (such as population growth and new trade agreements) and to predict the types of problem that are developing in the international community.

Using Gagné's framework along with models of teaching allows us to think about the knowledge and/or skills we want to teach, analyse them for the class of learning they require, then design our lessons to increase the probability that students will learn the curriculum content we have selected as most worthy.

Part 5

The leading edge

14 Learning through simulations

"This is a lot better than turning a real chopper upside down."

Army instructor to Bruce Joyce, more than a few years ago

From the behavioural systems family, we have selected simulation as our illustrative model. In this chapter, we briefly explore the principles of simulation and discuss examples of various kinds of simulation.

Scenario 1

In a school in Moscow, a primary class is watching a television screen. The programme announcer portrays a countdown as a rocket attempts to break free from the gravity of the moon but fails to do so. Class members then take the role of members of the spaceship crew. Instructions from the Russian Space Administration divide them into teams and they prepare to work together to conserve their life support systems and to manage their relationships in the rocket ship until repairs can be made.

Scenario 2

In another classroom, this time in the suburbs of Edinburgh, a class is watching a television show. The actors are portraying the members of the Scottish parliament facing a crisis. After examining the issues, the class reaches a conclusion. One student reaches for the telephone in the classroom, dials a number and speaks to the actors in the studio, suggesting how they might play their roles differently to resolve the crisis. Twenty-five other classrooms are simultaneously debating the issues seen on television and they, too, are communicating their views to the actors in the studio. The next day the show resumes. In various ways, the actors play out the suggestions made by the classes. The other members of the cabinet react. Students in the 25 classrooms not only see their ideas brought to life on the television screen, they also see the consequences of their recommendations.

Scenario 3

In a London school, two groups of children enter a room. One group represents the Alzoa culture, the other the Betam culture. Their task is to learn how to communicate with others who have learned rules and patterns of behaviour from a different society. Gradually, they learn to master communication patterns. Simultaneously, they become aware that, as members of a culture, they have inherited powerful patterns that strongly influence their personalities and their ways of communicating with other people.

Scenario 4

In Livingston, Montana, a class is engaged in a caribou hunt. As they progress through the hunt, which the Netsilik inuit operate, they learn behaviour patterns of the Netsilik and begin to compare those patterns with the ones they carry on in their everyday lives.

Scenario 5

In Lancaster, a group of students faces a problem posed by the minister of agriculture. Agronomists have developed a nutrient that, when added to the food of cattle, greatly increases their weight. Only a limited amount of this nutrient is available and the students must determine how the nutrient will be divided among the needy countries of the world. The minister has imposed the following restraints: recipient countries must have a reasonable supply of beef cattle, must not be aligned with support for terrorist organizations, must not be vegetarians and must have a population that exceeds a certain size.

The students debate the alternatives. Some countries are ruled out immediately. Of the remaining countries, some seem attractive at first, yet less attractive later. The students grapple with the problems of humanity and ideology and with practical situations. In this simulation, they face the problems of the committees of scientists who continually advise parliament on various courses of action.

Scenario 6

There are now a number of computer-based games that make it possible to individualize the simulation in terms of learning pace, scope, sequence and difficulty of material. Aside from this feature, the properties of the simulation remain the same as in noncomputer-based simulation games.

The possibilities for education were revealed 40 years ago. The Sumerian Game (developed by the Center for Educational Services and Research, Board of Cooperative Educational Services, 42 Triangle Center, Yorktown Heights, NY 10598, USA) instructs the student in the basic principles of economics as applied to three stages of a primitive economy – the prevalence of agriculture, the development of crafts and the introduction of trade and other changes. The game is set during the time of the Neolithic revolution in Mesopotamia, about 3500 BC. The student is asked to take the role of the ruler of the city state of Lagash. The ruler must make certain agricultural decisions for the kingdom at each 6-month harvest. For example, the ruler is presented with the following problematic situation: 'We have harvested 5,000 bushels of grain to take care of 500 people. How much of this grain will be set aside for next season's planting and how much will be stored in a warehouse?' (Boocock and Schild 1968: 156). The student is asked to decide how much grain to allocate for consumption, for production and for storage.

These situations become more complex as the game continues, for the student must take into account such circumstances as changes in population, the acquisition of new land and irrigation. Periodically, technological innovations and disasters alter the outcome of the ruler's decisions. The effect of each decision on the economic condition of the kingdom is shown in an immediate progress report. Students are apprised of certain quantitative changes – for example, in population, in the amount of harvested grain and in the amount of stored grain – and they are furnished with some substantive analyses of their decisions, for instance 'The quantity of food the people received last season was far too little' (Boocock and Schild 1968: 164). In phase 2 of the Sumerian Game, the student can apply his or her surplus grain to the development of arts and crafts.

Scenario 7

Again, more than 40 years ago, Harold Guetzkow and his associates have developed a very complex and interesting simulation for teaching secondary and high school students the principles of international relations (Guetzkow et al. 1963). This international simulation consists of five 'nation' units. In each of these nations, a group of participants acts as decision makers and 'aspiring decision makers'. The simulated relations among the nations are derived from the characteristics of nations and from principles that have been observed to operate among nations in the past. Each of the decision-making teams has available to it information about the country it represents. This information concerns the basic capability of the national economic systems, the consumer capability, force capability (the ability of the nation to develop military goods and services), and trade and aid information. Together, the nations play an international relations game that involves trading and the development of various agreements. International organizations can be established, for example, or mutual aid or trade agreements made. The nations can even make war on one another, the outcome being determined by the force capability of one group of allies relative to that of another group.

As students play the roles of national decision makers, they must make realistic negotiations such as those diplomats and other representatives make as nations interact with one another and they must refer to the countries' economic conditions as they do so. In the course of this game-type simulation, the students learn ways in which economic restraints operate on a country. For example, if they are members of the decision-making team of a small country and try to engage in a trade agreement, they find that they have to give something to get something. If their country has a largely agricultural economy and they are dealing with an industrialized nation, they find that their country is in a disadvantageous position unless the other nation badly needs the product they have to sell. By receiving feedback about the consequences of their decision, the students come to an understanding of the principles that operate in international relations.

Simulation as a model of learning and teaching

The seven scenarios given here describe simulations. Elements of the 'real world' have been simplified and presented in a form that can be contained inside a classroom, workroom or living room. The attempt is to simulate realistic conditions as much as possible so that the concepts learned and problem solutions generated are transferable to the real world and to understanding and performing tasks related to the content of the simulation.

Most simulations are constructed from descriptions of real-life situations, although modified for teaching purposes. Sometimes the renditions are quite elaborate (for example, flight and space flight simulators or simulations of international relations). The student engages in activity to achieve the goal of the simulation (to get the aircraft off the ground, perhaps, or to redevelop an urban area) and has to deal with realistic factors until the goal is mastered.

To progress through the tasks of the simulation, students develop concepts and skills necessary for performance in the specified area. In the simulations just described, the young caribou hunters have to learn concepts about a certain culture; the young members of the cabinet need to learn about international relations and the problems of governing a nation. Students also learn from the consequences of their actions. The students who do poorly in the caribou hunt learn what happens if the culture does not function efficiently, or if its members shrink from carrying out the tasks that enable them to survive.

Some simulations are games, some not; some are competitive, some cooperative; and some are played by individuals against their own standard. For example, competition is important in the familiar board game Monopoly. Monopoly simulates the activity of real-estate speculators and incorporates many elements of real-life speculation. The winning player learns the 'rules' of investment and speculation as embodied in the game.

In simulations such as the Life Career game, players attempt to reach their goals in a noncompetitive way. No score is kept, but interactions are recorded and analysed later. In the Life Career game, the students play out the lifecycle of a human being: they select mates, choose careers, decide whether to obtain various amounts of education and learn (through the consequences of their decisions) how these choices can affect their lives.

In the familiar computer simulations like Sim City and Sim Earth, students can play alone or together against their own standard for creating a good quality of life.

Nearly all simulations depend on software – that is, materials or paraphernalia of various kinds, from the driving simulator in the scenario above; to the information and materials about the life of Netsilik inuits; to the Monopoly board, money and symbols of property; to the computer and computer software program of Sim Earth.

Effective use of the simulation model in the classroom depends on how the teacher blends the already prepared simulation into the curriculum, highlighting and reinforcing the learning inherent in the game. Both the teacher's ability to make the activities truly meaningful and the self-instructional property of simulations are vital.

Computers and simulations

In the immediate future, the personal computer and an abundance of software are going to greatly increase the likelihood that simulations will be used in schools. Sorting out from the developing storehouse of software those items that will be useful is not easy and is worth a few words here.

The currently available software can be loosely divided into three categories:

1 games built around fantasy adventures
2 game-like simulations that tangentially involve curriculum-relevant content
3 simulations developed to accomplish educational purposes.

Fantasy adventures are not designed to teach real-life concepts and skills, but they do require logical thinking and may well promote it. Working one's way through Middle Earth or working through the levels of Dungeons and Dragons can certainly encourage logical thinking.

Game-like simulations, such as the Carmen San Diego Series, involving puzzles set in real-life terrain – such as the United States, Europe or a period in history – are not designed to teach geographical or historical concepts, but may well add to knowledge. Following the Carmen San Diego gang around the world will acquaint the player with information about our world, its geography and its economy, although not in depth.

Simulations that require learning academic concepts can be an important part of a curriculum. Examples in the Sim series include Sim City, where students construct communities and have to face the consequences of decisions. For instance, they learn that saving land for parks means a lessening of areas for residential, commercial or industrial use, balanced against quality-of-living considerations. When assessing software, finding simulations that require the learning and application of academic concepts should be a high priority.

Phases of the model

The simulation model has four phases: orientation, participant training, the simulation itself and debriefing.

During orientation, *phase 1*, the teacher presents the topic to be explored, the concepts that are embedded in the actual simulation, an explanation of 'simulation' if this is the students' first experience with it and an overview of the game itself. This first part should not be lengthy but can be an important context for the remainder of the learning activity.

During participant training, *phase 2*, the students begin to get into the simulation. At this point the teacher sets the scenario by introducing the students to the rules, roles, procedures, scoring, types of decisions to be made and goals of the simulation. He or she organizes the students into the various roles and conducts an abbreviated practice session to ensure that students have understood all the directions and can carry out their roles.

Phase 3 is the participation in the simulation. The students participate in the game or simulation and the teacher functions in his or her role as referee and coach. Periodically, the simulation may be stopped so that the students receive feedback, evaluate their performances and decisions and clarify any misconceptions.

Finally, *phase 4* consists of participant debriefing. Depending on the outcomes, the teacher may help the students focus on:

- events and their other perceptions and reactions
- analysing the process
- comparing the simulation to the real world
- relating the activity to course content
- appraising and redesigning the simulation.

From the point of view of the teacher, the use of simulations is deceptively simple. The process of debriefing, which surely occurs after each use and may occur periodically throughout the simulation, is the one most often neglected.

Reflections

Simulations have been used increasingly in education over the last 30 years, but the simulation model did not originate within the field of education. Rather, it is an application of the principles of *cybernetics*, a branch of psychology. Cybernetic psychologists, making an analogy between humans and machines, conceptualize the learner as a self-regulating feedback system. The central focus is the apparent similarity between the feedback control mechanisms of electromechanical and human systems. 'A feedback control system incorporates three primary functions: it generates movement of the system toward a target or defined path; it compares the effects of this action with the true path and detects error; and it utilizes this error signal to redirect the system' (Smith and Smith 1966: 203).

For example, the automatic pilot of a boat continually corrects the helm of the ship, depending on the readings of the compass. When the ship begins to swing in a certain direction and the compass moves off the desired heading more than a certain amount, a motor is switched on and the helm moves over. When the ship returns to its course, the helm straightens out again and the ship continues on its way. The automatic pilot operates in essentially the same way as a human pilot. Both watch the compass and both move the wheel to the left or right, depending on what is going on. Both initiate action in terms of a specified goal ('Let's go north') and, depending on the feedback or error signal, both redirect the initial action. Very complex self-regulating mechanical systems have been developed to control devices such as guided missiles, ocean liners and satellites.

Cybernetic psychologists interpret the human being as a control system that generates a course of action and then redirects or corrects the action by means of feedback. This can be a very complicated process (as when the secretary of state re-evaluates foreign policy) or a very simple one (as when we notice that our sailboat is heading into the wind too much and we ease off on our course just a little). In using the analogy of mechanical systems as a frame of reference for analysing human beings, psychologists came up with the central idea that 'performance and learning must be analysed in terms of the control relationships between a human operator and an instrumental situation'. That is, learning was understood to be determined by the nature of the individual, as well as by the design of the learning situation (Smith and Smith 1966: vii).

All human behaviour, according to cybernetic psychology, involves a perceptible pattern of motion. This includes both covert behaviour, such as thinking and symbolic behaviour, and overt behaviour. In any given situation, individuals modify their behaviour according to the feedback they receive from the environment. They organize their movements and their response patterns in relation to this feedback. Thus their own sensorimotor capabilities form the basis of their feedback systems. This ability to receive feedback constitutes the human system's mechanism for receiving and sending information. As human beings develop greater linguistic capability they are able to use indirect as well as direct feedback, thereby expanding their control over the physical and social environment. That is, they are less dependent on the concrete realities of the environment because they can use its symbolic representations.

The essence, then, of cybernetic psychology is the principle of sense-oriented feedback that is intrinsic to the individual (one 'feels' the effects of one's decisions) and is the basis for self-corrective choices. For example, in the driving simulation, if the driver heads into curves too rapidly and then has to jerk the wheel to avoid going off the road, this feedback permits the driver to adjust his or her behaviour so that when driving on a real road he or she will turn more gingerly when approaching sharp curves. The cybernetic psychologist designs simulators so that the feedback about the consequences of behaviour enables the learners to modify their responses and develop a repertoire of appropriate behaviours. According to this view, individuals can 'feel' the effects of their decisions because the environment responds *in full*, rather than simply 'You're right' or 'Wrong! Try again.' That is, the environmental consequences of their choices are played back to them. *Learning* in cybernetic terms is sensorially experiencing the environmental consequences of one's behaviour and engaging in self-corrective behaviour. Instruction in cybernetic terms is designed to create an environment for the learner in which this full feedback takes place.

15 Literacy in the early years: a report

This chapter is a modification of a report on a longitudinal study.

As presented, it was titled The Tending of Diversity Through a Robust Core Literacy Curriculum: Gender, Socioeconomic Status, Learning Disabilities, and Ethnicity.

The authors are:

Bruce Joyce, Booksend Laboratories
Saint Simons Island, Georgia, USA

Marilyn Hrycauk, The Northern Lights
School Division #69
Bonnyville, Alberta, Canada

Emily Calhoun, The Phoenix Alliance
Saint Simons Island, Georgia, USA

and

Walter Hrycauk, Chairman
Board of Trustees
The Northern Lights School Division
Bonnyville, Alberta, Canada

Abstract

The Tending of Diversity through a Robust Core Literacy Curriculum:

Gender, Socioeconomic Status, Learning Disabilities, and Ethnicity

This paper renders the case study of a school division – the Northern Lights School Division – in Bonnyville, Alberta – that developed a core primary grade literacy curriculum built on current research on the teaching of literacy and studied the effects on the diverse students that it serves in its 15 elementary schools. The emphasis is on the early years, particularly for students between 4½ years and 5½ years old as the study began in what are called the kindergarten years in Canada. The effects on student learning have been studied, at this point, through when the students are about 12 years old (sixth grade in Canada). The results support the proposition that a strong, multidimensional early years curriculum, focused on literacy and built around researched models of teaching, can meet the needs of diverse populations and reduce the need for specially targeted remedies later.

Approaches to tending diverse student populations

Generally, there are three approaches to meeting the needs of diverse student populations. In common, their emphasis has been on increasing the extent to which subpopulations have access to education that enables them to have achievement:

- The first emphasizes inclusion: ensuring that various types of student are not deprived of full participation in the mainstream schooling process and that equity in educational opportunity is achieved.
- The second emphasizes the development of programme variations to support the development of students with ethnic, socioeconomic or social/ psychological characteristics that are different from the 'mainstream' population.
- The third, the one reported here, builds on current research on the teaching of literacy and emphasizes the development of a robust core curriculum that has room for the development of the talents of nearly all students.

We have no intention of pitting the three approaches against one another.

Inclusion is important. There are many natural forces that separate students from one another. Prominently, neighbourhood differences in demography can generate inequalities related to SES and ethnic differences, differences that can have a lifelong effect. As difficult as it is, we need to seek ways to reduce the effects of de facto segregation and other forces that generate exclusion and inequality.

Targeted initiatives are important. We need to continue the search for ways of helping students whose characteristics make them candidates for low academic, social and personal achievement. Efforts of developers like the SIM group at the University of Kansas are vital (see Chapter 8). They are particularly important because most large-scale initiatives to target students hampered by low socioeconomic environments have, on the whole, been very unsuccessful as have many programmes that serve students with mild or moderate learning disabilities. Gender can be very important in the literacy areas. In many school districts, males lag seriously behind females from primary levels through high schools and, in the United States, college, where 60 per cent of the enrolment are females and, once there, they outperform males on average (see, for example, Brooks 2005).

The strength of the core curriculum is important. First, the core curriculum (in this case the literacy curriculum) serves all students. And, we can wonder, does a robust curriculum pull all students, not just mainstream students, into higher levels of achievement through instruction and building a culture of higher achievement?

A strengthened curriculum

In Northern Lights, we made a serious overhaul of our early years and primary grade curriculum. In previous papers we have reported the considerable general improvement in literacy learning that has resulted (see Hrycauk 2002; Joyce et al. 2001). Here we concentrate on the effects on diverse populations stemming from the implementation of a reading/literacy curriculum in the kindergarten.

We begin with a description of the curricular changes and its rationales, proceed to the provisions for staff development and the study of implementation and then to the evaluation of student effects, including effects on the diverse populations served by the school division. These populations include genders, SES differences, students diagnosed as having learning disabilities and ethnic differences (especially the progress of aboriginal students). While we have been able to report general effects on student learning, a recent change in provincial regulations now permits us to report data by SES and ethnicity.

First, a note on Northern Lights School Division #69.

The division is in northern Alberta and spans over 200 kilometres with a geographic area of 14,800 square kilometres. Schools are located in the major towns of Cold Lake, Bonnyville and Lac La Biche (these three towns have a combined population of about 21,000), the villages of Glendon and Plamondon, the hamlet of Casden and the rural areas of Ardmore, Iron River and Wandering River. The division operates a school on 4 Wing, a major air force installation near Cold Lake.

There are about 6,000 students. Students with mild to moderate learning disabilities comprise about 11 per cent of the student population and about 8 per cent are of interest here, because the diagnosed disabilities theoretically affect learning to read and write. Students whose parents identify them as aboriginal make up 28 per cent of the population (1,675 students). Of these, 230 are First Nations persons who live on reservations and have 'status rights', including the rights to treaty benefits and to inherit land. Sixty two are First Nations students who do not live on reservations and do not have status rights. There are about a thousand Metis (originally a mixture of French and aboriginal) or 16 per cent of the district student population. There is one Inuit student – origins are in the arctic areas of North America.

Historically, student achievement might be described as Canadian/US normal. Until the new curriculum was implemented, 'standard' test results have been relentlessly average. About two-thirds of the students appeared to learn adequately or better. About 30 per cent of the students did not learn to read or write well.

Designing the curriculums

Rationale issues: what is developmentally appropriate?

For years, the term 'developmentally appropriate' has been the dominating phrase in discussions about curriculum in the early years and even first grade curriculum. Not only professionals but laymen have come to use the phrase, partly because it was popularized by a leading psychologist who was also a columnist on child psychology for a popular magazine (Elkind 1987, 2001). To educators and laypeople alike, the term makes intuitive sense: 'Of course, we would hope that schooling would make contact with the student's developmental level.' However, the opponents of formal instruction polarized the issue. Again and again, the position was (and is) expressed that kindergarten-aged students are not developmentally ready to learn to read. And the picture drawn of teaching reading to young children often depicts the worst kind of meaningless drill and practice with flashcards representing abstract words or sounds, even with made-up rather than real words. The use of that horrific picture raises a second and confusing question: is the problem being raised one of developmental readiness or of an aversion to a miserable curriculum? The mantra of developmental readiness has become so entrenched that even a panel of the leading scholars of reading curriculum, charged with making a comprehensive analysis of research on reading, dismissed the idea of kindergarten readers without even a nod toward relevant research (Snow et al. 1998). They began their interpretations of research with first grade, apparently because the idea of teaching reading earlier was resoundingly dismissed by the 'experts'. The polarization – putting a 'play school' orientation against a harsh curriculum – is disseminated to the public regularly. The title of an April 2005 article in the *San Diego Union-Tribune*, 'Kindergarten or "Kindergrind" ' is an example. And the article reports that teachers scaled back literacy goals developed by school officials after a 2-year conflict on the grounds of developmental readiness confounded by the idea that if you teach reading you do so harshly. For many decades San Diego Unified has been one of the least troubled of the nation's large school systems, but a quarter or more of its students cannot read effectively as they exit the primary grades. But its kindergarten teachers construed an upgrade of their emergent literacy emphasis to be necessarily a move toward a harsh and rote curriculum (Gao 2005). By the way, they dismissed full-day school for 5 year olds as, in Elkind's words, 'too much, too soon'.

As we write, the position papers of the large curriculum organizations continue to come from a 'developmentally inappropriate' perspective (International Reading Association 1998; National Association for the Education of Young Children 1998). Some experts even question whether having 'full day' school for 5-year olds is too much, let alone a curriculum in reading (Natale 2001).

The categorical rejection of a formal literacy curriculum in kindergarten is odd for several reasons. One of the most respected scholars of early reading in the United States has presented an extensive argument (Durkin 1966) for beginning early and her rationale is essentially unquestioned by other scholars. Further, in a longitudinal study, Hanson and Farrell (1995) found that the effects of a reading curriculum in kindergarten could be seen in the academic achievement of graduating high school students. Finally, the 'father' of the idea of kindergarten, Fredrich Froebel, emphasized the need for a rich environment that would pull students into inquiry and development: neither a free-play school in a play-only environment nor a rough-edged curriculum.

From our perspective the real issue is whether a comprehensive reading curriculum can be developmentally appropriate.

By the way, we are acquainted with some really fine 'emergent literacy' classrooms where many fine things happen even without a formal literacy curriculum. In those classrooms, there are rich classroom libraries – collections the children can pore over themselves or ask the teacher to read to them. Interesting field trips are mined for new language, tied to real experiences. The science learning centre is a place for observation and experimentation. The students may not learn to read, but they surely grow in cognitions and language development. Unfortunately, when the developmentally appropriate theory is taken to mean staying within what the students bring to school rather than enriching their development, the result is what Mike Schmoker characterized as the 'Crayola Curriculum' (Schmoker 2001) and that is exactly what those San Diego teachers wanted to preserve. Sadly, it was their desire to stay within their existing repertoire that trumped their professional need to learn how to teach their little charges to read.

Curriculum design

Important for our early literacy curriculum was the emergence of the picture–word inductive model (see Chapter 6) from the tradition of the language experience frame of reference with the addition of concept formation and attainment models of teaching (Calhoun 1999). The picture–word inductive model designs cycles that begin with photographs of scenes whose content is within the ability of the students to describe. For example, photographs can be of aspects of the local community or they can take students around the world with photos of scenes they can relate to – the 'boat' picture in Chapter 6 is an example. The students take turns identifying objects and actions in the picture. The teacher spells the words, drawing lines from the words to the elements in the picture to which they refer, creating a picture dictionary (as on page 55). The students are given copies of the words and they identify them using the picture dictionary they have created. They proceed to classify the words using the well-tested inductive model of learning (see Chapter 3), noting their similarities and differences. The teacher selects some of their categories for extended study. The teacher models the creation of titles and sentences and the students create both, using the words 'shaken out' of the picture, dictating them and learning to read them. The students gradually learn to assemble titles and sentences into paragraphs about the content of the picture. The picture word cycles (inquiries into the pictures) generally take from 3 to 5 weeks.

A major assumption underpinning the curriculum is that students need to become inquirers into language, seeking to build their sight vocabularies and studying the characteristics of those words, trying to build generalizations about phonetic and structural characteristics.

Our image of a nurturant curriculum appears to differ widely from what many people imagine would be the shape of a curriculum for young children and which image causes those people to shy away from formal literacy instruction in the early years. As we indicated earlier, we believe that the developmentally appropriate issue is confounded by aversion to a harsh and rote curriculum. For our part, we did not imagine students with workbooks, alphabet flash cards or letter-by-letter phonics drills. We imagined an environment where students would progress from their developed listening/speaking vocabularies to the reading of words, sentences and longer text that they had created, where they would examine simple books in a relaxed atmosphere, where they would begin to write with scribbling and simple illustrations, where they would be read to regularly and where comprehension strategies would be modelled for them through the reading and study of charming fiction and non-fiction books. If the work of childhood is play, we imagined the students playfully working their way into literacy. Froebel envisioned capitalizing on children's natural propensity to play to enable them to mature socially and cognitively by engaging in increasingly complex activities. We wished to create an environment where students would learn to read in a joyful fashion. From the literature on early reading, we identified several dimensions of learning to read (see Calhoun, 1999):

- *The development of sight vocabulary.* At first, this would come through the analysis of pictures (a large picture, 24 by 30 inches or more, would be the basis of study for 3 to 5 weeks. Imagine the students studying a picture of a woman holding a child in a market in Kuala Lumpur. The students identify items and actions: 'banana', 'smile', 'cars', and so on. These words are printed and spelled by the teacher with lines going from the words to the objects in the picture. Thus the words are within the students' listening–speaking vocabulary. Additional words are studied as the teachers shares non-fiction and fiction books about markets around the world. Students visit these settings through their own exploration and reading of trade books.
- *The inductive study of words.* Students classify words, discovering phonetic and structural characteristics. They learn that the language is comprehensible – that words are almost always spelled the same, an onset in one word is likely to sound the same if it begins another word, that rhymes have a lot of regularity, that adding 's' to banana and smile will create a plural, and taking 's' from cars will get you a single car.
- *Wide reading at the developed level.* At the beginning, students can engage at the picture level (see later) and, gradually can deal with caption-level books as they learn how meaning is conveyed by the authors. They also learn to generate sentences from the words they have shaken out, at first dictating them: 'The woman is holding the boy'. And paragraphs are created from the sentences. The teachers model sentence and paragraph making. And, of course, the teachers read to the children regularly.
- *Regular (several times daily) writing.* At first they may just illustrate a word with a drawing. Gradually, students progress to writing picture-related sentences and paragraphs.
- *The study of comprehension strategies.* Although most of the research on comprehension is with older students, the search for meaning begins early and the modeling of comprehension strategies (explicit instruction in the literature) is important from the beginning (for greater detail, see Calhoun 1999; Joyce et al. 2001).

Implementation and student learning

The experiences described here and the presentations of data are from what we call the original implementers (TOI), composed of eight early years classes of 5 year olds in the Cold Lake area of the district.

The teachers participated in 12 days of staff development, five at the beginning of the school year and the others spread throughout the year. They were visited regularly by the consultants and coordinator and several principals and assistant principals participated in the training and practised with the teachers periodically. The study of implementation was accomplished through a combination of self-report logs and observations conducted by consultants and central office personnel.

Embedded studies of student learning, from the learning of the alphabet in the kindergarten classes to the study of the acquisition of sight vocabulary, were conducted on a regular (generally monthly) basis by each of the teachers.

A team of external assessors were trained to administer the Gunning procedure (see later) in the first year, and the Gray Oral Reading Test as the students proceeded through first to fifth grades.

The Gunning procedure, developed by Thomas Gunning (1998), presents to the students trade books that have been selected because they represent the following levels.

Gunning levels

Level 1: picture level. The vocabulary is very small – sometimes only a half dozen words – and is closely linked to pictures.

Level 2: caption level. There are a few more words and there is more action – more to comprehend. Each page has a phrase that moves the book along.

Level 3: easy sight level. Extended text is introduced. The student has to read text beyond what is illustrated.

Levels 4 to 6: beginning reading levels. The vocabularies increase, the complexity of the stories increases, and the understanding of even lavishly illustrated books depends on the reading of complex text.

Level 7: grade 2-A. These are larger, more complex books. The student who can read at this level can read a large number of books on many topics and do so independently.

The books are presented to the students and the cover pages are discussed briefly. Then the students read the books and answer questions designed to assess comprehension of the major aspects of the books. To ensure that the students are not familiar with the books, they were selected from titles published in Great Britain that have not yet been distributed in Canada.

In the following pages we will deal, first, with the general effects of an initial implementation of the curriculum in eight kindergarten sections. We then proceed to examine the effects on diverse populations.

Summative results for the initial eight sections –

The embedded studies of alphabet recognition and vocabulary acquisition are important, but, for our purposes here, the first question is how did those students fare initially, with the use of the Gunning procedure and, second, over the years, as represented by the fifth grade,

Table 15.1 presents the results for the initial cohort group at the end of the first year.

Table 15.1 Percentage of students reaching Gunning levels at end-of-year testing

Level	% reaching level
Picture (a few words, closely connected to pictures)	2
Caption (picture books, with text in captions)	26
Easy sight (simple text carries meaning)	30
Above easy sight (extended text in complex stories)	42

The students learned to read somewhat better than first grade students usually did in our school district with an important addition – they all learned to read at some level. In previous years, about 70 per cent of the students in those schools learned to read in the primary grades – first to third grade and about 30 per cent would have been at the picture level or below, about the same proportion as in United States primary grades in general as reported in the National Assessment of Educational Progress at fourth grade (Donahue 1999; NCES 1998).

All eight sections apparently succeeded in bringing all the students to some level of print literacy. About 40 per cent of the students appeared to be able to read extended text and another 30 per cent manifested emergent ability to read extended text. Twenty per cent reached the '2A' level, which includes long and complex passages and requires the exercise of complex skills both to decode and infer word meanings. All the students could manage at least the simplest level of books. Very important to us was that there were no students who experienced abject failure. Even the student who enters first grade reading independently at the picture level carries alphabet recognition, a substantial storehouse of sight words and an array of phonetic and structural concepts to the first grade experience. However, half a dozen students needed to be watched closely because, even if they were able to handle books at the caption level, they laboured at the task, manifesting difficulty either in recognizing text – graphics relationships or using their phonetic or structural generalizations to attack unfamiliar words.

Year 1: comfort and satisfaction

During the year parents voiced their opinions regularly and in May we prepared simple questionnaires for both parents and children. We asked the parents a series of questions about the progress of their children and whether they and the children believed they were developing satisfactorily. The children were just asked whether they were learning to read and how they felt about their progress. Primarily, we were trying to ferret out whether there were levels of discomfort that were not being detected. Apparently not. No student or parent manifested discomfort or dissatisfaction related to the curriculum. However, some parents were anxious at the beginning and still worried at the end of the year. Some were concerned that we had not taken a 'letter-by-letter' synthetic phonics approach and worried that future problems might develop as a consequence, but they appeared to believe that their children were progressing well 'so far'.

By the end of sixth grade, the national GORT average grade level equivalent score in comprehension is 7.0, which is about the average over the years for students in the division. For these students, the average is GLE 8.5. Contrary to the doctrine that teaching early years students with a formal literacy curriculum will be damaging later, it appears that these students have not been damaged but, rather, have prospered. Importantly, only four students are below the 6.0 level and just one of these is a struggling reader.

Diversity

We are concerned here with gender, socioeconomic status (SES), learning disabilities and ethnicity.

Gender

Gender did not influence levels of success from kindergarten through sixth grade. The distributions of scores for boys and girls were almost identical. Typically, in North America, males are at approximately the 30th percentile of the female distribution.

SES

The distributions of scores for students having or not having subsidies for lunch (the usual measure of socioeconomic status) were also approximately equal. Major initiatives in Canada and the United States have tried to reach all or most students from economically poor homes with indifferent results, despite providing additional resources to schools with sizeable populations of economically poor students.

Learning disabilities.

The special education 'specialists' believed that students about one-quarter of our 5 year olds had special needs, that is, learning disabilities. Ordinarily, all would have been given special training throughout their school career. Special needs instruction was discontinued for all but 5 per cent of these students.

Ethnicity

In our population area, the major concern is with the achievement of aboriginal students. In the district, nearly all the aboriginal students have done poorly. There were only eight aboriginal students in our population. Their average comprehension score at the end of the sixth grade was 8.0. Just one was below 7.0, the average score for graduating sixth grade students.

Summary

As achievement of these early years students rose with the implementation of the formal and more robust curriculum in literacy, it appears that the sub-populations benefited simultaneously. As we look at the students who have just graduated in sixth grade, the females are prospering, literacy wise, and so are the males. Mild to moderate learning disabilities appear to be diminishing. SES did not inhibit growth. And, in the area where we have the skimpiest evidence, ethnicity, in this case the progress of aboriginals, did not appear to have the dampening effect that ordinarily occurs.

The average GLE in comprehension at the end of sixth grade is 8.5. Our *ninth grade* students' mid-year average has been about 7.4 in the past!

Curriculum development, appropriately combining several models of teaching, may have bypassed the controversies as far as kindergarten is concerned. Beginning with the little people may be a nice way to leave none of them behind later.

CODA   How do we learn new models of learning?

"A school teaches in three ways: by what it teaches, by how it teaches, and by the kind of place it is."

Lawrence Downey (1967)

Inquiry into teaching and learning makes the professional life of educators. We create environments, study how our students respond and watch them learn how to learn. Our position is that reflection on teaching can be greatly enhanced through the study of models of learning and teaching that have been submitted to intense scrutiny and development. Practice, theory and research become intertwined and the body of professional knowledge becomes enhanced as each of us generates information about student learning.

Studies of teachers learning models of teaching indicate that there are three types of learning mingled together:

1   developing an understanding of the model, how it works, why it works and how it can be modulated to take individual differences into account
2   getting a picture of the model in action, envisioning what the teacher does and what the students do and how the instructional and social environments are managed
3   adapting the model to what one teaches – the goals of the parts of the curriculum for which one is responsible.

The first involves lots of reading and discussion – getting hold of the books and articles that describe the model and its rationale and analysing them thoroughly.

The second requires watching demonstrations and analysing them so that the process becomes clear. One begins to 'feel' the model in action and sense how to teach the students to use it as a tool for learning. Our rule of thumb is that one has to see a 'new' model about 20 times to get that feel.

The third is adaptation of the model to one's teaching situation – practising until executive control over the model is achieved. During that practice, one has to cope with the frustration that more trials are needed than one expects and the further the model is from one's developed repertoire, the greater the number before a comfort level is reached.

Optimally, these three learning processes are mixed. One reads, watches, reads some more, watches and practises, reads and watches and practises and so on ...

Working as an individual

Suppose that you (a head, teacher, adviser or academic) decide to study models of teaching and have no colleague willing to join you? (If there is someone available, then enlist that person immediately, for it will make the process much easier!) No matter, you can do it yourself. You just have to figure out how you can manage the three types of learning while working alone. Here are some of our 'tested' suggestions:

1   *Study* just one model at a time and keep at it until you have mastered it.
2   *Read* anything you can get your hands on pertinent to the model. *Models of Teaching* (Joyce et al. 2008) is a handy guide to the literature.
3   See if you can find a workshop conducted by someone who is an expert in using the model. Make sure the workshop includes lots of *demonstrations*. If you can't find a workshop, then obtain videotapes of the model in action and study them (a few tapes, watched again and again, help a lot).
4   *Practise like crazy*. Prepare short lessons and long units (both are necessary). After a few practices with your students, read some more and watch the tapes again and then practise. Make sure your practice is regular – don't let long periods go by between them – and that the practice is within your normal content area, where you have the greatest substantive control. You will feel uncomfortable at first. Ignore the discomfort and keep practising. After a few tries, you will begin to get the feel of the moves of the model and the adaptation to your curriculum area, or schemes of work, will become easier.
    Be sure to study what the students are learning, both substance and how to learn.

Working as a whole-school staff

Suppose you are working with a staff that is studying teaching strategies. How would you proceed, based on what we currently 'know' about school improvement and student achievement?

1   Organize peer coaching or partnership teaching groups. First, form partners from within the staff – one or two people, no more – who can work together to study the new teaching strategy or strategies. Develop a weekly schedule for peer coaching, or partnership teaching, close to an hour each week, when the partners can meet, preferably in the same setting at the same time, to share plans and progress.
2   The staff needs to study one model at a time, arrangements to do just one are difficult enough.

3   The rest of the process is the same as if you were working alone: studying the literature of the model, watching demonstrations and practising, except that you now have the companionship of others as you work toward effective implementation.

That's about it. No rocket science is needed, just bite the bullet and get at it.
Good luck!

APPENDIX: Peer coaching guides

The following pages contain peer coaching guides for the models of teaching contained in this book. These forms facilitate planning and communication between teachers who observe one another and try to profit from the observational experience. The forms can also be used to facilitate sharing of ideas by teachers, whether or not observation of one another's teaching is included.

Hence they are addressed to both parties in the peer coaching process: the teacher who is planning and directing the teaching episode and the partner who is studying the model. Both parties are involved in a continuing experiment on teaching. Each has the same purpose, which is to increase their ability to analyse the transactions between teacher and student and their ability to teach students how to learn information and concepts. The guide is used both to assist the planning of the teaching episode and in focusing the observation on key features of the model. The teacher prepares the observer by filling out the entries where indicated. The observer fills in the observation checklist and communicates the result to the teacher. Both parties will profit most by making a partnership that studies the student responses and plans how to help the students learn more effectively. The observer is not present to advise the teacher on how to teach better but, rather, to learn by observing and help the teacher by providing information about the students' responses.

The communication of the analysis should be conducted in a neutral tone, proceeding matter of factly through the phases of the model. The guide draws attention to the syntax of the model – the cognitive and social tasks that are presented to the students and how students respond and the principles of reaction – the guidelines for reacting to the students as they try to attain the concept. The teacher may want to direct the coaching partner to look closely at a specific phase of the model, such as student response to a particular cognitive or social task or reactions to student responses. The coaching partner should avoid giving gratuitous advice. Normally the communication about a teaching episode should be completed in 5 minutes or less. For self-coaching, teachers should use videotape when possible and, during playback, enter the role of partner, analysing the transactions as dispassionately as possible.

Peer Coaching Guide for the Inductive Model

Learning to think inductively

This guide is designed to assist peer coaching of the inductive thinking model of learning and teaching. When planning questions, skip through the guide to the entries marked 'Teacher' and fill them in as needed. They will guide you through the model. Observers can use the guide to familiarize themselves with the plans of the teacher and to make notes about what is observed. Remember, observers, that your primary function is not to give 'expert advice' to your colleague, but to observe the students as requested by the teacher and to observe the whole process so that you can gain ideas for your own teaching. The teacher is the coach in the sense that he or she is demonstrating a teaching episode for you. When you teach and are observed, you become the coach.

The teacher or student teacher being observed needs to identify the phases of the model that will be present in this teaching episode; not all lessons will include all phases. More often, the full inductive model will take several days and with extensive datasets – such as poems, paragraphs on text structures or statistical/textual databases on countries or regions – the class may spend several weeks productively moving through and back and forth among the six phases of the inductive model. Along with the phases for the lesson to be observed, the teacher may want to identify a particular area of concern, such as how the students study the dataset.

Teacher Do you want to suggest a focus for the analysis? If so, what is it?

_____

_____

THE TEACHING PROCESS

Most lessons you teach will have both content and process objectives. *Content* objectives identify subject matter (facts, concepts, generalizations, relationships) and content-related skills to be mastered by students, while *process* objectives specify skills and procedures students need in order to achieve content objectives or auxiliary social objectives (e.g. cooperation in a learning task).

The content objectives for inductive thinking reside in the information and concepts embedded in the dataset. Students categorize items in the dataset by attributes held in common by subsets of items. For example, if the dataset consisted of a collection of plants, students might classify plants by types of leaf (size, texture, patterns of veins, shape, connection of leaves to stems, etc.). Content objectives for this dataset might include both information about specific plants and the building of a typology. Process objectives might include learning the scientific skill of the discipline (observation and classification) as well as the social skills of cooperative problem solving.

Content objective(s)

Teacher What knowledge or skill do you want students to gain from today's tasks?

_____

_____

Process objective(s)

Teacher Are the students familiar with the model? Do they need special assistance or training with respect to any aspect of the process? (For example, do students understand how to group items by common attributes? Can they work cooperatively with partners on a classification task?)

_____

_____

PHASE 1: DOMAIN IDENTIFICATION

Teacher What domain is being explored? What are the long-term objectives of this exploration?

_____

_____

PHASE 2: COLLECTION, PRESENTATION AND ENUMERATION OF DATA

The primary activity of Phase 2 of the inductive model involves collection or presentation of a dataset. The teacher may provide a dataset or instruct students to collect the data that will be categorized. The data that will be scrutinized by the students are extremely important, for they represent much of the information the students will learn from this phase. The choice between data collection or presentation is also important. To continue this example, if students collect leaves, a different set of data will result than if they had been presented with them.

Data are easier to discuss and to group if enumerated. Continuing with our example of plants, the teacher might place a numbered card under each plant so that students may discuss plants number 1, 4, 7 and 14 as sharing a common attribute rather than by plant names (which students may not yet know). However, when young children are dealing with a dataset of letter names, numerals or word cards, enumeration may not be necessary.

Teacher Please describe the dataset to be used in this lesson. Will you provide the dataset or have students collect data? If the latter, what will be the sources of information they will use?

_____

_____

Teacher What, in your opinion, are the critical attributes of the dataset? What categories do *you* bring to the set?

_____

_____

Observer Did the teacher/students enumerate the data before attempting to categorize it?

Yes ☐   No ☐

PHASE 3: EXAMINATION OF DATA

Once a dataset has been presented to students or collected by them, the teacher needs to direct students to review (read, examine, study) all items in the dataset.

Teacher What will you say to students to engage them in a full review of the dataset before they begin categorizing the items?

_____

_____

Observer Did the students examine the items in the dataset before they proceeded to classification?

_____

_____

PHASE 4: FORMATION OF CONCEPTS BY CLASSIFYING

Once a dataset has been collected by or presented to students, the teacher may want to set parameters for the classification activity by orienting students to relevant attributes. For example, if the data are plants, the teacher may wish to narrow the field of observation by having students classify by 'types of leaf'. By the same token, the teacher may wish to leave the parameters open and simply instruct students to classify by common attributes. Generally speaking, the more open-ended the instructions the better the results and the broader the cognitive engagement of the students.

Items from a dataset may be included in only one category or they may be in multiple categories. You may want to experiment with different instructions regarding the classification of data and observe differences in the categories that result. Generally speaking, leaving open the possibility of multiple category membership for items from the dataset provides more energy.

Once students have been instructed on procedures for grouping the data, the teacher will need to attend to the mechanics of the grouping activity. Students may work alone, in pairs, in small groups or as one large group. Working alone requires the least social skill and working in small groups the greatest social skill. If one process objective is to develop students' abilities to work cooperatively, assertively defending their groupings but compromising when appropriate for group consensus, then students will need instruction and practice to develop these skills. If the teacher chooses to work with the entire class as a single group for the categorizing activity, they will need to exercise caution so that categories are not inadvertently provided for the students. Structuring students into pairs for the categorizing activity is the simplest way to have all students actively engaged in the task, although the teacher must again use considerable skill in keeping everyone involved while recording and synthesizing reports from the pairs. Teachers will probably want to experiment with different ways of structuring this activity, and pros and cons of each process can be discussed with peer coaches.

Teacher Please describe how you will instruct the students to classify the data that you have provided or that they have collected.

_____

_____

Observer In your opinion, did the students understand the criteria and procedures they were to employ during the categorizing activity? Did the teacher inadvertently give clues about what the 'right' groups would be?

_____

_____

Teacher Please describe how you will organize students for the categorizing activity.

_____

_____

Observer Did the students work productively on the categorizing activity?

Yes ☐   No ☐   Partially ☐

_____

_____

If the teacher had the students work in pairs or small groups, did the students listen as other groups shared their categories?

Yes ☐   No ☐   Partially ☐

Were students able to explain the attributes on which they grouped items within categories?

Yes ☐   No ☐   Partially ☐

Were students able to provide labels or descriptive phrases for their groups which reflected the attributes on which the groups were formed?

Yes ☐   No ☐

Note: the names or labels students attach to groups of items within a dataset will often accurately describe the group but not coincide with a technical or scientific name, and this is fine. For example, students may label a group of leaves 'jagged edges' while the technical term would be 'serrated edges'. The teacher may choose to provide technical or scientific terms when appropriate, but not before students have attempted to provide their own labels.

COMMENTS ON PHASES 1–4

For some lessons, the content objectives will be accomplished at the conclusion of phase 4. When the teacher wishes to have students learn information by organizing it into categories and labelling it in order to gain conceptual control of the material, they may choose to stop here. Or when the objective is to learn what students see within a dataset and what attributes they are unaware of, the grouping activity will accomplish that objective. When, however, the objective is the application of concepts that have been formed through phase 4, the remainder of the inductive model is appropriate. Phases 5 and 6 result in further processing of the information and ownership of the concepts embedded in the dataset and should usually be completed.

PHASE 5: GENERATION AND TESTING OF HYPOTHESES

The purpose of phase 5 is to help students develop an understanding of possible relationships between and among categories that they have formed in phase 4 and how (and in what instances) the different categories are useful. The class will need a common set of categories in order to work productively in this kind of discussion. Working off the groups that students developed in phase 4, the teacher asks questions that focus students' thinking on similarities and differences between the groups. By asking 'why' questions, the teacher attempts to develop cause and effect relationships between the groups. The success of this phase depends on a thorough categorizing activity in phase 4 and the length of phase 5 is relatively short compared with the time required for phase 4.

Teacher   Although you will not know during your planning what groups the students will form, make a guess about possible categories they might construct and then write two sample questions that would explore relationships between those groups.

_____

_____

_____

Observer   Were the students able to discuss possible relationships among the groups?

Yes ☐   No ☐   Partially ☐

Did the teacher ask the students to go beyond the data and make inferences about the appropriate use of different groups?

Yes ☐   No ☐

If yes, were the students able to do so?

Yes ☐   No ☐

If students were unable to make inferences or conclusions, can you think of any ideas to share with your partner that might help them do so?

_____

_____

Teacher   If students were successful in making inferences and conclusions about their data, you may wish to push them a step further and ask them to predict consequences from their data by asking 'What would happen if ...' kinds of question. Please write one or two examples of hypothetical questions you might ask students about this dataset.

_____

_____

_____

Observer   Were students able to make logical predictions based on the foregoing categorization and discussion of relationships?

Yes ☐   No ☐

Did the teacher ask the students to explain and support their predictions?

Yes ☐   No ☐

If students were unable to make logical predictions based on their previous work with their categories, can you think of questions or examples that might assist students in doing so?

PHASE 6: CONSOLIDATION AND TRANSFER

The goal of this phase is for students to use the concepts (knowledge and skills) they have been forming. Can they find and create new items that belong to the different groups/categories? Can they write knowledgeably about or use these concepts? Application of the categories and practice in using them through discussion, writing and/or performance comprise the major portion of this phase.

Teacher Think about one or two of the categories you believe students will form. Create a writing assignment that would require the application of the content objectives/concepts that have been explored through this dataset (or domain, if appropriate).

_____

_____

_____

Observer Are there other writing assignments or activities that would be appropriate for consolidation and transfer?

_____

_____

_____

FOR TEACHER AND OBSERVER DISCUSSION

In order to improve student performance with a model, the first option we explore is whether their performance will improve with practice. That is, will simple repetition of the model give the students a chance to learn to respond more appropriately. Second, we directly teach the students the skills they need to manage the cognitive and social tasks of the model.

Observer Please comment on the skills with which the students engaged in the activities and suggest any areas where you believe demonstrations by the teacher or further training might be useful. Think especially of the students' ability to group by attributes, to provide labels for groups that accurately described the groups or synthesized attributes characteristic of a given group, to articulate possible relation-ships among groups, to make inferences regarding use of the different categories and to use (discuss, write about, demonstrate) the concepts being explored.

_____

_____

_____

_____

Peer Coaching Guide for Concept Attainment

Learning to explore concepts

This guide is designed to assist peer coaching of the concept attainment model of learning and teaching. When planning, skip through the guide to the entries marked 'Teacher' and fill them in as needed. They will guide you through the model. Observers can use the guide to familiarize themselves with the plans of the teacher and to make notes about what is observed. Remember, observers, that your primary function is not to give 'expert advice' to your colleague, but to observe the students as requested by the teacher and to observe the whole process so that you can gain ideas for your own teaching. The teacher is the coach in the sense that he or she is demonstrating a teaching episode for you. When you teach and are observed, you become the coach.

Teacher   Do you want to suggest a focus for the analysis? If so, what is it?

_____

_____

THE TEACHING PROCESS

Most lessons have both content and process objectives. Content objectives identify subject matter (facts, concepts, generalizations, relationships) to be mastered by students, while process objectives specify skills and procedures students need in order to achieve content objectives or auxiliary social objectives (for example, cooperation in a learning task).

Content objective

Teacher   Please state the concept that is the objective of the lesson. What are its defining attributes? What kind of data will be presented to the students? Is the information or concept new to the students?

_____

_____

Process objective

Teacher   Are the students familiar with the model? Do they need special assistance or training with respect to any aspect of the process?

Focus

The focus defines the field of search for the students. It may eliminate non-relevant lines of inquiry. Often it is pitched at a level of abstraction just above the exemplars (i.e. 'a literary device' might serve as a focus for the concept of metaphor).

Teacher   Please write the focus statement here.

Observer   Did the teacher deliver the focus statement?

Yes ☐   No ☐

In your opinion, was it clear to the students and did it function to help them focus on the central content of the lesson?

Completely ☐   Partially ☐   No ☐

PHASE 1: PRESENTATION OF DATA AND IDENTIFICATION OF THE CONCEPT

The dataset should be planned in pairs of positive and negative exemplars, ordered to enable the students – by comparing the positive exemplars and contrasting them with the negative ones – to distinguish the defining attributes of the concept.

Teacher   Please describe the nature of the exemplars. (Are they words, phrases, documents, etc.? For example: 'These are reproductions of nineteenth-century paintings. Half of them are from the impressionists [Renoir, Monet, Degas] and the other half are realistic, romantic or abstract painters.')

The set

Observer Were approximately equal numbers of positive and negative exemplars presented?

Yes ☐   No ☐

Were the early positive exemplars clear and unambiguous?

Yes ☐   No ☐

Did the dataset contain at least 15 each of positive and negative exemplars?

Yes ☐   No ☐

How was the set presented?

A labelled pair at a time?

All at once, with labels following?

Other (please describe)

_____

_____

Did the teacher provide the labels for the first eight or 10 pairs before asking the students to suggest a label?

Yes ☐   No ☐

PHASE 2: TESTING ATTAINMENT OF THE CONCEPT

As the students work through the dataset, they are to examine each exemplar and develop hypotheses about the concept. They need to ask themselves what attributes the positive exemplars have in common. It is those attributes that define the concept.

Teacher How are you going to do this?

_____

_____

Observer Were the students asked to generate hypotheses but to avoid sharing them?

Yes ☐   No ☐

Sometimes students are asked to record the progression of their thinking.

Teacher Do you want to do this?

_____

_____

Observer   Were the students asked to record their thinking as the episode progressed?

Yes ☐   No ☐

As the lesson progresses, we need to get information about whether the students are formulating and testing ideas.

PHASE 3: ANALYSIS OF THINKING STRATEGIES

When it appears that the students have developed hypotheses that they are fairly sure of, they are asked to describe the progression of their thinking and the concept they have arrived at.

Teacher   When to do this is a matter of judgement. How will you decide and what will you say?

_____

_____

_____

Observer   Did the teacher ask the students to share their thinking?

Yes ☐   No ☐

Were the students able to express their hypotheses?

Yes ☐   No ☐

If there were several hypotheses, could the students justify or reconcile them?

Yes ☐   No ☐

Naming and applying the concept

Once concepts have been agreed on (or different ones justified), they need names. After students have generated names, the teacher may need to supply the technical or common term (i.e. 'We call this style "impressionism" '). Application requires that students determine whether further exemplars fit the concept and, perhaps, find examples of their own.

Teacher   Is there a technical or common term the students need to know? How will you provide further experience with the concept?

_____

_____

_____

Observer   Were the students able to name the concept?

Yes ☐   No ☐

Was a technical or common term for the concept supplied (if needed)?

Yes ☐   No ☐

Were additional exemplars provided?

Yes ☐   No ☐

Were the students asked to supply their own?

Yes ☐   No ☐

As the students examined new material, supplying their own exemplars, did they appear to know the concept?

Yes ☐   No ☐

An assignment to follow the lesson often involves the application of the concept to fresh material. For example, if the concept of *metaphor* had been introduced, the students might be asked to read a literary passage and identify the uses of metaphor in it.

Teacher   Are you planning such an assignment? If so, please describe it briefly.

_____

_____

_____

COMMENTS ON STUDENT TRAINING NEEDS

In order to improve student performance, the first option we explore is whether it will improve with practice. That is, simple repetition of the model gives the students a chance to learn to respond more appropriately. Second, we directly teach the students the skills they need to manage the cognitive and social tasks of the model.

A discussion including the following topics might ensure.

How the students responded to phase 1

Did they pay close attention to the focus statement and apply it to the examination of the exemplars? If not, is it worthwhile to give specific instruction and what might that be?

_____

_____

_____

How the students responded to phase 2

Did they compare and contrast the exemplars? Did they make hypotheses with the expectations that they might have to change them? Were they using the negative exemplars to eliminate alternatives? Is it worthwhile to provide specific training, and what might that be?

_____

_____

_____

How the students responded to phase 3

Were they able to debrief their thinking? Were they able to see how different lines of thinking gave similar or different results? Were they able to generate labels that express the concept? Do they understand how to seek exemplars on their own and apply what they have learned? Is it worthwhile to provide specific training and what might that be?

_____

_____

_____

Peer Coaching Guide for Synectics

Learning to think metaphorically

This guide is designed to assist peer coaching of the synectics model of learning and teaching. When planning questions, skip through the guide to the entries marked 'Teacher' and fill them in as needed. They will guide you through the model. Observers can use the guide to familiarize themselves with the plans of the teacher and to make notes about what is observed. Remember, observers, that your primary function is not to give 'expert advice' to your colleague, but to observe the students as requested by the teacher and to observe the whole process so that you can gain ideas for your own teaching. The teacher is the coach in the sense that he or she is demonstrating a teaching episode for you. When you teach and are observed, you become the coach.

Teacher   Do you want to suggest a focus for the observer? If so, what is it?

_____

_____

THE TEACHING PROCESS

Most teaching episodes have both content and process objectives. Content objectives include the substance (information, concepts, generalizations, relationships, skills) to be mastered by students. Process objectives include skills or procedures the students need in order to learn productively from the cognitive and social tasks of the model.

Content objective(s)

Teacher   Please state the content objectives of the episode. What kind of learning will come from the activity? What is the nature of the area to be explored?

_____

_____

_____

Process objective(s)

Teacher Are the students familiar with the model? Is there some aspect of its process where they need practice or instruction and will you be concentrating on it in this lesson?

_____

_____

Observer Please comment on the students' response to the model. Do they appear to need specific help with some aspect of the process?

_____

_____

_____

PHASE 1: DESCRIPTION OF PRESENT CONDITION

Commonly, synectics is used to generate fresh perspectives on a topic or problem either for clarification or to permit alternative conceptions or solutions to be explored. Thus it generally begins by soliciting from students a product representing their current thinking. They can formulate the problem, speak or write about the topic, enact a problem, draw a representation of a relationship – there are many alternatives. The function of this phase is to enable them to capture their current thoughts about the subject at hand.

Teacher Please describe how you will elicit the students' conceptions of the area to be explored. What will you say or do to orientate them?

_____

_____

_____

Observer Please comment on the students' response to the originating task. What is the nature of their conceptions?

_____

_____

_____

PHASES 2 AND 3: DIRECT AND PERSONAL ANALOGIES

The core of the model requires the development of distance from the original product through exercises inducing the students to make comparisons between sets of stimuli that are presented to them (direct analogy exercises) and to place themselves, symbolically, in the position of various persons, places and things (personal analogy exercises). The analogies material generated in these exercises will be used later in the creation of further analogies called 'compressed conflicts'.

Teacher What stimuli will you use to induce the students to make the direct and personal analogies? Please describe the material and the order in which you will proceed to stretch the students toward the more unusual and surprising comparisons.

_____

_____

_____

Observer Please comment on the stimuli and the student responses. Did the students get 'up in the air' metaphorically and generate less literal and more analogistic comparisons?

_____

_____

_____

PHASES 4 AND 5: COMPRESSED CONFLICT AND DIRECT ANALOGY

The next task is to induce the students to operate on the material generated in phases 2 and 3 and create compressed conflicts. You need to be prepared to define compressed conflict, even if the students have familiarity with the model, and to continue eliciting material until a number of examples clearly contain the logical (illogical?) tension that characterizes a high-quality oxymoron.

Teacher Please describe how you will initiate phases 4 and 5 and how you will explain compressed conflict if you need to.

_____

_____

_____

Observer Please comment on the students' response to the task. How rich was the product?

_____

_____

_____

Now we ask the students to select some pairs that manifest great tension and to generate some analogies that represent the tension. For example, we might ask them to provide some examples of 'exquisite torture'.

Teacher Please describe briefly how you will present these tasks to the students.

Observer Please discuss the students' understanding of the concept 'compressed conflict' and their ability to select the higher quality ones. Also, comment on the product of their attempt to generate oxymoronic analogies.

PHASE 6: RE-EXAMINATION OF THE ORIGINAL TASK

The compressed conflicts and the analogies to them provide material from which to revisit the original problem or topic. Sometimes we select or have the students select just one analogy with which to revisit the original material. At other times multiple perspectives are useful. What course to take depends on a combination of the complexity of the original problem or concept and the students' ability to handle new perspectives. For example, if a secondary social studies class has been trying to formulate potential solutions to a problem in international relations, we are dealing with a very complex problem for which multiple analogies are probably both appropriate and necessary. However, the task – helping the students share and assess a variety of analogies that can be used to redefine the problem and generate alternative solutions – is complex indeed.

Teacher Please describe how you will present the task of revisiting the original product. What will you ask the students to do?

Observer   Please comment on the student products. What do you think has been the effect of the metaphoric exercises?

_____

_____

_____

_____

Now the new product needs to be examined. If the student worked as an individual or in a subgroup, the separate products need to be shared. If a problem is to be solved, new definitions and solutions need to be arranged. If written expression emerged, possibly it needs further editing. Unless the teaching episode is the conclusion of a topic of study, it generally leads to further study.

Teacher   Please describe how the synectics products are to be shared and used. Will they lead to further reading and writing, data collection or experimentation?

_____

_____

_____

_____

Observer   Please comment on the use of the new products. Are the students able to see the effects of the metaphoric activity? If they are asked to participate in further activities or to generate them, are they bringing to those tasks a 'set' toward the development of alternative perspectives or avenues?

_____

_____

_____

_____

COMMENTS ON STUDENT TRAINING NEEDS

It is the student who does the learning and the greater the skill of the student in responding to the cognitive and social tasks of the model, the greater the learning is likely to be. Practice alone will build skill and we want to provide plenty of it. After students are thoroughly familiar with the structure of the model, we can begin to develop specific training to improve their ability to perform.

Observer   Please comment on the skills with which the students engaged in the activities and suggest any areas where you believe training might be useful. Think especially of their ability to make comparisons, their ability to take the roles required to make 'personal analogies' and their understanding of the structure of compressed conflicts and how to use them. Thinking back on the entire experience, is there any area where specific process training should be considered?

_____

_____

_____

_____

Peer Coaching Guide for Mnemonics

Learning mnemonically

During the last 15 years there has been renewed research and development on strategies for assisting students to master and retain information. The science of mnemonics, as it is called, has produced some dramatic results (Pressley et al. 1981a, 1981b).

Rote repetition (rehearsing something over and over until it is retained) has until recently been the primary method taught to students for memorizing information and the primary method used by teachers as they interact with students. In fact, rote methods have become so used that they have become identified in many people's minds with the act of memorization. To memorize, it is often thought, is to repeat by rote.

MEMORIZATION STRATEGIES

However, although rehearsal of material continues to be one aspect of most mnemonic strategies, a number of other procedures are employed that greatly increase the probability that material will be learned and retained. These procedures are combined in various ways, depending on the material to be learned. Most of the procedures help build associations between the new material and familiar material. Some of the procedures include the following.

Organizing information to be learned

The more information is organized the easier it is to learn and retain. Information can be organized by categories. The concept attainment, inductive and advanced organizer models assist memory by helping students associate the material in the categories. Consider the following list of words from a popular spelling series, in the order the spelling book presents them to the children:

soft	plus	cloth	frost	song
trust	luck	club	sock	pop
cost	lot	son		won

Suppose we ask the children to classify them by beginnings, endings and the presence of vowels. The act of classification requires the children to scrutinize the words and associate words containing similar elements. They can then name the categories in each classification (the *c* group and the *st* group), calling further attention to the common attributes of the group. They can also connect words that fit together (*pop song*, *soft cloth*, etc.). They can then proceed to rehearse the spelling of one category at a time. The same principle operates over other types of material – say, number facts, etc. Whether categories are provided to students or whether they create them, the purpose is the same. Also information can be selected with categories in mind. Our list is, to outward appearances, almost random. A list that deliberately and systematically provides variations would be easier to organize (it would already have at least implicit categories within it).

Ordering information to be learned

Information learned in series, especially if there is meaning to the series, is easier to assimilate and retain. For example, if we wish to learn the names of the states of Australia it is easier if we always start with the same one (say, the largest) and proceed in the same order. Historical events by chronology are more easily learned than events sorted randomly. Order is simply another way of organizing information. We could have the students alphabetize their list of spelling words.

Linking information to familiar sounds

Suppose we are learning the names of the states of America. We can connect *Georgia* to *George*, *Louisiana* to *Louis*, *Maryland* to *Marry* or *Merry* and so on. Categorizing the names of the states or ordering them by size, or ordering them within region, provides more associations.

Linking information to visual representations

Maryland can be linked to a picture of a marriage, Oregon to a picture of a gun, Maine to a burst water main and so forth. Letters and numerals can be linked to something that evokes both familiar sounds and images. For example, *one* can be linked to *bun* and a picture of a boy eating a bun, *b* to *bee* and a picture of a bee. Those links can be used over and over again. 'April is the cruellest month, breeding lilacs out of the dead land' is easier remembered thinking of an ominous spring, bending malevolently over the spring flowers.

Linking information to associated information

A person's name, linked to information such as a well-known person having the same name, a soundalike and some personal information, is easier to remember than the name rehearsed by itself. Louis (Louis Armstrong) 'looms' over Jacksonville (his place of birth). Learning the states of Australia while thinking of the points of the compass and the British origins of many of the names (New South Wales) is easier than learning them in order alone.

Making the information vivid

Devices that make the information vivid are also useful. Lorayne and Lucas (1966) favour 'ridiculous association', where information is linked to absurd associations. ('The silly two carries his twin two on his back so they are really four' and such.) Others favour the use of dramatization and vivid illustrations (such as counting the basketball players on two teams to illustrate that five and five equals 10).

Rehearsing

Rehearsal (practice) is always useful and students benefit from knowledge of results. Students who have not had past success with tasks requiring memorization will benefit by having relatively short assignments and clear, timely feedback linked to their success.

PLANNING WITH MEMORIZATION IN MIND

The task of the teacher is to think up activities that help the students benefit from these principles.

A teaching episode or learning task that can be organized at least partly by these principles contains information to be learned. Both teacher and students should be clear that a very high degree of mastery is desired. (The students need to be trying to learn all the information and to retain it permanently.)

Teacher Please identify the information to be learned by your students in some curriculum area within a specified period of time.

_____

_____

_____

Which principles will you emphasize in order to facilitate memorization?

_____

_____

Will these principles be used as the information is presented to the students? If yes, how?

_____

_____

_____

Which principles will be used as the students operate on the information? How?

_____

_____

_____

How will rehearsal and feedback be managed?

Observer During the teaching/learning episode, situate yourself so that you can observe the behaviour of a small number of children (about half a dozen). Concentrate on their response to the tasks they are given.

Comment on their response. Do they appear to be clear about the objectives? Do they engage in the cognitive tasks that have been provided to them? Can they undertake these tasks successfully? Do they appear to be aware of progress?

_____

_____

_____

_____

_____

DISCUSSION

The observer should report the results of the observation to the teacher. Then the discussion should focus on how the students responded and on ways of helping them respond more effectively, if that is desirable.

Practice frequently enables students to respond more productively without further instruction. Where instruction is needed, demonstration is useful. That is, the teacher may lead the students through the tasks over small amounts of material.

Tasks can be simplified in order to bring them within the reach of the students. We want the students to develop a repertoire of techniques that enable them to apply the mnemonic principles to learning tasks. Making the process conscious is a step toward independence, so we seek ways of helping the students understand the nature of the tasks and why these should work for them.

Peer Coaching Guide for the Role-playing

Learning to study values

The guide is designed to assist peer coaching of the role-playing model of learning and teaching. When planning questions, skip through the guide to the entries marked 'Teacher' and fill them in as needed. They will guide you through the model. Observers can use the guide to familiarize themselves with the plans of the teacher and to make notes about what is observed. Remember, observers, that your primary function is not to give 'expert advice' to your colleague, but to observe the students as requested by the teacher and to observe the whole process so that you can gain ideas for your own teaching. The teacher is the coach in the sense that he or she is demonstrating a teaching episode for you. When you teach and are observed, you become the coach.

Teacher   Do you want to suggest a focus for the analysis? If so, what is it?

THE TEACHING PROCESS

Most lessons have both content and process objectives. Content objectives identify subject matter (facts, concepts, generalizations, relationships) to be mastered by students, while process objectives specify skills and procedures students need in order to achieve content objectives or auxiliary social objectives (for example, cooperation in a learning task).

Content objective

Teacher   Please state the objective of the lesson. What problem will be presented to the students, or in what domain will they construct a problem? Is the problem or domain of values new to the students?

Process objective

Teacher Are the students familiar with the model? Do they need special assistance or training with respect to any aspect of the process?

_____

_____

_____

PHASE 1: WARMING UP THE GROUP

Role playing begins with a social problem. The problem may be from a prepared study of a human relations situation or an aspect of human relations may be presented to the students so they can generate situations involving it. Possibly the problem is one in their lives that simply needs recapitulation.

Teacher How will you present the problem to the students or help them develop it?

_____

_____

_____

Observer In your opinion, was the problem clear to the students? Were they able to understand the nature of the problem and the type of human relationships problem it represents? Could they identify the players in the situation and how they act? Can they see the several sides of the problem?

_____

_____

_____

PHASE 2: SELECTING THE PARTICIPANTS (ROLE PLAYERS AND OBSERVERS)

Teacher Please describe how the participants will be selected.

_____

_____

_____

PHASE 3: SETTING THE STAGE

Teacher   How are you going to do this? Do you wish the first enactment to highlight certain aspects of values?

_____

_____

_____

Observer   Were they able to generate a plausible and meaningful story line? Please note any difficulties they had.

_____

_____

_____

PHASE 4: PREPARING THE OBSERVERS

Once the characters have been identified and the story line generated the observers (students) are prepared.

Teacher   What will you ask the observers to focus on?

_____

_____

_____

Sometimes the observers are asked to record the progression of their impressions.

Teacher   Do you want to do this?

_____

_____

PHASE 5: THE ENACTMENT

Now the students enact the problem for the first time.

Observer   How well did the students enact the roles? Did they appear to empathize with the positions they were to take? Were the observers attentive and serious? Comment on any problems either role players or observers had.

_____

_____

_____

PHASE 6: DISCUSSION

Observer Were the students able to analyse the nature of the conflict and the values that were involved? Did they reveal their own value positions? Did they have any confusion about tactics of argumentation, skill and values?

_____

_____

_____

PHASES 7, 8 AND 9

From this point, phases 1 to 3 are repeated through several enactments. The teacher guides the students to ensure that the value questions are brought out.

Observer Please comment on the student performance in the ensuing cycles of enactments and discussions. Did the students increasingly become able to distinguish value positions?

_____

_____

_____

ANALYSIS

When the teacher judges that sufficient material has been generated, a discussion is held (a cooperative learning format can be used for this phase to maximize participation, if desired). This ensures that the value positions are brought out; the discussion also puts forward positions about what can be done to deal with the particular type of problem from a valuing basis rather than one involving adversarial uses of argumentation and conflict.

Teacher Please prepare the instructions you will give the students to inaugurate phase 4.

_____

_____

_____

Observer   Please comment on the students' ability to handle the tasks involved in phase 4.

_____

_____

_____

DISCUSSION

Following the teaching episode, the coaching partners might discuss ways of helping the students respond more effectively to the model. Remember that the early trials are bound to be awkward and that practice often does the trick. Also problems can be adjusted to simplify the issues that have to be dealt with at any one time. Demonstrating the phases of the model to the students is also useful. The coaching partners can play the role of observer or even role player to give the students a model. Or the two teachers can demonstrate together.

Please summarize the results of the discussion – the one or two chief conclusions you have reached – to guide what you will next do as you use the model.

_____

_____

_____

_____

Peer Coaching Guide for Nondirective Counselling

Learning through counselling

The guide is designed to assist peer coaching of the nondirective counselling model of learning and teaching. When planning questions, skip through the guide to the entries marked 'Teacher' and fill them in as needed. They will guide you through the model. Observers can use the guide to familiarize themselves with the plans of the teacher and to make notes about what is observed. Remember, observers, that your primary function is not to give 'expert advice' to your colleague, but to observe the students as requested by the teacher and to observe the whole process so that you can gain ideas for your own teaching. The teacher is the coach in the sense that he or she is demonstrating a teaching episode for you. When you teach and are observed, you become the coach.

When first practising this model, we suggest that you work with individual students or very small groups.

Teacher Do you want to suggest a focus for the observer? If so, what is it?

_____

_____

_____

THE TEACHING PROCESS

The most common use of the nondirective model is to help a student or a group of students (perhaps the entire class or even an entire student body) to understand their behaviour and take charge of some aspect of their development. The guide will focus on this type of use and will assume that the teaching episodes are to be built around helping the students approach an aspect of social development or an aspect of an academic area they are having trouble with. In other words, the guide assumes that you are contriving an encounter with the content to be studied.

Objectives

Teacher Please indicate the area of development you are focusing on during these episodes.

_____

_____

_____

_____

PHASES 1 AND 2: DEFINING THE HELPING SITUATION AND EXPLORING THE PROBLEM

Teacher You need to open the discussion. How are you going to do this? Are you going to simply begin the discussion or are you going to set up an encounter with the area, such as showing a film, giving an assignment, asking the students to perform a task or setting up a role-playing enactment?

_____

_____

_____

Observer How did the students respond? Did they appear to express themselves openly? For example, if the teacher is concentrating on students' anxiety in approaching problem solving in mathematics, was the anxiety expressed, albeit 'covered' by a rationale based on external causes?

_____

_____

_____

Observer Was the teacher able to reflect to the students on their expressions, and develop a preliminary picture of their conceptions, keeping individual differences in expression alive?

_____

_____

_____

PHASE 3: DEVELOPING INSIGHT

Teacher You need to figure out how you will induce the students to focus on an aspect of their behaviour and begin the process of accepting responsibility for changing themselves. How will you set up this aspect of the discussions?

_____

_____

Observer Please comment on the discussion. Were the students able to focus on some aspect of their behaviour? How did they handle the suggestion that they would have to make a change?

PHASE 4: PLANNING AND DECISION MAKING

Teacher You now need to induce the students to make a hypothesis that, if they change something, their situation will change. For example, if they have anxiety about some aspect of school work or some aspect of social interaction, they need to pick something they can do and practise doing it. How are you going to induce them to focus and develop their hypotheses?

Observer Please indicate how the students responded. Do they have a course of action?

PHASE 5: INTEGRATION

Now we work with the students to explore whether they are making progress. If their hypotheses aren't working, we help them develop new ones.

   The phases are recycled as necessary. If phase 3 breaks down, move back to phase 1 or 2 and try again.

Observer What do you think? Are the students making progress, both with the problem area and with their ability to respond to the tasks of the model?

Peer Coaching Guide for the Simultions

Learning through simulations

The guide is designed to assist peer coaching of the simulation model of learning and teaching. When planning questions, skip through the guide to the entries marked 'Teacher' and fill them in as needed. They will guide you through the model. Observers can use the guide to familiarize themselves with the plans of the teacher and to make notes about what is observed. Remember, observers, that your primary function is not to give 'expert advice' to your colleague, but to observe the students as requested by the teacher and to observe the whole process so that you can gain ideas for your own teaching. The teacher is the coach in the sense that he or she is demonstrating a teaching episode for you. When you teach and are observed, you become the coach.

Most simulations are embodied in print material or computer software. For most people, using such packaged simulations is the easiest way to begin the mastery of the model.

The structure of the guide assumes that students are just learning to use simulations and, therefore, pays attention to the process of teaching the students to use simulations.

Teacher   Do you want to suggest a focus for the analysis? If so, what is it?

_____

_____

_____

_____

_____

THE TEACHING PROCESS

Simulations provide tasks and feedback so that, by behaving and observing the results, the student can alter behaviour. The tasks and feedback cycles are arranged to help the students learn the structure of concepts in an area and the skills necessary for achieving particular objectives. Therefore, on completing a simulation exercise successfully, the students have acquired concepts and skills that need to be consolidated and brought under symbolic control. The students need to be able to articulate the concepts and describe the skills. In the best applications, they are asked to use them as they study other domains or areas of study.

Setting up the objectives requires that the teacher understands the simulation thoroughly. The teacher needs to engage in it personally in order to comprehend it fully.

Content objectives

Teacher   Please describe the major concepts and skills that the students are to learn.

_____

_____

_____

_____

Process objectives

Teacher   Are the students familiar with the process of the model? Do they need special help with any aspect of the process?

_____

_____

_____

_____

PHASE 1: ORIENTATION

The students need to know the kind of objectives they are to achieve with the particular simulation. One does not tell them the specific objectives and skills they will learn, but rather the kinds of concepts and skills they will learn.

Teacher   How will you do this? What major points will you emphasize?

_____

_____

_____

Observer   Do you think the students understand the kinds of things they are to learn?

_____

_____

_____

_____

PHASE 2: PARTICIPANT TRAINING

This phase may take several sessions. The teacher's role is to help the students get going and to help them solve problems.

Teacher What kinds of help do you anticipate having to provide?

_____

_____

_____

_____

Observer Did the students appear able to take on the tasks? How did they respond to feedback? Do they appear to understand what they are to learn?

_____

_____

_____

_____

PHASE 3: SIMULATION OPERATIONS

In this phase, the students reach the end of a segment of the simulation or the entire simulation. They need to reflect on what they have learned – what worked and didn't work – and establish conscious control over the concepts and skills.

Teacher How will you conduct this session or these sessions? What will you ask the students? How will the information be recorded?

_____

_____

_____

_____

Observer How effectively were the students able to articulate the concepts and skills essential to successful performance?

_____

_____

_____

PHASE 4: PARTICIPANT DEBRIEFING

We suggest that the students write about the area they have studied or develop written/oral presentations, including graphics, that describe the learning.

Teacher   Please describe the task you will give the students and how the products of the task will be shared.

_____

_____

_____

_____

Observer   Did the students understand the task? Did they engage in it knowledge-ably? What further help do they need to consolidate their learning?

_____

_____

_____

_____

COMMENTARY

These phases can be recycled and repeated as necessary. A long simulation may require several revisitations of various phases and may actually be conducted as a series of segments that include all the phases.

Peer Coaching Guide for Picture–Word Inductive Model

Learning to read and write with the picture–word inductive model

School or agency _____ Name _____

Grade level/position _____ Beginning date of PWIM cycle ____

Description of class (grade level, no. of students, specials needs) ____

    A Describe your picture.

    B List of words shaken out of the picture.

Words added to the picture-word chart and word sets after the first round.

    C Examples of categories of words or phrases generated by students.

    D Examples of categories or concepts selected by you for instructional emphasis.

Phonetic analysis categories or concepts.

Structural analysis categories or concepts.

Content categories or concepts.

Other.

    E Examples of titles generated by students.

From the picture.

From the picture–word chart.

From sentence groups or categories.

    F Examples of sentences generated by students.

    G One of the informative paragraphs composed by you from student ideas.

Be sure to do a think aloud with your students about how you put the ideas together to convey your message.

H Sample(s) of student work.

You may want to simply attach examples of student work to the guide.

Be sure to take samples of student work, when they are available, to your sessions with your peer-coaching partner and to designated sessions with the team as a learning community. You may take work from your whole class or group; however, I suggest you take, for collective study, the work of six students whose responses you are monitoring more formally and maybe more analytically than those of the whole class.

I If you used trade books with the PWIM cycle, list the title, author and other literary strategies used (if applicable).

Title	Author	Fiction or non-fiction	Strategy (read aloud, talk aloud, think aloud, explicit instruction)
1			
2			
3			
4			
5			
6			
7			
8			
9			
10			
11			
12			
13			

Strategies	Total no. during PWIM cycle
Read aloud	
Talk aloud	
Think aloud (reading)	
Think aloud (composing)	
Explicit instruction	

Comments.

_____

_____

_____

_____

Questions.

_____

_____

_____

_____

Numbers of lessons/days in PWIM cycle _____

Ending date of PWIM cycle _____

Number of times you planned with your peer coach in this PWIM cycle _____

Number of times you demonstrated with your peer coach in this PWIM cycle _____

Number of times you debriefed with your peer coach in this PWIM cycle _____

PWIM: studying student performance emphasis: vocabulary development

School or agency _____ Name _____

Grade level/position _____ Beginning date of PWIM cycle _____

A Description of class (grade level, no. of students, special needs).

B Description of six students whose learning is being studied formally as part of studying the PWIM.

1 Name _____ Birthdate _____ Gender: F M

Other information that would be useful to understanding the student, such as learning history, etc.

2 Name _____ Birthdate _____ Gender: F M

Other information that would be useful to understanding the student, such as learning history, etc.

3 Name _____ Birthdate _____ Gender: F M

Other information that would be useful to understanding the student, such as learning history, etc.

4 Name _____ Birthdate _____ Gender: F M

Other information that would be useful to understanding the student, such as learning history, etc.

5 Name _____ Birthdate _____ Gender: F M

Other information that would be useful to understanding the student, such as learning history, etc.

6 Name _____ Birthdate _____ Gender: F M

Other information that would be useful to understanding the student, such as learning history, etc.

Gender of student	Total no. words	Date asst.	No. words read		Total no. words	Date asst.	No. words read	GAIN
1								
2								
3								
4								
5								
6								

Comments and reflections.

_____

_____

_____

_____

Questions.

_____

_____

_____

_____

Remember to take your assessment of student performance to sessions with your peer-coaching partner and to designated sessions with the team as a learning community.

Peer Coaching Guide for the Planning and Observation of Other Models of Teaching

Learning through cooperative disciplined inquiry

Unlike the other guides in this series, this form to assist in the planning and observation of teaching is not built around a model of teaching. The substance is the organization of students into study groups and partnerships. It does not deal with the specific cooperative learning strategies developed by Robert Slavin and his associates (Slavin et al. 1996) or Roger Johnson and David Johnson (1994), although the philosophy of the approach is similar. Neither does it deal specifically with group investigation (Sharan and Hertz-Lazarowitz 1980a, 1980b; Thelen 1960).

Rather, cooperative learning organization provides a setting for cooperative study that can be employed in combination with many approaches to teaching.

This guide describes some options and asks the teacher to select from them or to generate others. The observer analyses the students' productivity and attempts to identify ways of helping the students engage in more productive behaviour. The examples that follow are in reference to the inductive model of teaching. Using the two guides simultaneously may be useful.

When other models are being used, analogous use can be made of cooperative learning.

OPTIONS FOR ORGANIZATION

The underlying idea is to organize the students so that everyone in the class has a partner with whom they can work on instructional tasks. For example, pairs of students can operate throughout the inductive model, collecting information, developing categories and making inferences about causal relationships. The partnerships (which need not be long term, although they can be) are collected in teams. For example, if there are 30 students in the class, there can be five teams of six. We do not recommend team size any larger than six. These teams can also work alongside the partnership structure. The partnerships provide an easy organization through which teams can divide labour. For example, each partnership can collect information from certain sources and then the information can be accumulated into a dataset for the team. Similarly, team sets can be accumulated into a class set of data. Teams can then operate on these datasets and compare and contrast the results with those of other teams.

Team membership and partnerships can be organized in a number of ways, ranging from student selection, random selection, or teacher-guided choices to maximize heterogeneity and potential synergy.

Instruction of teams can range from explicit procedures to guide them through the learning activities to general procedures that leave much of the organization to the students.

Organization

Teacher How will you organize the class for this teaching episode? How many groups of what sizes will be selected?

_____

_____

_____

_____

How will memberships be determined?

_____

_____

_____

_____

What approach to teaching/learning will be used? If you are not using a specific model of teaching, what will be your instructional strategy?

_____

_____

_____

_____

How will cooperative groups be used throughout the teaching episode? What cooperative tasks will be given to pairs, study groups or the whole class? For example, if this were an inductive lesson, partnerships might collect data, classify it and make inferences. Or partnerships might collect data, but it might be assembled by the entire class prior to the classification activity. Partnerships might study words, poems, maps, number facts and operations or other material. What is your plan?

_____

_____

_____

_____

Observer After you have familiarized yourself with the plan, situate yourself in the room so that you can observe about six students closely. Throughout the teaching episode, concentrate on the behaviour of those students, whether they are working in partnerships, study groups or any other organization. Then comment on their performance.

Did they appear to be clear about the tasks they were to accomplish? If not, can you identify what they were not clear about?

_____

_____

_____

_____

Did they appear to know how to cooperate to accomplish the tasks assigned to them? Is there anything they appear to need to know in order to be more productive?

_____

_____

_____

_____

Do they regulate their own behaviour, keeping on task, dividing labour, taking turns? Could they profit from having any aspect of group management modelled for them?

_____

_____

_____

_____

What sort of leadership patterns did they employ? Did they acknowledge one or more leaders? Did they discuss process? Were they respectful to one another?

_____

_____

_____

_____

Discussion

Following the episode, discuss the operation of the groups in which the six students were members. Is their productivity satisfactory? Their relationships? If not, see if you can develop a plan for helping the students become more productive. Remember that:

1   Providing practice is the simplest and most powerful way to help students learn to work productively. This is especially true if they have not had much experience working in cooperative groups.

2   The smaller the group, the more easily students can regulate their own behaviour. Reducing the size of study groups often allows students to solve their own problems.

3   Demonstration gets more mileage than exhortation. A teacher can join a group and show the students how to work together. In fact, the observer can be a participant in a study group in future sessions.

4   Simpler tasks are easier for students to manage. Breaking complex tasks into several smaller ones often allows students to build their skills through practice.

5   Praising appropriate behaviour gets results. If two groups are performing at different levels, it often helps to praise the productive group and then quietly join the less productive one and provide leadership.

Literature

Adams, A., Johnson, M. and Connors, J. (1980) *Success in Kindergarten Reading and Writing*. Glenview, IL: Good Year Books.

Adams, M. J. and Huggins, A. W. F. (1985) The growth of children's sight vocabulary: a quick test with educational and theoretical implications. *Reading Research Quarterly, 20(3): 262–81.*

Adey, P., with Hewitt, G., Hewitt, J. and Landau, N. (2004) *The Professional Development of Teachers: Practice and Theory*. London and Boston: Kluwer.

Adger, C., Hoyle, S. and Dickinson, D. (2004) Locating learning in in-service education for preservice teachers. *American Educational Research Journal*, 41(4): 867–900.

Alkin, M. (ed.) (1992) *Encyclopedia of Educational Research*, 6th edn. New York: Macmillan.

American Institutes for Research (1999) *Designing Effective Professional Development: Lessons from the Eisenhower Program, Executive Summary*. Washington, DC: American Institutes for Research.

Applebee, A., Langer, J., Jenkins, L., Mullis, I. and Foertsch, M. (1990) *Learning to Write in our Nation's Schools*. Washington, DC: US Department of Education.

Aronson, E., Blaney, N., Stephan, C., Sikes, J. and Snapp, M. (1978) *The Jigsaw Classroom*. Beverly Hills, CA: Sage.

Association for Supervision and Curriculum Development (2005) *Professional Development Online: Professional Development for Educators*. Alexandria, VA: Association for Supervision and Curriculum Development.

Association for Supervision and Curriculum Development (2005) *Professional Development Online: Course Catalog*. Alexandria, VA: Association for Supervision and Curriculum Development.

Atkinson, J. W. (1966) *Achievement Motivation*. New York: John Wiley & Sons.

Ausubel, D. P. (1960) The use of advance organizers in the learning and retention of meaningful verbal material. *Journal of Educational Psychology*, 51: 267–72.

Ball, S. and Bogatz, G. A. (1970) *The First Year of Sesame Street*. Princeton, NJ: Educational Testing Service.

Bartell, C. (2005) *Cultivating High-Quality Teaching through Induction and Mentoring*. Thousand Oaks, CA: Corwin Press.

Baveja, B. (1988) An exploratory study of the use of information-processing models of teaching in secondary school biology science classes (PhD thesis). Delhi: New Delhi University.

Baveja, B., Showers, B. and Joyce, B. (1985) *An Experiment in Conceptually-based Teaching Strategies*. Eugene, OR: Booksend Laboratories.

Becker, W. and Gersten, R. (1982) A follow-up of Follow Through: the later effects of the direct instruction model on children in the fifth and sixth grades. *American Educational Research Journal*, 19(1): 75–92.

Bereiter, C. (1984) Constructivism, socioculturalism, and Popper's world. *Educational Researcher*, 23(7): 21–3.

Bereiter, C. (1997) Situated cognition and how to overcome it. In Kirshner, D. and Whitson, W. (eds) *Situated Cognition: Social, Semiotic, and Psychological Perspectives*. Hillsdale, NJ: Lawrence Erlbaum Associates, Inc.

Bloom, B. S. (1984) The 2 sigma problem: the search for group instruction as effective as one-to-one tutoring. *Educational Researcher*, 13: 4–16.

Boocock, S. S. and Schild, E. (1968) *Simulation Games in Learning*. Beverly Hills, CA: Sage.

Borman, G. D., Slavin, R. E., Cheung, A., Chamberlain, A., Madden, N. A. and

Bredderman, T. (1983) Effects of activity-based elementary science on student outcomes: a quantitative synthesis. *Review of Educational Research*, 53(4): 499–518.

Borman, G. D., Slavin, R. E., Cheung, A., Chamberlain, A., Madden, N. and Chambers, B. (2005) Success for All: first year results from the National Randomized Field Trial. *Educational Evaluation and Policy Analysis*, 27(1): 1–22.

Brooks, D. (2005). Mind over muscle. *New York Times*, October 16: A12.

Bruner, J. (1961) *The Process of Education*. Cambridge, MA: Harvard University Press.

Bruner, J. (1966) *Toward a Theory of Instruction*. Cambridge, MA: Harvard University Press.

Bruner, J., Goodnow, J. J. and Austin, G. A. (1967) *A Study of Thinking*. New York: Science Editions.

Calhoun, E. (1997) *Literacy for All*. Saint Simons Island, GA: The Phoenix Alliance.

Calhoun, E. (1999) *Teaching Beginning Reading and Writing with the Picture Word Inductive Model*. Alexandria, VA: Association for Supervision and Curriculum Development.

Central Advisory Council for Education (1967) *Children and their Primary Schools* (Plowden Report). London: HMSO.

Chall, J. S. (1983) *Learning to Read: The Great Debate*. New York: McGraw-Hill.

Chamberlin, C. and Chamberlin, E. (1943) *Did They Succeed in College?* New York: Harper & Row.

Chambers, B. (in press) The National Randomized Field Trial of Success for All: second-year outcomes. *American Educational Research Journal*.

Chesler, M. and Fox, R. (1966) *Role-playing Methods in the Classroom*. Chicago: Science Research Associates.

Chin, R. and Benne, K. (1969) General strategies for effecting change in human systems. In Bennis, W., Benne, K. and Chin, R. (eds) *The Planning of Change*. New York: Holt, Rinehart & Winston.

Clark, H. H. and Clark, E. V. (1977) *Psychology and Language: An Introduction to Psycholinguistics*. New York: Harcourt Brace Jovanovich.

Cornelius-White, J. (2007) Learner-centered teacher–student relationships are effective: a meta-analysis. *Review of Educational Research*, 77(1): 113–43.

Dale, P. (1988) *Ten in the Bed*. London: Walker Books.

Deshler, D. and Schumaker, J. (2006) *Teaching Adolescents with Disabilities*. Thousand Oaks, CA: Corwin Press.

Dewey, J. (1916) *Democracy in Education*. New York: Macmillan.

Donahue, P. (1999) *1998 NAEP Reading Report Card for the Nation and the States*. Washington, DC: U.S. Department of Education.

Downey, L. (1967) *The Secondary Phase of Education*. Boston, MA: Ginn.

Duke, N. and Pearson, P. D. (undated) *Effective Practices for Developing Reading Comprehension*. East Lansing, MI: College of Education, Michigan State University.

Durkin, D. (1966) *Children Who Read Early*. New York: Teachers College Press.

Eastman, P. D. (1961) *Go, Dog, Go!* New York: Random House.

Edmonds, R. (1979) Effective schools for the urban poor. *Educational Leadership*, 37(1): 15–27.

Ehri, L. C. (1994) Phases of acquisition in learning to read words and instructional implications. Paper presented to the annual meeting of the American Educational Research Association, Montreal.

Elkind, D. (1987) *Miseducation: Preschoolers at Risk*. New York: Knopf.

Elkind, D. (2001) *Much Too Early*. Palo Alto, CA: Hoover Institute at Stanford University.

El-Nemr, M. A. (1979) Meta-analysis of the outcomes of teaching biology as inquiry (unpublished doctoral dissertation). Boulder, CO: University of Colorado.

Englert, C. and Raphael, T. (1989) Developing successful writers through cognitive strategy instruction. In Brophy, J. (ed.) *Advances in Research in Teaching*. Greenwich, CT: JAI Press.

Englert, C. S., Raphael, T. E., Anderson, L. M., Anthony, H. M. and Stevens, D. D. (1991) Making strategies and self talk visible: writing instruction in regular and special education classrooms. *American Educational Research Journal*, 28(2): 337–72.

Estes, W. E. (ed.) (1976) *Handbook of Learning and Cognitive Processes, Vol. IV. Attention and Memory*. Hillsdale, NJ: Lawrence Erlbaum Associates, Inc.

Gagné R. (1965) *The Conditions of Learning*. New York: Holt, Rinehart & Winston.

Gao, H. (2005) Kindergarten or 'kindergrind'? School getting tougher for kids. *San Diego Union-Tribune*, April 11, 2005.

Garner, R. (1987) *Metacognition and Reading Comprehension*. Norwood, NJ: Ablex.

Gerbner, G. (1974) Teacher images in mass culture: symbolic functions of the 'hidden curriculum'. In *Media and Symbols*, 73rd yearbook of the National Society for the Study of Education. Chicago: University of Chicago Press.

Glass, G. V. (1982) Meta-analysis: an approach to the synthesis of research results. *Journal of Research in Science Teaching*, 19(2): 93–112.

Glynn, S. M. (1994) *Teaching Science with Analogies*. Athens, GA: National Reading Research Center, University of Georgia.

Goffman, I. (1982) *Gender Advertisements*. New York: Harper & Row.

Goodlad, J. and Klein, F. (1970) *Looking behind the Classroom Door*. Worthington, OH: Charles A. Jones.

Gordon, W. J. J. (1961) *Synectics*. New York: Harper & Row.

Gordon, W. J. J. (1970) The metaphorical development of man. In Brooks, C. (ed.) *The Changing World and Man*. New York: New York University Press.

Gordon, W. J. J. (1971) Architecture – the making of metaphors. *Main Currents in Modern Thought*, 28(1).

Graves, M. F. (1992) The elementary vocabulary curriculum: what should it be? In Dreher, M. J. and Slater, W. H. (eds) *Elementary School Literacy: Critical Issues*. Norwood, NJ: Christopher Gordon.

Guetzkow H., Alger, C. F., Brody, R. A., Noel, R. C. and Snyder R. C. (1963) *Simulation in International Relations*. Englewood Cliffs, NJ: Prentice- Hall.

Gunning, T. (1998) *Best Books for Beginning Readers*. Boston, MA: Allyn & Bacon.

Hanson, R. and Farrell, D. (1995) The long-term effects on high school seniors of learning to read in kindergarten. *Reading Research Quarterly*, 30(4): 908–33.

Hillocks, G. (1987) Synthesis of research on teaching writing. *Educational Leadership*, 44(8): 71–82.

Hopkins, D. (1987) *Knowledge, Information Skills and the Curriculum*. London: British Library.

Hopkins, D. (1998) *Theories of Development, Strategies for Growth. Tensions in and Prospects for School Improvement* (International Handbook on Education: Volume IV). Dordrecht, Netherlands: Kluwer Academic.

Hopkins, D. (2001) *School Improvement for Real*. London: Routledge Falmer.

Hopkins, D. (2002a) *Improving the Quality of Education for All*, 2nd edn. London: David Fulton.

Hopkins, D. (2002b) *A Teacher's Guide to Classroom Research*, 3rd edn. Buckingham: Open University Press.

Hopkins, D., Ainscow, M. and West, M. (1994) *School Improvement in an Era of Change*. London: Cassell.

Hrycauk, M. (2002) District weaves safety net. *Journal of Staff Development*, 23(1): 55–8.

Hunt, D. E. (1971) *Matching Models in Education*. Toronto: Ontario Institute for Studies in Education.

Hunter, I. M. L. (1964) *Memory*. London: Penguin.

International Reading Association (1998) *Position Statement on Phonemic Awareness and the Teaching of Reading*. Newark, DE: International Reading Association

International Reading Association (2004) Coaches, controversy, consensus. *Reading Today*, 21(5): 1.

International Reading Association and the National Association for the Education of Young Children (1998) *Position Statement on Learning to Read and Write: Developmentally Appropriate Practices for Young Children*. Newark, DE: International Reading Association.

Iowa School Boards Association (2001) The lighthouse enquiry: school board/ superintendent behaviors in school districts with extreme differences in student achievement. Paper presented to the annual meeting of the American Educational Research Association, Seattle.

Johnson, D. W. and Johnson, R. T. (1974) Instructional goal structure: cooperative, competitive, or individualistic. *Review of Educational Research*, 44: 213–40.

Johnson, D. W. and Johnson, R. T. (1981) Effects of cooperative and individualistic learning experiences on inter-ethnic interaction. *Journal of Educational Psychology*, 73(3): 444–9.

Johnson, D. W. and Johnson, R. T. (1990) *Cooperation and Competition: Theory and Research*. Edina, MN: Interaction Book Company.

Johnson, D. W. and Johnson, R. T. (1993) *Circles of Learning*. Englewood Cliffs, NJ: Prentice-Hall.

Johnson, D. W. and Johnson, R. T. (1994) *Learning Together and Alone*. Englewood Cliffs, NJ: Prentice-Hall.

Joyce, B. (1991) Common misconceptions about cooperative learning and gifted students. *Educational Leadership*, 48(6): 72–4.

Joyce, B. (1999) Reading about reading. *The Reading Teacher*, 52(7): 662–71.

Joyce, B. (2004) How are professional learning communities created? History has a few messages. *Phi Delta Kappan*, 86(1): 76–83.

Joyce, B. and Calhoun, E. (eds) (1996) *Learning Experiences in School Renewal*. Eugene, OR: ERIC Clearinghouse.

Joyce, B. and Calhoun, E. (1998) *Learning to Teach Inductively*. Needham, MA: Allyn & Bacon.

Joyce, B. and Showers, B. (1983) *Power in Staff Development through Research on Training*. Washington, DC: Association for Supervision and Curriculum Development.

Joyce, B. and Showers, B. (2002) *Student Achievement through Staff Development*, 3rd edn. Alexandria, VA: The Association for Supervision and Curriculum Development.

Joyce, B. and Wolf, J. M. (1996) Readersville: building a culture of readers and writers. In Joyce, B. and Calhoun, E. (eds) *Learning Experiences in School Renewal: An Exploration of Five Successful Programs*. Eugene, OR: ERIC Clearinghouse.

Joyce, B., Calhoun, E., Halliburton, C., Simser, J., Rust, D. and Carran, N. (1994) The Ames Community Schools staff development program. Paper presented to the annual meeting of the Association for Supervision and Curriculum Development, Chicago.

Joyce, B., Calhoun, E., Halliburton, C., Simser, J., Rust, D. and Carran, N. (1996) University town. In Joyce, B. and Calhoun, E. (eds) *Learning Experiences in School Renewal*. Eugene, OR: ERIC Clearinghouse.

Joyce, B., Calhoun, E. and Hopkins, D. (2000) *The New Structure of School Improvement*. Buckingham: Open University Press.

Joyce, B., Calhoun, E. and Hrycauk, M. (2003) Learning to read in kindergarten. *Phi Delta Kappan*, 85(2): 126–32.

Joyce, B., Calhoun, E. and Weil, M. (2008) *Models of Teaching*, 8th edn. Needham, MA: Allyn & Bacon.

Joyce, B., Hrycauk, M. and Calhoun, E. (2001) A second chance for struggling readers. *Educational Leadership*, 58(6): 42–7.

Joyce, B., Showers, B., Murphy, C. and Murphy, J. (1989) Reconstructing the workplace: school renewal as cultural change. *Educational Leadership*, 47(3): 70–8.

Juel, C. (1992) Longitudinal research on learning to read and write with at risk students. In Dreher, M. S. and Slater, W. H. (eds) *Elementary School Literacy: Critical Issues*. Norwood, NJ: Christopher Gordon.

Kagan, S. (1990) *Cooperative Learning Resources for Teachers*. San Juan Capistrano, CA: Resources for Teachers.

Kamii, C. (1994) *Young Children Reinvent Arithmetic*. New York: Teachers College Press.

Kaplan, A. (1964) *The Conduct of Inquiry*. San Francisco: Chandler.

Keyes, D. K. (2006) *Metaphorical Voices* (doctor of education dissertation). Houston, TX: University of Houston.

Kohlberg, L. (1981) *The Philosophy of Moral Development*. New York: Harper & Row.

Kövacses, Z. (2002) *Metaphor: A Practical Introduction*. New York: Oxford University Press.

Krashen, S. (2005) Is in-school reading free reading good for children? Why the National Reading Panel Report is (still) wrong. *Phi Delta Kappan*, 85(6): 444–7.

Kuhn, T. (1962) *The Structure of Scientific Revolutions*. Chicago: University of Chicago Press.

Levin, M. E. and Levin, J. R. (1990) Scientific mnemonics: methods for maximizing more than memory. *American Educational Research Journal*, 27: 301–21.

Levine, D. Y. and Lezotte, L. W. (1990) *Unusually Effective Schools: A Review and Analysis of Research and Practice*. Madison, WI: The National Center for Effective Schools Research and Development.

Lorayne, H. and Lucas, J. (1966) *The Memory Book*. New York: Briercliff Manor.

Loucks-Horsley, S. (2003) *Designing Professional Development for Teachers of Science and Mathematics*. Thousand Oaks, CA: Corwin Press.

Lyons, C. and Pinnell, G. (2001) *Systems for Change in Literacy Education: A Guide to Professional Development*. Portsmouth, NH: Heinemann.

MacGilchrist, B., Mortimer, P., Savage, J. and Beresford, C. (1995) *Planning Matters*. London: Paul Chapman.

McGill-Franzen, A. and Allington, R. L. (1991) Every child's right: literacy. *The Reading Teacher*, 45: 86–90.

McKinney, C., Warren, A., Larkins, G., Ford, M. J. and Davis, J. C. III (1983) The effectiveness of three methods of teaching social studies concepts to fourth-grade students: an aptitude treatment interaction study. *American Educational Research Journal*, 20: 663–70.

Mevarech, Z. (1995) Teachers' paths on the way to and from the professional development forum. In Guskey, T. and Huberman, M. (eds) *Professional Development in Education*. New York: Teachers College Press.

Morris, R. (1997) How research on brain development will influence educational policy. Paper presented to the Policymakers Institute, Georgia Center for Advanced Telecommunications Technology, Atlanta.

Mortimore, P., Sammons, P., Stoll, L., Lewis, D. and Ecols, R. (1988) *School Matters*. London: Open Books.

Nagy, W. and Anderson. P. (1987) Breadth and depth in vocabulary knowledge. *Reading Research Quarterly*, 19: 304–30.

Natale, J. (2001) Early learners: are full day academic kindergartens too much, too soon. *American School Board Journal*, 188(3): 22–5.

National Assessment of Educational Progress (2004) *Reading Highlights, 2003*. Washington, DC: National Center for Educational Statistics.

National Center for Educational Statistics (1998) *Long-Term Trends in Reading Performance, NAEP Facts*. Washington, DC: Office of Educational Research and Improvement, US Department of Education.

National Council for Staff Development (2001) *E-Learning for Educators: Implementing the Standards for Staff Development*. Oxford, OH: NSDC and National Institute for Community Innovations.

National Institute of Child Health and Human Development (2000) *Report of the National Reading Panel: Teaching Children to Read: An Evidence-based Assessment of the Scientific Research Literature on Reading and its Implications for Reading Instruction*. Rockville, MD: National Institute of Child Health and Human Development.

Newby, T. J. and Ertner, P. A. (1994) Instructional analogies and the learning of concepts. Paper delivered to the annual meeting of the American Educational Research Association, New Orleans.

Oakes, J. (1986) *Keeping Track: How Schools Structure Inequality*. New Haven, CT: Yale University Press.

Pardini, P. (1999) Making time for adult learning. *Journal of Staff Development*, 20(2).

PBS Teacherline (2005) *An Introduction to Underlying Principles and Research for Effective Literacy Instruction*. PBS Electronic Catalog. Washington, DC: PBS.

Phillips, D. (1983) After the wake: postpositivistic educational throught. *Educational Researcher*, 12(5): 4–12.

Piaget, J. and Inhelder, B. (2000) *The Psychology of the Child*. New York: Basic Books.

Pinnell, G. S. (1989) Helping at-risk children learn to read. *Elementary School Journal*, 90(2): 161–84.

Popper, K. (1935) *The Logic of Scientific Discovery*. London and New York: Routledge.

Pressley, M. (1977) Children's use of the keyword method to learn simple Spanish vocabulary words. *Journal of Educational Psychology*, 69(5): 465–72.

Pressley, M. (1995) *Cognitive Strategy Instruction that Really Improves Student Performance*. Cambridge, MA: Brookline.

Pressley, M. and Dennis-Rounds, J. (1980) Transfer of a mnemonic keyword strategy at two age levels, *Journal of Educational Psychology*, 72(4): 575–82.

Pressley, M., Levin, J. R. and Delaney, H. D. (1982) The mnemonic keyword method. *Review of Educational Research*, 52 (1): 61–91.

Pressley, M., Levin, J. and Miller, G. (1981a) How does the keyword method affect vocabulary, comprehension, and usage? *Reading Research Quarterly*, 16: 213–26.

Pressley, M., Levin, J. and Miller, G. (1981b) The keyword method and children's learning of foreign vocabulary with abstract meanings. *Canadian Psychology*, 35(3): 283–7.

Qin, Z., Johnson, D. W. and Johnson, R. T. (1995) Cooperative versus competitive efforts and problem solving. *Review of Educational Research*, 65(2).

Quellmatz, E. S. and Burry, J. (1983) *Analytic Scales for Assessing Students' Expository and Narrative Writing Skills*, CSE Resource Paper No. 5. Los Angeles: Center for the Study of Evaluation, UCLA Graduate School of Education.

Richardson, V. and Placier, P. (2001) Teacher change. In Richardson, V. (ed.) *Handbook of Research on Teaching*, 4th edn. Washington, DC: American Educational Research Association.

Roebuck, F., Buhler, J. and Aspy, D. (1976) A comparison of high and low levels of humane teaching/learning conditions on the subsequent achievement of students identified as having learning difficulties. Final report: Order No. PLD 6816–76 re. the National Institute of Mental Health. Denton, TX: Texas Woman's University Press.

Rogers, C. (1961) *On Becoming a Person*. Boston, MA: Houghton-Mifflin.

Rogers, C. (1982) *Freedom to Learn for the Eighties*. Columbus, OH: Charles E. Merrill.

Rudduck, J. and Hopkins, D. (eds) (1985) *Research and Basis for Teaching, Readings from the Work of Lawrence Stenhouse*. London: Heinemann.

Rutter, M., Maughan, B., Mortimer, P. and Ouston, J. (1979) *Fifteen Thousand Hours*. London: Open Books.

Sanders, D. A. and Sanders, J. A. (1984) *Teaching Creativity through Metaphor*. New York: Longman.

Sarason, S. (1982) *The Culture of the School and the Problem of Change*, 2nd edn. Boston, MA: Allyn & Bacon.

Scherer, M. (2005) Perspectives. *Educational Leadership*, 82(8): 7.

Schmoker, M. (2004) The tipping point: from feckless reform to substantive instructional improvement. *Phi Delta Kappan*, February: 424–32.

Schmoker, M. (2001) The 'Crayola Curriculum'. *Education Week*, October 24.

Schwab, J. (1965) *Biological Sciences Curriculum Study: Biology Teachers' Handbook*. New York: John Wiley & Sons.

Schwab, J. (1982) *Science, Curriculum and Liberal Education: Science Essays*. Chicago: University of Chicago Press.

Shaftel, F. and Shaftel, G. (1967) *Role Playing for Social Values: Decision Making in the Social Studies*. Englewood Cliffs, NJ: Prentice-Hall.

Shaftel, F. and Shaftel, G. (1982) *Role Playing in the Curriculum*. Englewood Cliffs, NJ: Prentice-Hall.

Sharan, S. (1980) Cooperative learning in small groups: recent methods and effects on achievement, attitudes, and ethnic relations. *Review of Educational Research*, 50(2): 241–71.

Sharan, S. (1990) *Cooperative Learning: Theory and Research*. New York: Praeger.

Sharan, S. and Hertz-Lazarowitz, R. (1980a) Academic achievement of elementary school children in small group versus whole-class instruction. *Journal of Experimental Education*, 48(2): 120–9.

Sharan, S. and Hertz-Lazarowitz, R. (1980b) A group investigation method of cooperative learning in the classroom. In Sharan, S., Hare, P., Webb C. and Hertz-Lazarowitz, R. (eds) *Cooperation in Education*. Provo, UT: Brigham Young University Press.

Sharan, S. and Shachar, H. (1988) *Language and Learning in the Cooperative Classroom*. New York: Springer-Verlag.

Showers, B., Joyce, B., Scanlon, M. and Schnaubelt, C. (1998) A second chance to learn to read. *Educational Leadership*, 55(6): 27–31.

Sigel, I. R. (1985) *Advances in Applied Developmental Psychology*. Westport, NJ: Ablex.

Skinner, B. F. (1953) *Science and Human Behavior*. New York: Macmillan.

Slavin, R. E. (1983) *Cooperative Learning*. New York: Longman.

Slavin, R. E. (1990) Achievement effects of ability grouping in secondary schools. *Review of Educational Research*, 60(3): 471–500.

Slavin, R. E. (1991) Are cooperative learning and 'untracking' harmful to the gifted? *Educational Leadership*, 48(6): 68–70.

Slavin, R. E. (1996) *Education for All*. Lisse, Netherlands: Swets & Zertlinger.

Slavin, R. E. and Madden, N. (2001) *One Million Children: Success for All*. Thousand Oaks, CA: Corwin Press.

Slavin, R., Madden, N., Dolan, L. and Wasik, B. (1996) *Every Child, Every School: Success for All*. Thousand Oaks, CA: Corwin.

Slavin, R., Madden, N., Karweit, N., Dolan, L., & Wasik, B. (1996) *Success for All: Effects of Variations in Duration and Resources of a Statewide Elementary Restructuring Program*. Baltimore, MD: Center for Research on Effective Schooling for Disadvantaged Students, Johns Hopkins University.

Slavin, R. E., Madden, N. A., Karweit, N., Livermon, B. J. and Dolan, L. (1990) Success for all: first-year outcomes of a comprehensive plan for reforming urban education. *American Educational Research Journal*, 27: 255–78.

Smith, K. and Smith, M. (1966) *Cybernetic Principles of Learning and Educational Design*. New York: Holt, Rinehart & Winston.

Smith, M. L. (1980) *Effects of Aesthetics Education on Basic Skills Learning*. Boulder, CO: Laboratory of Educational Research, University of Colorado.

Smith, T. and Ingersall, R. ((2004) What are the effects of induction and mentoring on beginning teacher turnover? *American Educational Research Journal*, 41(3): 681–714.

Snow, C., Burns, M. and Griffin, P. (1998) *Preventing Reading Difficulties in Young Children*. Washington, DC: National Academy Press.

Spaulding, R. (1970) *Early Intervention Program*. Durham, NC: Duke University Press.

Stauffer, R. (1969) *Directing Reading Maturity as a Cognitive-Learning Process*. New York: Harper & Row.

Stauffer, R. (1970) *The Language-Experience Approach to the Teaching of Reading*. New York: Harper & Row.

Stenhouse, L. (1975) *An Introduction to Curriculum Research and Development*. London: Heinemann.

Stenhouse, L. (ed.) (1980) *Curriculum Research and Development in Action*. London: Heinemann.

Stevenson, H. and Stigler, J. (1992) *The Learning Gap*. New York: Summit Books.

Suchman, R. J. (1964) Studies in inquiry training. In Ripple, R. and Bookcastle, V. (eds) *Piaget Reconsidered*. Ithaca, NY: Cornell University Press.

Sullivan, E. V. (1990) *Critical Psychology and Pedagogy*. New York: Bergin & Garvey.

Swanborn, M. S. J. and de Glopper, K. (1999) Incidental word learning while reading: a meta analysis. *Review of Educational Research*, 69(3): 261–85.

Taba, H. (1966) *Teaching Strategies and Cognitive Functioning in Elementary School Children* (Cooperative Research Project 2404). San Francisco: San Francisco State College.

Taba, H. (1967) *Teachers' Handbook for Elementary School Social Studies*. Reading, MA: Addison-Wesley.

Tennyson, R. D. and Cocchiarella, M. (1986) An empirically based instructional design theory for teaching concepts. *Review of Educational Research*, 56: 40–71.

Thelen, H. (1954) *Dynamics of Groups at Work*. Chicago: University of Chicago Press.

Thelen, H. (1960) *Education and the Human Quest*. New York: Harper & Row.

Thelen, H. (1967) *Classroom Grouping for Teachability*. New York: John Wiley & Sons.

White, W. A. T. (1986) The effects of direct instruction in special education: a meta-analysis (PhD thesis). Eugene, OR: University of Oregon.

Wiederholt, J. L. and Bryant, B. (2001) *Gray Oral Reading Tests*. Austin, TX: Pro-Ed.

Wolpe, J. and Lazarus, A. (1966) *Behavior Therapy Techniques: A Guide to the Treatment of Neuroses*. Oxford: Pergamon Press.

Wood, K. and Tinajero, J. (2002) Using pictures to teach content to second language learners. *Middle School Journal*, May: 47–51.

Index